THE CELTIC MOON SIGN KIT

. . . .

BOOK TWO

THE LUNAR HOROSCOPE READINGS

. . . .

HELENA PATERSON

A Fireside Book
Published by Simon & Schuster

In memory of my father. A man of the sea, whose working life
followed the flow of the tides and the position of the stars.

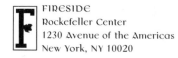

FIRESIDE
Rockefeller Center
1230 Avenue of the Americas
New York, NY 10020

Text copyright © 1999 by Helena Paterson
Illustrations copyright © 1999 by Danuta Mayer
This edition copyright © 1999 by Eddison Sadd Editions

Adapted from
The Handbook of Celtic Astrology
Copyright © 1994 Helena Paterson
Published by Llewellyn Publications
St. Paul, MN 55164 USA

1 3 5 7 9 10 8 6 4 2

Library of Congress Cataloging-in-Publication Data

Paterson, Helena, [1945]
    The Celtic moon sign kit / Helena Paterson.
        p.   cm.
    Includes bibliographical references.
    1. Astrology, Celtic. 2. Horoscopes. 3. Moon—Miscellanea.
    I. Title.
BF1714.C44P384 1999
133.5'93916—dc21   99–17392
                                                                    CIP

ISBN 0-684-86218-2

AN EDDISON•SADD EDITION
Edited, designed and produced by
Eddison Sadd Editions Limited
St Chad's House, 148 King's Cross Road
London WC1X 9DH

Phototypeset in Colmcille MT using QuarkXPress on Apple Macintosh
Manufactured in China by Leo Paper Products

CONTENTS

Basic Paragraphs....4

Paragraphs of conjunctions and aspects....156

Basic Paragraphs

The following interpretive paragraphs refer both to solar position (tree sign) and lunar position (zodiac sign). First read the general information on your lunar symbol and tree-sign character, and then turn to the reference number relating to your lunar position to complete your Basic Paragraph. The interpretive paragraphs for the planetary conjunctions and aspects begin on page 156.

Celtic moon sign: Birch

Lunar Symbol: White Stag

The lunar symbol of the *White Stag* represented the beginning of the seven-month reign of the Sun-king in the ancient Celtic lunar calendar. Reference to 'the white stag of seven tines' (months) is found in the *Song of Amergin,* an archaic poem and incantation said to have been chanted by the Chief Bard of the Celts when they first set foot in Ireland around 1200 BC.

The birch tree is the first tree sign in the Celtic lunar zodiac, and during the first lunar month of the year the Druids used birch rods to drive out the spirit of the old year, a ritual known as the 'beating of the bounds'. Its purpose was to re-establish tribal boundaries and the order of the seasons.

The Druid's mystical zodiac, based upon their lunar calendar, symbolized the journey of the soul as it followed the spiralling light of the Sun through the different phases of the Moon: the integrated harmony of day and night, Sun and Moon. The Druids therefore placed the Sun at the beginning of their zodiac, a position where it begins its return – or rebirth – after the Winter Solstice. The annual rebirth of the Sun affirmed the Druid's belief in reincarnation, the Sun being an ancient symbol of life and eternity. The actual name of the Sun-king varied among Celtic tribes, but the one great 'Over-lord' claimed by all Celts is King Arthur.

Birch Tree character

You were born at the time of the year when dark winter nights prevailed over the light of day. Psychologically, this can initially inhibit much of your personality and individual potential. Contained within your psyche, however, is a powerful source of inner strength that enables you to overcome any personal limitations or humble origins; this relates to King Arthur, your archetypal character. Like a moth is drawn towards a light, so you will begin to discover the light of your true potential. As a result you will learn to direct your energy with great self-discipline and ambitious strategy. Basically, you have the mentality and persistence of a long-distance runner, which tends to isolate you from others. Family obligations or responsibilities are a cross to bear at times, and personal relationships can take a similar toll. Time is on your side, however, and the seed potential associated with your sign should begin to grow just as the Sun increases during the first half of the year.

You have inherited some distinct family traits of character that reveal a sense of morality and high ideals, and thus you will experience many inner battles of conscience; how you resolve these issues is the key to your evolving psyche.

Birch Tree character holds the seed potential of all the signs, and therefore the virtue of patience is attributed to your sign. There is also a second-child aspect in the mythology associated with your sign that has an interesting psychological reaction: you may have to take on the role as head of the family, not through seniority of birth but because you take family responsibilities more seriously than your brothers or sisters. It is often the case that you are also the most successful family member in financial terms, but you are not inclined to flaunt your success or spend your money unwisely. There is a sense of loneliness operating within your psyche that manifests as a difficulty in expressing feelings. Successful marriages or partnerships may, as a result, occur later in life.

With 160, 167 or 186 your moral character is strengthened, and in business dealings you are regarded as a person of honesty and personal integrity. Your self-confidence and general vitality are also increased. While goals will be easier to achieve, you must beware of becoming too superior-minded. With 161, 182 or 198 your basic nature of looking inwards is activated, and although you should reach a high degree of material success, you may find yourself in an increasingly isolated position. With 158, 165, 179, 189, 195, 217, 219 or 273 your personal feelings are more easily expressed, and the chances are that you will eventually enjoy a happy and contented love life. The difficulty experienced in personal relationships is, however, your Achilles Heel, and the position of your Moon will clarify this aspect of character with greater insight into your whole psyche. Your Basic Paragraph is thus extended.

1

Birch
....
Moon in Aries

You have great self-determination, a force to be reckoned with once you have decided on your course of action. Your weak point, which can become an undermining influence, is a tendency to lose enthusiasm or self-confidence if others, especially partners, do not fully support your ideas. Nevertheless, you have strong leadership abilities that can win the day providing you don't resort to bullying tactics. Your Shadow self is a mirror image of your unconscious mind, a lunar dimension of character that reflects a compulsive inner need to compete and win at all costs. As a Birch Tree character, your natural reserve or cautious approach to life is often a source of irritation, best summed up as 'if only'. This type of negative response reveals a form of 'double thinking', which you use when referring to why you did not take the initiative sooner or why you made an impulsive decision or took a risky gamble against your better judgement. With 160 or 167 luck is on your side. It deflects any second thoughts and helps to promote an optimistic response with an enduring sense of humour. It also encourages fair-mindedness and high moral standards. With 159, 166, 180, 185, 196 or 202 your need for independence is marked and you have tremendous personal drive, but watch that quick temper. With 179, 212, or 217 you are a passionate lover, and though you may be reluctant to give up your freedom, when you do you will make someone a faithful and loyal partner. Overall, you lunar placing indicates powerful feelings that ensure an active love life.

Hidden agenda

Your hidden agenda is to initiate greater ideals in others, and by accomplishing this task you will resolve your battles of conscience and fulfil your karmic lesson. In past lives you have reached high office, but remained unmoved by the suffering of others and jealously guarded your authority. This residual memory haunts your dreams as you try hard to break away from the cold nature still inherent in you. During your lifetime you may have to make some personal sacrifices, but this must not be at the expense of other people's feelings or affections. In psychological terms you still have much to learn from working more closely with others and, by acknowledging their loyalty as well as their shortcomings, your innermost fear of loneliness can be allayed. Your robust physical and mental energy usually ensures excellent health and you are not likely to suffer from ill health or nervous complaints. If you do, however, it is likely to manifest as feverish complaints or migraines.

You are a thoroughly practical individual. You make your way through life quietly and effectively, creating your own lifestyle of comfort and security. You relate strongly to the arts, and your own creative skills have considerable merit either in business or as an artist. Your Shadow self is an enchanting lunar dimension of character, a projection of your unconscious mind that reveals a sensual nature and deep emotions. As a Birch Tree character you are therefore more demonstrative in expressing your feelings, but you must allow others to have their own dreams or personal desires, as you are inclined to be possessive. You are, however, a generous and well-intentioned person, and a caring parent and partner. With 165 or 167 this magnanimous character trait is both a blessing and a curse, as you may find it can become almost impossible to enjoy a private life of your own, especially if your career places you under the spotlight in fields such as politics or entertainment.

With 164 or 181 you will adapt more quickly to outward pressures and generally outwit any opponents. With 159 or 180 you will respond more aggressively and not suffer fools gladly. With 165 or 170 you are a romantic, and these aspects bode well for finding happiness in a relationship with a partner. Overall, your lunar position is a very stable influence regarding emotions, so personal relationships should be easier to handle. The only weakness is a jealous nature that can emerge if you sense that your partner is losing interest.

Hidden agenda

Your hidden agenda is to develop your creative talents and encourage others to be more appreciative of beauty and nature. This is your karmic lesson, and through teaching by example you will resolve the inner emptiness that has haunted your childhood, which has nothing to do with being materially rich or poor. This is a residual memory of past

2

Birch
....
Moon in
Taurus

lives when you never had time to wander around the countryside for pleasure, but had to earn a living by working hard on the land. In your current life you probably still enjoy gardening or growing exotic flowers. During your lifetime you will meet many unusually gifted people who have experienced both success and failure. Psychologically speaking, they represent a part of your personality that needs to evolve – a splinter fragment that needs to be fully integrated.

3
Birch
....
Moon in Gemini

You are a complex individual, prone to acting out of character every so often just for the sheer hell of it. But underneath that charade you have every intention of being taken seriously – at least when it suits you. You may have discovered early on in life that people are more amenable or approachable when they don't take you too seriously, for you have a more formidable side to your nature that places others at a disadvantage. Your Shadow self is a mirror image of your unconscious mind, a lunar dimension of character that flickers on and off like a faulty light bulb. While it can be a distraction for others, in that they are never quite sure of which way you will respond, if at all, you are learning a great deal about them. With 160, 167, 181, 186 or 203 your boundless curiosity of human nature embraces philosophical attitudes and indicates intellectual skills and interests. With 161 or 175 you have had to work hard to overcome your own doubts and fears, but will gain great knowledge in the process. With 165, 179, 201 or 217 your restless nature can be tamed with the right partner. Your lunar placing overall indicates an emotional need for movement or change, and this can put a strain on all personal relationships. But your gregarious personality attracts many admirers who enjoy your company, and this is perhaps your way of expressing your true nature.

Hidden agenda
Your hidden agenda is to be able to communicate freely and honestly. In past lives you were clever at weaving the truth to suit yourself or creating a false image in order to impress others. In your current life this residual memory still corrupts your thought pattern. During your lifetime you may have to start all over again in order to find your true bearings, for you are inclined to believe your own propaganda. Your karmic lesson is to transform your lower mind or base instincts into higher-mind morality. In psychological terms you respond to negative influences that can create a basic instability of character. But you may also discover a source of truth that lies within: *know thyself* should become your watchword.

You operate from polarizing your objectives into two main areas in your life, namely your career and family. Anything else is either irrelevant or not worth mentioning. The extreme nature of this approach to life can, however, place you on a knife-edge, both emotionally and materially. While you strive hard in order to reach a senior position in your career and make sure your partner and family are well provided for, you are in danger of denying your own needs and self-identity. Your Shadow self dwells within your unconscious mind, a lunar dimension of character that also needs to be nourished and understood. The love of your family is not enough, nor the recognition or success achieved in your work area. With 168 or 187 you have learned to believe in yourself, and with 170, 189 or 206 you have created a wonderful retreat away from the outside pressures of work. With 160 or 167 you have a wider outlook and generosity of spirit. With 161 or 175 you take life far too seriously on occasions, and you are prone to worry unduly about your health and family. Both aspects indicate the self-made man/woman. Overall, your lunar placing is a powerful influence and any aspects in your chart will emphasize significant character traits.

Hidden agenda

Your hidden agenda is to support others in their hour of need, but at the same time you must not let them drain you. Although you have great inner reserves and you are a resourceful person, especially in times of crisis, no one has an inexhaustible supply on tap. Your lunar position marks the turning of the solar year after the Summer Solstice, a time when the Druids believed the soul began to experience strange dreams. Your unconscious mind, therefore, is psychically active, especially at night, which is when dreams of past lives occur. While you may be aware of some details, your karmic lesson in your current life is to give with an open heart and avoid resentment. Your psychological profile suggests that as a child you may have been denied affection from your parents or perhaps they were overly protective, which can have the adverse effect of creating a claustrophobic atmosphere in the home. Either way, you must allow your own children and partner more space.

4

Birch
....
Moon in
Cancer

You have no trouble believing in yourself and this positive approach can inspire others, providing you don't cramp their style. As a Birch Tree character you are a warm and sincere person, but you can too easily become a snob or 'vain glorious', a term the Romans used when describing the first Celts they encountered in Gaul. You are therefore naturally drawn to public office or a high social position in your community. Your Shadow self projects a high profile, a lunar dimension of character that normally operates on a low-key frequency in your unconscious mind. This suggests that initially you were a shy child, who decided to attract attention by adopting a more glamorous or flamboyant image. With

5

Birch
....
Moon in
Leo

167 you inherited your good looks and social position. With 159, 166 or 185 your energy and personal motivation is an overpowering formula for success generally. With 160, 174 or 191 you will push your luck to the limit, but the combination of your Celtic Moon sign and lunar position indicates the ability of quickly reorganizing any setbacks to a future advantage. Your lunar position reflects a great deal of self-confidence. With regard to personal relationships, you will probably marry well, but while you have mutual respect and affection for each other, you must be careful not to adopt a domineering role with your partner and children.

Hidden agenda

Your hidden agenda is simply to take charge of your life and lead by example.

In past lives you were reluctant to involve yourself in other people's affairs and remained a self-contained individual who sat on the sidelines as an observer. Your karmic lesson, therefore, is to consciously develop humanitarian feelings and principles. During your lifetime you may wish that things were less hectic on the social scene, but you thrive on winning exclusive business contracts or achieving your goals by sheer will power and impressive tactics – the ultimate executive mind that relies on self-taught expertise. In psychological terms you may be a little too near the edge of unreasonable behaviour at times as a result of having an insatiable appetite for public acclaim. If you learn to step back every so often you may find that you have missed a great deal along the way.

6

Birch
··············
Moon in
Virgo

You are a person who prefers to work quietly in the background. This suits your need for personal privacy and the nature of your work, which requires complete concentration. Everything you do is highly focused, and this can result in the creation of a narrow perspective on life. No doubt you see it differently, and you will analyse this reading very carefully. Your Shadow self is a mirror image of your unconscious mind, a lunar dimension of character that reflects a probing mentality which can find the 'needle in the haystack'. It also reveals a depth of character not easily perceived by most people, only by close friends and family, and shows a great capacity for devotion or serving the community. With 208 you are

inclined to use this talent on a more superficial level, but it is an excellent aspect for dealing with or working for the media. With 204 you are a serious and dedicated researcher. With 170 or 269 your instinct or intuitive insight enables you to find obscure information missed by others. Your lunar position indicates measured emotions, which can be rather off-putting in all personal relationships. With 165, 167, 179 or 195, however, you express your feelings more readily. If with 161 or 182, you may suffer from an inferiority complex or find it difficult relating with others generally. On the other hand your lunar placing could be termed a most discriminating instinct when it comes to choosing a partner.

Hidden agenda

Your hidden agenda is to delve into unresolved issues in life while at the same time maintaining an open mind. Your karmic lesson is to follow the pathway relating to the narrow 'line of liberty' that the Druids identified with the equinoxes, which in the Celtic lunar zodiac traditionally indicated a need for balance and harmony at a time when the evolving soul was faced with critical decisions. During your lifetime you will therefore be confronted with much opposition from others if you pursue a line of no compromise. Your psychological profile indicates that you are a born worrier, but you are also prepared to stand your ground and keep cool if challenged. This type of siege mentality can, however, become counter-productive. It needs to be fully integrated into your psyche as a personal asset, not a persistent dissenting voice.

You are one of those people who knows how to work hard and play hard. It's quite a juggling act, but this is key to your success in life. You are also a smooth salesperson and a skilful negotiator, able to remain totally uncommitted or compromised. You are, nevertheless, a sentimental person when it comes to family loyalties and this can cost you dearly in terms of emotions and finances. Your Shadow self is a projection of your unconscious mind, a lunar dimension of character that prefers the easy middle path through life. But this can cause a few problems for someone who is determined to achieve a successful career or pursue ambitious objectives. With 174 or 208 you will fritter away money and become involved in frivolous schemes, while with 167, 181 or 186 you are generous to charities or people less fortunate than yourself. With 161, 168 or 204 you will budget more wisely and be less inclined to sit on the fence. In affairs of the heart it should also make you less gullible. Overall, your lunar placing indicates hot and cold emotions – changeable loyalties that can be a source of discontent in all personal relationships. You are also inclined to manipulate people. Look for positive aspects to Jupiter, Venus and Saturn to mitigate these traits.

Hidden agenda

Your hidden agenda is to maintain a harmonious balance or moderation in all things. This is your karmic lesson, a difficult and thankless task at times which relates to the Autumnal Equinox when the Druids decreed a state of truce if battles were being waged. During your lifetime you will probably be called upon to act as a neutral adviser or someone qualified to make a fair judgement. In past lives you tended to sit on the fence or avoid making moral judgements. Your psychological profile suggests a person equal to this task and, when your conscious mind is fully integrated into your own psyche, you may then understand that to err is a human frailty not an unforgivable sin. In your current life you are inclined to moralize without being aware of all the facts; this can stem from parents who were either rather puritanical or lacking moral courage.

7

Birch
. . . .
**Moon in
Libra**

8

Birch

....

Moon in Scorpio

You are into power games in a big way. Whether employed as a clerk or an executive, the area where you work is your personal arena of contest and trial. Your attitudes are often obsessive to the point of fanatical zeal. While you are indeed a dangerous adversary, you are also unswerving in your loyalty to friends. This aspect of character, however, has an unrelenting nature and it can be two-sided. You are capable of working for or against the law or society in general. Your Shadow self is a mirror image of your unconscious mind, a lunar dimension of character that strikes like a cobra. It can also soar like an eagle if in pursuit of justice. With 266 or 268 you will suppress your personal feelings and emotions and act outwardly with nerves of steel and chilling indifference. With 267 you will use your remarkable powers for the general good and if also with 279 you could help to create a fairer society. Your lunar placing shows intensely passionate emotions, which some people may find intimidating. In personal relationships either 160, 165, 167 or 170 will help you to express your true feelings without being overly aggressive or demanding. Overall, your lunar placing provides a strong survival instinct that enables you to create

new beginnings and rise to the top again should events take a downward turn.

Hidden agenda

Your hidden agenda is to consciously develop your analytical skills and intuitive insight so you can uncover hidden truths, not only within your psyche but also in relation to information that needs to be accessible in the public domain. Your fearless approach is not enough, however, and by helping other people to overcome their innermost fears in life, you will conquer many of your own demons. You have the power to influence others, and this must be scrupulously controlled on your part. During your lifetime you will experience every kind of personal trauma, but you are at your best when it comes to winning against impossible odds. In psychological terms you can be your own worst enemy at times. When you begin to realize that personal victories are meaningless if they are at the expense of destroying innocent or worthy opponents, then your sense of purpose is truly activated and your karmic lesson near completion. The combination of your Celtic Moon sign and lunar position indicates that your ideal vocation, if other aspects concur, is in the field of psychology or psychiatry.

9

Birch

....

Moon in Sagittarius

You have poise and self-confidence that is most impressive. You also possess a humorous wit, and despite being bluntly honest people warm to you, and this allows you to do business on a global scale. You have probably enjoyed travelling from an early age, which may be due to parents

working abroad or spending time with people who opened your mind to wider horizons. Your Shadow self is a projection of your unconscious mind, a lunar dimension of character that is a free spirit, albeit a restless influence which can undermine your innate sense of responsibility. Your concentration can therefore wax and wane depending on how you are feeling emotionally. With 160 or 181 this restless trait is more pronounced, but it has the effect of expanding your personal ambitions and making you think on many levels other than simply material objectives. With 166 or 167 your energy and enterprise is well directed, but with 174 you should seek advice if investing money. With 161 or 182 you can become bitterly frustrated by your own personal limitations. Your lunar placing indicates a need for freedom in any personal relationships, and you would be wise in not marrying too hastily or too early in life. You are likely to find someone from abroad or while on your travels who matches your ideal partner. Overall, your lunar position provides a boost of vibrant energy and raises your level of intellect.

Hidden agenda

Your hidden agenda is to develop your knowledge to a higher-mind level, and by accomplishing this task you may begin to comprehend the nature of the universal spirit that inspires humankind, a divine wisdom which the Druids referred to as *Awen*. In your last incarnation you experienced a spiritual conversion, but in your current life this light is still very dim; your karmic lesson is to re-kindle it and thus inspire others. During your lifetime you will seek answers to your many questions. While this does indicate travelling to other countries, it can also mean the self-exploration of your mind. Whatever the case may be, you will discover that what you are searching for lies much closer to home, but your experiences on the way are invaluable lessons, nevertheless. Your psychological profile suggests that you require a certain amount of personal freedom or space in which to operate, and providing you extend this independence to others, especially members of the family, then your sense of fair play is justified.

Your philosophy of life is simple: no pain, no gain. You have, however, set yourself up to be knocked down. While this harsh line probably stems from suffering certain indignities from an early age, by building an emotional fortress around yourself you have unwittingly shut the door on people who could really teach you otherwise. Your Shadow self, a projection of your unconscious mind, is a lunar dimension of character that has reverted to defensive measures in order to draw you backward into a spiralling descent of darkness where you feel safe.

This is not a wholly a negative experience, as it puts you in contact with the primal energies associated with the Winter Solstice that the Druids considered regenerative. But it's really a matter of *mistiming* or misinterpreting your true potential. With 161 or 182 you may remain locked into this emotional vacuum until the next return of Saturn, which occurs around your twenty-eighth birthday. With 167 or 168 you have every chance of overcoming the severity of this lunar placing. The inner strength of these two aspects promotes self-confidence, optimism and – most

10

Birch
....
Moon in
Capricorn

important of all – a self-determination that does not concede defeat. Overall, your lunar position indicates controlled emotions that can lack warmth or sincerity. Personal relationships are therefore difficult to maintain, as you dislike sentimentality in any form. Look for positive aspects to Venus and Neptune that will help to soften your nature.

Hidden agenda

Your hidden agenda is to break out of a mould of character that is both spiritually and mentally obsolete – a karmic lesson that requires a total transformation of heart and mind. By accomplishing this task you will inevitably help others along the way because you epitomize a 'pillar of strength' in your community. During your lifetime you may experience periods of darkness or bouts of despair, but remember that by looking into the abyss, the abyss will look back at you. Your psychological profile indicates a strength of mind that can conquer all, but its rigid nature must learn to bend like the birch tree. While the mighty oak tree has greater growth and longevity, the birch tree will grow on stony ground where oaks can never flourish.

11

Birch

··············

Moon in Aquarius

You are a visionary with the stamina and will power to influence generations to come. No matter how controversial your ideas or behaviour, you will attract the attention of other brilliant minds including the respect of people who see you as a dangerous radical. Your outspoken views will bring hope to people who have suffered great injustices. Although you may remain an aloof individual in public, those closest to you have witnessed first-hand your kindness and compassion. Your Shadow self is a mirror image of your unconscious mind, a lunar dimension of character that reflects a high level of natural intelligence not learned from books or conventional wisdom. Though you may gain some academic qualifications, it is more likely that you are self-taught when it comes to understanding the complex problems in life, which remain largely unresolved. They can cover a whole range of things, but in the scientific or mathematical world you have a unique insight. With 162 or 169 you may contribute many brilliant theories that are too bizarre or unconventional for others to grasp. If also with 161 or 175 you are more consistent and constructive in your efforts and will prove your theories with solid supportive evidence. With 176 you have a rebellious streak that can remain a stumbling block to achieving your goals. With 157 you are quick on the draw when it comes to public speaking or handling the media. With 170 you are a cultured and charming individual. Your lunar position overall indicates cool emotions that are nevertheless responsive to the needs of others.

Hidden agenda

Your hidden agenda is to become aware of the endless possibilities in life instead of accepting the narrow confines imposed by people who fear change. Your karmic lesson is not an easy task, as you have to overcome ignorance and bigotry while maintaining a compassionate nature at the same time. In past lives you were too proud to compromise. During your current lifetime, though, you may experience hostility or indifferent attitudes, but if you keep your faith you can win the argument.

You are highly intuitive and use your keen insight for practical purposes. Like a dowser looking for water that can be used for irrigation, this sixth sense enables you to make the right decisions in life. But life is never that simple, and you may have already found that what is right for you is not necessarily right for others, particularly those closest to you. You may therefore have to make concessions that are difficult to realize. Your Shadow self is a projected image of your unconscious mind, a lunar dimension of character that reveals a compassionate individual with a highly sensitive nature. With 163 you must be careful not to confuse the realities with personal fantasies, though with this aspect your intuition is at times extremely accurate. With 170 your appreciation of the arts and music stems from an inner sense of harmony or balance. With 267 your intuitive nature is highly focused and deeply penetrating. With 161 or 175 you may have to guard against developing neurotic tendencies, especially when emotionally upset. Overall, your lunar placing shows that emotional relationships are more sensitively handled and you

Your psychological profile reveals a high degree of nervous energy that requires firm control. Your need for independence can also increase the sense of isolation associated with your tree sign. If you learn to develop a more rational outlook you will find that people may not reject you or your ideas out of hand.

prefer to keep your private or family life as far away from your public life or career obligations as possible.

Hidden agenda
Your hidden agenda is to come to terms with what it is you really value most in life. In past lives you were a person of strong ideals who could not accept less than perfect standards. This residual memory carried over into your current life, hence your aversion to ugliness or pollution. It can also affect you physically, which results in strange allergies. During your lifetime you may often feel let down regarding close personal relationships, but this is largely due to your emotional nature which overreacts to any form of criticism or censure. Your psychological profile is one of alternating strengths and weaknesses – shifting waves of consciousness that spring from a basic duality of character. But you can adapt very quickly to changing circumstances in your life and your genuine concern for others will bring its own rewards. Your karmic lesson is to is to inspire others to have greater faith in themselves.

12

Birch
....
Moon in Pisces

Celtic moon sign: Rowan

Lunar symbol: Green Dragon

The *Green Dragon* is a Celtic lunar symbol of spiritual regeneration at the time of the year when light begins spiralling out again from darkness. In world myths, dragons represent the supernatural forces that usually guard great secrets and treasures. In Celtic myth the magical rowan tree was known as the 'tree of life', and each berry eaten was said to add a year to one's life and also heal the wounded. It was guarded by a fiery green dragon because its gift of immortality belonged to the gods. During the second lunar month the druids made rowan wands and ritually used them for divining the future. The rowan was also planted around dwellings and in lonely places as protection against evil spirits and the awesome force of lightning.

The Fire Festival of Brigantia was celebrated at the time of the New Moon during the rowan month, the name being derived from Brighid or Brigid, a young-maiden aspect of a Celtic triune goddess. She represented the power of the New Moon, spring, and the flowing sea. At the first glimmer of dawn the following day, the Cailleach, representing the old-crone aspect, was transformed into a fair young bride. According to the Arthurian legend, Candlemas, the Christianized version of this ancient ceremony, was the time when the Celtic knights and barons gathered around the stone holding the sword that would proclaim their rightful king. Arthur Pendragon was thus armed with a symbol of divine right at the time of the year when the penetrating light of the Sun was beginning to pierce the darkness of winter. The power of the Sun at this time relates to the planet Uranus, which represents the power of vision or progressive thinking that holds the key to humankind's own divinity.

Rowan Tree character

You were born at the time of the year when the sky was full of omens and a strange new light that took the force and form of lightning – a restless and stormy influence. Psychologically, it creates a radical response to life – a state of mind that can be at odds with conventional thinking. Basically, you have a different set of values to the rest of society because you are a visionary, which relates to your archetypal character Brigantia. The germination process of all thought yields original ideas, but the real measure of their worth is sometimes indefinable on a practical level. This can make you a target for ridicule or, in the extreme, someone who is regarded as a dangerous subversive. So while you may project an air of indifference, inwardly you are experiencing a sense of frustration that can become a major source of eccentric behavioural patterns. The significance of lighting the candles and torches at midnight, the 'magical hour of darkness' in honour of Brigantia, symbolically marks an 'awakening' of the whole psyche, a transformation that alters your state of consciousness. Your awareness or perception of life thus runs its own course.

Your ability to perceive a different and diverse set of ideals also stems from inherited or strong family influences – a different mind set that marks a line of highly inventive individuals who challenge stagnant ideologies and intransigent thinking. This innate sense of independent thinking is usually inherited from your grandmother, or possibly a great-grandmother, and it can be either a maternal or paternal link. You have also inherited her sense of frustration, and how you deal with it is the key to understanding and evolving your conscious self.

With 178, while you are tolerant of the ideas of others you can become totally transfixed by your own ideas, which curtails your argument. With 179 or 189 you are a persuasive and ardent campaigner who attracts loyal followers; it also denotes a warmer response in personal relationships. Generally speaking, your need for personal space and independence doesn't lean towards making permanent commitments of any kind. With 180 or 185 you are an activist in every sense of the word. With 181 or 186 your charitable nature and keen sense of justice is well directed and that inner sense of frustration less marked. Your drive and vitality is impressive. With 182 or 192 your lack of self-confidence is revealed in an inability to express your feelings and communicate generally, but while intensifying that inner frustration, your self-reliance becomes a formidable strength of character. With 183 or 193 your rebellious nature is fully empowered, and this requires more stable aspects. If with 186, 187, 242, 243, 250 or 264 your unconventional ideas will inspire others and your unique potential steadily evolves. The harmony or disharmony operating within your psyche is further clarified with the position of your Moon. Your Basic Paragraph is thus extended.

You have the fighting spirit of an intellectual gladiator. This can place you at the top of your profession almost overnight, as your direct approach cuts through red tape or normal procedures of promotion. While you will have the backing or loyalty of old friends in all your endeavours, you will also incur envy, jealousy and treachery behind the scenes so watch your back. Your Shadow self dwells in your unconscious mind, a lunar dimension of character that reveals a passionate commitment to forcing change through original ideas and objectives, which can be quite unnerving for people who lack your imagination or vision. Your response to their intransigence can make you more determined and less sympathetic at times, but then again you tend to thrive on challenges and innovation. A need for caution is, however, paramount when dealing with people who appear to back you without question; they are playing a more sinister game in which you may become expendable. With 160 or 167 you know how to win over the most difficult adversaries

13

Rowan
....
Moon in Aries

because you have strong morals and noble ideals. With 159 or 173 your physical and mental stamina places you in a superior position, but your long-term staying power is less predictable. With 158 or 165 you can win the hearts and minds of the most cynical souls, but don't play this social charm card too often – only in an emergency. With 162 or 169 your visionary mind has tapped into a source of scientific discovery that denotes a New Age pioneer. Your lunar placing overall has fired your emotions and ideals, but while you will attract loyal friendships, your love life or personal affairs are more erratic and thus less stable.

Hidden agenda

Your hidden agenda is complex. You are destined to create waves which can have a habit of swamping your own back yard every so often. In past lives you were a law until yourself and this residual memory has reared its head in your current life. During your lifetime you will confront bigotry and ignorance, but the most important issue is coming to terms with your inner frustrations, which are capable of undermining your unique talents. This is part of your karmic lesson, and when you can extend it to expressing your feelings with more sensitivity to your partner you will experience an inner harmony that can transform your whole psyche. Your psychological profile suggests an inner battle for supremacy between your heart and mind. This can lead to a constant state of mental trauma. The key to finding a solution is learning to think more compassionately and to act less impulsively.

14

Rowan
· · · · · · · · · · · ·
Moon in Taurus

You have an agreeable disposition which makes you a popular companion and work colleague, but as a Rowan Tree character you also have some strong opinions that can be controversial. You have discovered early on in life that by remaining calm and apparently conciliatory you can change the attitudes of others, albeit a gradual process. So while you appear to remain consistent, you are absorbing and reconstructing a great deal of information. Your Shadow self is a mirror image of your unconscious mind, a lunar dimension of character that reveals deeply rooted convictions and motives. You work from an inner sense of knowing exactly where you are going in life. This can, however, create a false sense of security in a rapidly changing world. With 179 or 217 you have artistic talents and you enjoy socializing; these aspects are also excellent for loving relationships. With 159 or 166 you are quicker off the mark, and with 160 or 167 you have a magnetic personality and many influential friends. With 161 or 175 you have a predisposition to learning things the hard way, though on the whole this serves to strengthen your convictions and motivation. With 162 or 169 you are a complete individualist with highly specialized talents – ideal for work involved with New Age research. With 176 your headstrong opinions can cause unnecessary conflict in both your personal and professional life. Nevertheless, overall your lunar position is a stable influence emotionally and encourages highly creative but practical ideas.

Hidden agenda
Your hidden agenda is an instructive programme of building bridges or conscious awareness. Providing you don't become too complacent you can evolve away from your own inner fear of insecurity, which may be both emotional and financial. Your karmic lesson is to develop your inner strength of self-reliance. In a recent past life you decided to compromise your ideals for others who let you down. During your lifetime you may travel widely, but you are reluctant to move away from your home base once established. Psychologically speaking, though you enjoy meeting people and learning new skills, you require a consistent routine in order to feel truly at one with yourself. Your strong need to establish a self-identity once again stems from past lives experience, a residual lunar memory that currently enforces a sense of personal commitment.

15

Rowan
. . . .
Moon in Gemini

You are a hyperactive individual, always involved with new projects and generally keeping abreast of any pending changes because you are well informed. As a Rowan Tree character your whirlwind mind and highly charged energy are designed to combat apathy and stir up controversy wherever you go. The only trouble is you are so prone to change your own mind that others are never sure what you are really trying to say. Your Shadow self is a projection of your unconscious mind, a lunar dimension of character that is multi-faceted; consequently, you are a consummate actor of many parts. But while it may be very entertaining and at times highly provocative, you are on a steep learning curve when it comes to understanding the rest of humanity. With 161 or 175 you may start to take yourself too seriously. With 165 you are a snake charmer: a fascinating act to watch. With 159 your independent viewpoints win respect. With 160 or 167 you may become a champion of worthy causes, though inclined to overact on occasion. With 162 you have a highly charged emotional nature, which can become explosive and irrational, but your intellectual abilities are astounding. With 176 your lack of tact wins few friends, but with 168 or 169 your approach is more constructive and you can handle any criticism with a skilful defence. Overall, your lunar position indicates numerous friendships and love affairs.

Hidden agenda
Your hidden agenda is to find a cohesive strategy in order to utilize your unusual and unique potential. Your articulate powers of speech and coherent thinking are a great personal asset, but this is not enough. During your current life you are inclined to court controversy, and the course of rebound is therefore self-created. In past lives you absorbed a great deal of knowledge without realizing its worth or merit, and this residual memory is a constant reminder to raise your superficial

level of intelligence to a more profound understanding. Your psychological profile reveals a high degree of nervous tension, which can lead to many forms of neuroses. On the other hand you are a highly intelligent individual who needs a great deal of personal space in which to operate. If this criteria is met, your current journey of self-discovery will expand on all levels, and this is your karmic lesson.

16

Rowan
....
Moon in
Cancer

Your sensitivity and compassionate nature is an endearing character trait. You have highly psychic powers and a canny insight combined with a thoroughly modern or advanced method of analysing information or new technology. Your association with the paranormal indicates group-mind activity where you can provide a healing touch. Your Shadow self dwells within your conscious mind, a lunar dimension of character that reveals a need for respect and recognition. But, this residual emotion must evolve into giving freely without any ulterior motives or self-centred expectations. The lunar aspects are particularly significant with this placing. With 160 or 167 you have the ability to make a powerful impact for the good or benefit of others. With 164 or 169 you are highly intelligent and in control of your emotions, adaptable and quick-witted. With 161 or 175 your need for respect stems from basic lack of self-confidence and hypersensitivity to personal criticism. In time, however, your mental and psychic abilities become formidable strengths. With 162 you are prone to unpredictable mood swings and bizarre behaviour. With 163 your intuition is less reliable, but if with 170 or 288 you have remarkable powers that are positively directed. Overall, your lunar position shows a sympathetic nature that strengthens family ties and personal relationships.

Hidden agenda

Your hidden agenda is to learn a sense of responsibility. In past lives you followed a fine line between genuine compassion and self-created martyrdom. Your karmic lesson in your current life, therefore, is to avoid false sentiments that compromise your integrity. During your lifetime you will witness many strange or bizarre incidents, due to your highly developed psychic abilities. But your belief system is by no means conventional, and can at some stage be completely centred on either materialism or spiritual matters. Your psychological profile reveals a strong resistance to taking advice, and also an inability to accept failure. Consequently, you must learn to develop a totally new emotional response pattern if you are to raise your consciousness to new dimensions of self-awareness.

The strength of your convictions works overtime. You are basically a proud and self-reliant individual who works from the premise that everything in life is on offer for those willing to make the effort. Your energy and enthusiasm for life makes you a natural leader in any chosen profession or sphere of influence. Your Shadow self, a lunar dimension of character, projects a powerful personal aura that attracts a wide audience, with you taking a centre-stage role. On a personal level, however, you are not the easiest person to live with, despite your affectionate nature, as you are inclined to subjugate those closest to you. With 160 or 167 you are more magnanimous, and your passionate desire to help others is reflected in everyday living. With 159 or 166 you are hooked on power-games and you are an aggressive activist in any arena. With 168 your intellectual capacity is well directed and your emotions are more controlled. With 161 or 175 your authoritative manner can become dictatorial, but you make up for it with total honesty and practical solutions. With 162 or 169 you are a brilliant strategist and a highly intelligent and inventive individual. With 163 or 177 you are inclined to have unrealistic ideas or ambitions that lack practical application. With 170 your intuitive insight is a powerful aid in achieving worthwhile objectives. Overall, your lunar position adds a touch of glamour to your life.

Hidden agenda
Your hidden agenda is to develop strength from within and transform your consciousness and personal principles to a higher level. During your lifetime you may experience long periods of self-imposed isolation or self-doubt, but ultimately you will discover that your own sense of individuality has unique value. In past lives you developed a powerful ego that demanded attention and respect. This residual memory can still manifest as arrogant or pompous behaviour, hence your periods of reflection. Your psychological profile also shows a need to impose your own will on others, but while this is rarely for personal gain, it does reveal an inborn sense of superiority. This pronounced characteristic can become unacceptable socially, but among your closest friends it strikes a different chord of leadership and personal integrity that wins their respect, and this is your karmic lesson in life.

You have a mission in life. You are a single-minded individual with an analytical approach to complex issues or subjects. Your emotional feelings also come under close scrutiny to such an extent that any personal demonstrative acts appear to be carefully calculated beforehand. Your Shadow self, which dwells in your unconscious mind, is a lunar dimension of character that has a suspicious nature when it comes to dealing with other people's motivations or apparent interest. You have what can best be described as the 'sleuth' mentality – a profoundly curious mind combined with astute powers of observation and attention

17

Rowan
. . . .
Moon in Leo

18

Rowan
. . . .
Moon in Virgo

to minute detail. You also have personal eccentricities that can manifest in strange ideas or remedies for health problems. With 162, 169 or 188 you may become a science-fiction writer or perhaps some kind of science adviser. You are a brilliant researcher with interests in the paranormal or in the revolutionary methods used in modern science. With 164 or 167 your curious mind is well channelled into practical but expansive projects. These aspects also denote a high degree of intelligence. Your lunar position generally, however, casts a difficult influence for personal relationships. With 165 or 170 your ability to express genuine emotions is activated and should continue to evolve throughout life. But with 161, 172 or 175 you may choose to remain unmarried or uncommitted, and genuine friendships may better suit your temperament. With 160 you may even decide to become a missionary.

Hidden agenda

Your hidden agenda is to develop your self-confidence and allow the external pain or sorrows of others to touch your heart and mind; this is your karmic lesson to learn. In past lives you were a compassionate thinker and practical administrator regarding human affairs, but you were always more comfortable evaluating people's needs at a distance. During your current life you will become involved firsthand with many human sagas and tragedies. Your cool and controlled emotional nature is very well suited to helping people on a practical and humanitarian level. During this progressive period in your life you should begin to emerge as a truly rare humanitarian. If you read the mythology of the Vine sign, your lunar dimension of character is further defined. Psychologically speaking, you tend to worry about your health and this can take the form of hypochondria.

19

Rowan
....
Moon in
Libra

You are a persuasive and articulate communicator. Your staying power or personal stamina can, however, be difficult to maintain at times, and you can become both unpredictable and quickly disillusioned. This applies to current projects as well as personal relationships. While you have an inner sense of harmony and tolerance, you are easily knocked off balance when people or situations do not comply with your own ideals. Your Shadow self is a projection of your unconscious mind, a lunar dimension of character that recoils from unpleasant or distasteful confrontations. On the other hand you can become extremely manipulative when it suits you, and thus you may find that you unwittingly create a source of friction. With 164 or 166 you are clever enough to cover your tracks. With 165 or 179 your powers of persuasion are finely balanced with genuine concern for the feelings and welfare of others. With 159 your razor-sharp wit is both provocative and flippant. With 160 or 167 you have great humour and intelligence. With 162 you never make compromises, and with 161 you are given to erratic mood swings of depression and elation. Your lunar position overall signifies a powerful rapport operating within your psyche that creates a basic harmony of personality and character.

Hidden agenda

Your hidden agenda is to maintain your position in life without becoming too contrary or inclined to change your allegiances. In past lives you learned some very subtle lessons of diplomacy and compromise, but during your current life you may experience painful adjustments, which can dent your ego. Your karmic lesson, therefore, is to guard against bitter recriminations so you can achieve the cooperation and love from others that has always eluded you – a personal quest that relates, metaphysically speaking, to the disappearing light in winter. In psychological terms you are a person with an identity crisis. Personal relationships hold the key to your spiritual development as well as your conscious sense of identity. Your partners therefore have strong karmic links, which usually go back many centuries.

You are a revolutionary thinker who believes in the power and freedom of the individual. You have great passions and emotions but these are often repressed on the surface, belying an inner turbulence of mighty proportions – almost like an explosive cocktail waiting to be served. The all-important timing mechanism is, however, as complex as your mentality and visionary ideals. Your Shadow self is a mirror image of your unconscious mind, a lunar dimension of character that dramatically responds to the phases of the Moon, with the New Moon initiating fundamental decisions and changes and the Full Moon exposing turbulent or unfulfilled emotions. It is your inner sense of failure that has created a stormy reservoir of emotion. With 266 or 273 the depths of your emotions can only be plumbed by your unconditional love of another. With 268 or 277 your need for independence exposes a ruthless streak that will sever any ties or personal relationships which stand in the way. With 264 or 267 your feelings are warmly expressed and your general approach to life is more conciliatory and thoughtful. With 164, 165, 166 or 167 your emotions are more controlled and you can achieve your goals with less struggle or rancour. With 159, 173 or 176 your explosive temper is too frequently released with damaging consequences. With 168 or 204 you take life more seriously, and these aspects provide stability in any chart. The overall influence of your lunar position has intensified your emotions and ideals.

Hidden agenda

Your hidden agenda is to learn self-discipline by objectively studying and reflecting upon your passionate innermost desires. In past lives you have consciously created a need to feel powerful as a result of feeling emotionally insecure. This residual memory remains an aggressive thought pattern which must be transformed. As part of your karmic lesson, therefore, during your lifetime you will

20

Rowan
....
Moon in
Scorpio

experience a number of personal transformations – a rebirthing, which relates to the Celtic Fire Festival of Samhain. If you read the mythology of the Reed sign you should be able to connect your personal experiences to the continuous cycle of spiritual regeneration associated with the Druid's belief in reincarnation. Your psychological profile suggests a need to probe into the deeper mysteries of life, primarily because of your need to see yourself clearly on the deepest levels, and this is the second part of your karmic lesson. The occult or esoteric teachings found in ancient philosophies will provide the necessary keys.

21

Rowan
············
Moon in Sagittarius

You are a world citizen with no particular allegiances, save your own ideals and original philosophies. You are basically a progressive thinker who readily adapts and absorbs new techniques as a matter of course. Your Shadow self dwells in your unconscious mind, a lunar dimension of character that instils a sense of eternal optimism in everything you do. While others find you a source of encouragement and stimulation, your need for total independence can limit the potential for intimate relationships. However, there is a powerful emotional need for friendships of like-minded people, which in time may lead you to discover a kindred spirit who fits your ideal partner. With 165 or 170 you are a secret romantic, and often find personal happiness unexpectedly or during the course of a journey. With 160 or 167 you are drawn to partners with whom you have an intellectual rapport. With 162 or 220 you are inclined to unconventional relationships that suit both parties. With 164 or 186 you have a generous spirit and greater tolerance in general. With 166 you are an ardent lover and a passionate campaigner for animal rights. Your lunar position overall identifies with the spiritual liberation of humankind that goes hand in hand with environmental issues and protecting wildlife.

Hidden agenda

Your hidden agenda is to raise your consciousness from superficial standards or ideals by learning the art of discrimination. In past lives your refusal to commit yourself wholeheartedly, either personally or professionally, developed into a form of hypocrisy as you strove to maintain your position in life. During your lifetime, therefore, your karmic lesson is being confronted with having to make truthful statements as a result of talking yourself into untenable situations. Your psychological profile indicates a highly nervous and restless individual who can nevertheless achieve a high success rate in all personal endeavours. Overall, you possess a highly charged energy that requires positive control and direction. Your greatest personal asset is an inborn sense of humour.

You have an inborn sense of duty that can be at odds with your need for independence. You are also a very private individual despite being drawn towards positions of authority, which inevitably attract attention. Your Shadow self is a mirror image of your unconscious mind, a lunar dimension of character that is highly sensitive to criticism or rejection by others. There is usually a strong inner need for a father figure with this lunar placing, due either to a lack of contact or never having time to establish a father–child relationship. The reasons may vary from premature death to divorce or absences from home, or perhaps your father was not an easy man with whom to establish close ties of affection. For men, it can manifest later as a strong conscious need to become a father. With 175, 182 or 192 parental influence has been demanding – even harsh at times. With 160, 167, 181 or 186 you have benefited from a responsible and favourable upbringing. With 165 or 170 you have been endowed with good looks and a natural grace that attracts many admirers. With 161, 182 or 209 you are inclined to brood about past injustices or personal slights. With 159 or 166 your aggressive nature hides an inferiority complex. With 162 or 169 you have inherited a brilliant and enquiring mind. With 163 or 184 you have inherited highly psychic abilities. Overall, your lunar position adds a more cautious approach to life and represses emotions. On the positive side it provides great inner strength and self-discipline.

Hidden agenda

Your hidden agenda is to stand alone in the sense of being responsible for your own actions, and thus evolve an inner maturity. This is a karmic lesson, and therefore in your current life you will experience the harsh realities of life to an extreme degree. Your lunar position marks the time of the Winter Solstice, a testing time which, according to the Druids, marked the evolutionary progress of the individual and humankind universally. In past lives, due to your highly sensitive nature you were inclined to retreat from situations that threatened your emotional and financial security. Consequently, your psychological profile indicates a certain resignation to fate having dealt you a hard hand to play in life. This can, if you are not careful, take the form of negative thinking or accepting your lot too readily.

22

Rowan
....
Moon in Capricorn

You are a unique individualist, born at the time of the New Moon that marked the Celtic Fire Festival of Brigantia. The ritual use of fire to symbolize light is a very ancient custom, and is still practised in most religions around the world. The significance of the Fire Festival of Brigantia was to evoke the spirit of light at a time of winter darkness, and it also marks the New Year in China. Your Shadow self is a projection of your unconscious mind, a lunar dimension of character that can remain a latent influence for many years. Basically, it symbolizes

23

Rowan
....
Moon in Aquarius

advanced knowledge or inventive genius, which is difficult for others to comprehend – including yourself. As a result you can become extremely frustrated as to why you perceive things differently to the rest of society. It can also compound learning difficulties, but there will come a time when you begin to recognize its true value. With 157 or 171 you may try to be too clever, and your quick-wit out-runs your real depth of knowledge. With or 164 or 167 you are able to communicate your ideas freely and intelligently. With 158 you rely on charm, and with 159 you rely on personal authority. With 160 or 167 you adopt the ethical or moralist approach, and with 161 you pursue your goals with chilling indifference. With 163 or 177 you are intuitively guided but inclined to follow false prophets. With 169 your visionary mind finds creative and highly lucrative outlets, and with 168 or 170 you are a dedicated humanitarian. With 162 you are a supreme antagonist, a born revolutionary and egocentric. Your lunar placing overall indicates an egocentric

behavioural pattern coupled with a lack of emotions, which can limit any form of personal intimacy. Look for positive aspects to Venus and Jupiter, or positive aspects between Venus, Jupiter and Neptune.

Hidden agenda

Your hidden agenda is to recognize your own divinity as part of a collective whole, not the other way round. A great many people born with your lunar combination of position and place in the Celtic lunar zodiac are inclined to be dispassionate agnostics or confirmed atheists. Your karmic lesson in your current life is to discover first-hand that scientific knowledge and modern technologies become mindless and dangerous if controlled by soulless people. Your psychological profile reveals an intense pride which inflates your ego. There is, however, another side which has all the hallmarks of an extraordinary and exceptional humanitarian. These special qualities are your guiding light for inspiration and eventual spiritual growth.

24

Rowan
············
Moon in
Pisces

You have the soul of a mystic and the visionary mind of an intellectual. While you can intuitively find your way through the labyrinth of life, you also manage to make rational deductions from the irrational or the bizarre. Your Shadow self dwells in your unconscious mind, a lunar dimension of character that has formed a bridge with your conscious self. It not only provides a rare insight into your own destiny, but it may also provide a keen observation of the

changing world as we approach the twenty-first century. With 163 your intuitive nature though inspired, especially through artistic talents, can become unstable and weaken your strength of mind. With 177 you lean towards unreality at crucial times in your life when more caution is required. With 170 you are receptive to ideas and have a vivid imagination that can be positively channelled into the arts or writing fictional stories of a high calibre. You also enjoy your own company for long periods at a time. With 157 there is a danger you can become too inward-thinking, but with 166 you are quick to learn new skills and have an intuitive knowledge of many subjects. With 158 or 165 you are a born romantic and poet. With 166 you are more direct in your speech or attitude, and with 167 you have a deep compassion and reverence for all living creatures. With 162 you are a highly intelligent individual whose ideas, though brilliantly conceived and expressed, are far beyond the understanding of others. With 169 your highly original thinking is more readily expressed and received. With 175 or 205 you are – not to put too fine a point on it – a self-taught genius. With 168 you may well become a formidable expert in your chosen field. Your lunar placing overall requires mental stability, so if with 164, 242, 243, 251 or 258 you are likely to achieve a high degree of success in all personal endeavours.

Hidden agenda

Your hidden agenda is to find order in your own personal scheme of things, as you work from the premise that the world around you is in chaos. While it may appear so, chaos begins from within and projects outwardly. This is not to say that chaos does not exist in the outer world, but its source is intrinsically linked to the primordial depths of human nature. Your karmic lesson during your current life is to try to solve many puzzles and, although you may lose your perspective from time to time, you are destined to perceive with great clarity of thought and vision. Your psychological profile indicates great vulnerability and sensitivity, which can have the effect of shutting down your psychic circuits as a protection against forming neuroses. You may therefore seek solitude or retreat in order to recharge your batteries. Your perfect transition or personal development rests with confronting the truth within.

Celtic moon sign: Ash

Lunar Symbol: Sea-horse

The lunar symbol of the *Sea-horse* is a Celtic zoomorphic art symbol associated with Sea-gods, having been devised as part horse and part fish. The importance of archetypal symbolism was later incorporated in heraldry, and the symbol of the Sea-horse, representing the Irish Sea-god Lir, forms the ancient crest of the city of Belfast in Northern Ireland.

Lir can be identified with the Greek Sea-god Poseidon or the Roman counterpart Neptune. Astrologically speaking, the mystical qualities associated with all Sea-gods represent the unknown and as yet unformed forces or energies that greatly influence the Ash Tree character. The planet Neptune is not easily defined, even to this day, as it represents a nebulous stage of evolution that contains a chaos aspect, but its sublime or ultimate goal is in raising humankind's level of consciousness above the subjective state of desire. In Celtic myth the ash tree was primarily associated with powerful Sea-gods and with enchantment. During the third lunar month of the year the Druids made magical wands from its slender young spiral branches, and its wood was used as a talisman against drowning. In Arthurian legend Lir's counterpart is the mystical Fisher King, whom Sir Galahad healed after receiving the Holy Grail.

Ash Tree character

You were born at the time of the year when the awesome power of the sea pounded the shorelines around Ireland and Britain. Though a natural phenomenon, to the ancient Celts it represented a force of nature that humans had little or no control over, hence they identified it with the restless spirit of their Sea-god Lir. The month of the ash is the last lunar month of winter in the Celtic calendar, and symbolizes a turbulent confrontation of light and dark. Psychologically it has a polarizing effect that manifests within your psyche as a basic duality of character. So while you may have an artistic and sensitive nature, you can suddenly change course like a tempest and appear relatively calm and pragmatic. Nevertheless there remains an inner depth of emotion or sensitivity which makes you vulnerable to external influences. It is difficult, therefore, to assess your true nature or motives. However, you understand the more base elements of humankind as well as its

spiritual nature, and as a result you tend to adopt an amoral viewpoint when trying to establish your own personal boundaries or ethics.

You have inherited psychic gifts that can lie dormant for many years. There are strong links with the maritime world and the medical profession; your archetypal influence is associated with the Fisher King, placing an emphasis on healing and nautical skills. The mystical spiritual link may also manifest with a strong attraction towards religion or spiritual matters. While this is usually associated with your father's side of the family, the Moon exerts a powerful ancestral feminine influence, which indicates a lineage of strong matriarchal characters on both sides.

With 178 you are a dreamer and poet. With 179 you have the romantic soul of an idealist. With 180 you respond to challenges with a subtle wit. With 181 you are a compassionate healer and generous to a fault. With 182 you tend to bottle up your emotions, but you are generally more self-reliant. With 183 you respond erratically but with great humanity. With 184 you are a true mystic, though always in danger of being affected by the unstable or negative energies that you tend to attract. With 185 your physical and mental energy is well directed. With 186 or 187 you will fully develop your personal skills. With 188 you are a brilliant strategist. With 189 you have a calm and pleasant temperament. With 194 you can become overly fascinated by strange cults or morally weakening influences. With 204, 234 or 242 you have a strong free will, and physical and mental stamina that directs you to the top of your profession. Overall, the strengths and weaknesses of your sign are usually well-balanced compensating features, but the position of your Moon will determine whether your depth of emotion can be reasonably controlled. Your Basic Paragraph is thus extended.

You are a self-sufficient person who shows great initiative in times of personal crises. You are also receptive to the ideas of others, but will retain your independence. While you can become impatient – mainly with yourself – when things don't always go according to plan, it is only because you are inclined to overlook the finer details in an effort to gain an advantage. Your Shadow self is a projection of your unconscious mind, a lunar dimension of character that reveals a need to set new standards, particularly in the arts or entertainment industry. Whatever your chosen field (there is also a strong association with the medical profession), you will be drawn to areas that require a complete update or a new look. With 165 or 179 your artistic skills are highly creative and original. With 159 you may attract public acclaim at some stage. With 160 or 167 you are more likely to become involved with the medical profession as a surgeon or a psychiatrist, since you are a natural healer and technician. With 161 or 175 your ability to learn from painful experiences will contribute great practical knowledge. With 162 your courage, though admirable, can become foolhardy. With 176 your emotional temperament has a short fuse, but you are a passionate campaigner for human rights.

With 163 your psychic nature is highly advanced, but you lack sound common sense. With 170 you have great charm and personal magnetism, and with 164 or 166 you know how to communicate your ideas with artistry, intelligence and controlled passions. Your lunar influence overall requires control and more stability. If with 204, 232, 251 or 258 your creative skills and ideas, though often inspired, are carefully stage-managed to perfection.

Hidden agenda

Your hidden agenda is to develop a singular purpose and self-identity that is in harmony with your emotions and mind. In past lives you were highly susceptible to personal flattery that misdirected your time and energy – a residual karmic memory which influences your current life. During your lifetime you will therefore have to come to terms with feelings of guilt or indecisiveness. Your psychological profile indicates certain inhibitions, which stem from a lack of coherent objectives. Yours is truly a voyage of self-discovery, which can become an exciting challenge if properly addressed. Basically, you have an inner vitality that can be transformed into highly creative skills and compassionate ideals, and this is your karmic lesson to learn.

25

Ash
....
Moon in
Aries

26

Ash

....

Moon in Taurus

You are a gentle and well-mannered individual, and there is a quality about you that people find most attractive and reassuring. But you are not a pushover when it comes to standing your ground against injustices or interference from others; underneath that calm exterior beats a passionate heart and mind, whose ideals are not easily compromised or undermined. Your Shadow self is a mirror image of your unconscious mind, a lunar dimension of character that exerts a powerful emotive influence over everything you do or become involved with. While you have an inner need for emotional and financial security, you are likely to be drawn to vocational careers which can lack reliable or profitable material rewards. With 165 your appreciation of the arts shows refined tastes and financial security is assured. With 160 you have noble ideals and your popularity and luck is an enduring factor. With 161 you are inclined to make harsh judgements, but with 167 you have greater integrity. With 162 you have original style, but with 163 your creative skills require discipline. With 172 you are too easily discouraged, but with 179 you have a natural radiance that inspires others – an excellent aspect for artistic achievement and lucky breaks.

With 166 your energy and enthusiasm never falters, but with 173 or 177 your concentration and motivation can dissolve in an instant. Your lunar position is deemed to be a most beneficial influence, and therefore any negative aspects are considered less effective and can be seen as necessary reminders not to become too complacent or idle. Personal relationships are also less likely to fail.

Hidden agenda

Your hidden agenda is to reach a state of contentment by realizing your needs rather than your desires. This is your karmic lesson, and therefore means developing a new set of values and letting go of any emotional jealousies that may be aroused from time to time; in past lives you were inclined to store up resentment if thwarted in love. During your lifetime you may experience some very basic struggles for survival, and this will make you more determined than ever to create a safer environment around yourself. Your psychological profile, not surprisingly, reveals a behavioural pattern that is largely controlled by your conscious mind as you rarely act on impulse. Your basic instincts, however, are uncannily accurate and a measure of your inner knowledge.

27

Ash

....

Moon in Gemini

You are a fluent conversationalist and an eager participant of life. However, because you have a low boredom threshold you rarely make any lasting contributions – but then again your vivid imagination means that your fascinating ideas are often picked up and promoted

by others who can see their true potential. Your Shadow self is a projection of your unconscious mind, a lunar dimension of character that never sleeps, always alert to the possibilities in life. It results in an insatiable curiosity that stems from a high degree of nervous energy and conflicting emotions. So changeable are your opinions and feelings that others can find you hard to keep up with and even harder to really know. With 166 your agile mind and butterfly emotions are unrestrained. With 165 you have a magnetic personality and you are a leading light in your social scene. With 159 your sharp wit and artistic ability combine to make you a natural comedian or actor. With 160 you are a multi-talented individual, and with 167 your humanitarian ideals indicate a vocational career. With 161 you are more seriously minded, though inclined to sudden depressions. With 162 you have a rare genius bordering on the bizarre. With 163 you are highly psychic, but such gifts require self-discipline as well as training. With 164 you absorb facts and figures easily and have a more focused mind. With 170 you may even find your true soul mate. Your lunar position overall requires stability and positive direction if you are to harness fully your unusual talents. With 168 or 169 you can be highly successful, but with 175 you are capable of truly great things. With 173 or 177, however, you are too easily disillusioned and are inclined to rely a little too heavily on your charm.

Hidden agenda

Your hidden agenda is to learn to appreciate the opinions and talents of others. In past lives you insisted on retaining your sense of freedom at all costs, which made it almost impossible for others to get close enough to love and understand you. It also had the effect of making you fail to appreciate the contributions made by others. During your current lifetime this residual memory encourages you to move around from place to place seeking an ideal location. Psychologically speaking, this reflects a search for your own identity. There is, however, a mystical reason for your restlessness: you have much to say that has a special message or meaning for a great many people. It is likely, therefore, that even if you do settle down in one place you will continue to travel, as this need for movement and freedom is essential for your self-growth and well-being. It is also your karmic lesson.

Y ou are a sympathetic listener and confidante. While inclined to over-dramatize your own problems, you are nevertheless extremely sensitive to the feelings of others. You are also a natural medium who can pick up distress signals from complete strangers, and within your own close circle of friends and family your ability is quite amazingly accurate. Your Shadow self is a projection of your unconscious mind, a lunar dimension of character that is doubly emphasized with the position of your Moon. The lunar cycles therefore greatly influence your mood swings, which can reach extreme highs and lows. Starting with the New Moon, your initiative and sense of optimism is activated, reaching a crescendo around the Full Moon, and then it can suddenly dissolve into bouts of depression or a lack of self-confidence. It may not always follow such an extreme course – it all

28

Ash
....
Moon in Cancer

depends on what is going on in your life. If under stress it is usually fully activated, but even during periods of relative normality you will find that your energy and motivation continues to rise and fall with the waxing and waning cycle of the Moon. With 160 it promotes your higher mind ideals, but with 161 it shows pessimistic moods. With 163 it evokes your intuitive powers and with 266 intensifies your feelings of insecurity. With 164 or 167 it helps to evolve a high degree of intelligence. With 165 or 170 it enhances your expression of feelings and artistic talents. With 168 it adds greater stability all round. With 169 your sympathetic nature is combined with intelligent analysis and original solutions. With 159 or 174 you are less willing to support others and can become too self-centred. With 175, although you are still prone to mood swings, you will gradually learn to organize your lifestyle through persistent effort and will power.

Hidden agenda

Your hidden agenda is to learn to let go of the emotional baggage that you have accumulated from your earliest memories. In past lives you were prone to making yourself physically and emotionally ill in order to gain sympathy or avoid having to face up to difficult situations. During your lifetime, as part of your karmic lesson, you will experience more than your fair share of family burdens or responsibilities, but it will have the effect of strengthening your character and stabilizing your highly sensitive emotions. Your psychological profile reveals a hypersensitivity to arguments or harsh conditions, which suggests that you have been emotionally bruised or suffered a deprived childhood. Part of your inner drive for security and recognition certainly stems from feelings of inadequacy. As a result you should become a loving – if overly indulgent – parent, and by cherishing others you will fulfil your karma.

29

Ash
....
Moon in Leo

You are a born actor, a glamorous individual who projects an air of self-confidence – despite the fact that behind the scenes you are a very shy and private person. You are an artiste, however, with a fiery temperament ideally suited for playing passionate roles. The more sensitive part of your nature adds a touch of genuine sympathy and human frailty. Your Shadow self dwells in your unconscious mind, a lunar dimension of character that reveals a need to be loved and admired. In turn you are an affectionate and generous person who responds well

in emergencies and difficult situations. Your weak points can be self-pride or vanity, but overall your lunar position denotes a very likeable individual who has integrity. With 257 your energy and vitality is easily drained, but with 258 you have a serenity or natural poise which comes from a harmonious inner strength. With 259 you are quick to take offence and inclined to be impatient for rapid results. With 165 or 179 your artistic talents and social skills may provide the means of fame and fortune. With 160 or 167 these aspects indicate associations with the medical and legal professions. with 162 you are a prima donna, and with 163 a true mystic. Overall, your lunar position reveals creative enterprise that requires positive direction from an early age. If with 164, 168 or 175 you will eventually excel in any chosen profession. But if with 173, 174 or 177 your grandiose plans can go badly wrong.

Hidden agenda
Your hidden agenda is to achieve your objectives through your own merit rather than relying on influential friends, and this is your karmic lesson to learn. In past lives you learned the hard way that these types of friendship actually weaken your self-resolve and do little to build your self-confidence. During your current lifetime you will therefore experience disloyalties from unexpected quarters. Your psychological profile indicates that while you are a person of principles, you also dislike people who appear to cramp your style. Your natural flamboyance is a personal statement to that effect, but it also serves to provide a constant source of optimism and good humour.

You come from a long line of ancestors who served their community or country, hence your dedication in helping others. The medical profession or health clinics are top of the list. The combination of your lunar position and Celtic tree sign also indicates that your artistic skills could be equally directed into exquisite fine art or crafts, interior design or architecture. Your Shadow self is a projection of your unconscious mind, a lunar dimension of character that reveals cool and restrained emotions. This is primarily due to an analytical and subjective response system operating, which has its own strengths and weaknesses. Basically, you are a highly sensitive and gentle individual learning the art of discrimination in order to survive emotionally and psychologically in an uncertain world or environment. With 171 though you may lack a formal education, you have a natural wit and capacity for public speaking. With 164 or 167 you have an open mind and marked intelligence – excellent aspects for a writer or journalist. With 179 you have a more charismatic personality and should be fortunate in love. With 159 you are highly motivated, but with 161 you tend to demand respect. With 163 you are a spiritual healer, and with 169 you will quickly realize your true potential. With 168 or 175 success in life comes late but is extremely profitable. With 162 you are an independent free spirit. Your lunar position is, however, not a radical influence, and though some aspects may emphasize controversial behaviour or opinions, the moderating and discriminatory nature of your Moon remains a powerful influence.

Hidden agenda
Your hidden agenda is to speak your mind more openly and honestly. In past lives you were inclined to make critical observations rather than statements, having developed the art of subtlety as opposed to open discussion or consensus. During

your lifetime your karmic lesson entails developing an insight into the pain of others and, coupled with your desire for helping humanity, you will try and perfect a method of natural healing. Your psychological profile reveals some emotional scar tissue that suggests you have suffered painful experiences from an early age, or they can be attributed to residual memories of past lives. As a result you may become a hypochondriac or health fanatic unless you moderate your strict health regime.

31

Ash
············
Moon in Libra

You have great style and panache – an exotic individual who not only stands out in a crowd but appears to lead a highly glamorous lifestyle. But then you are a master of illusion and magic. Your Shadow self is a projection of your unconscious mind, a lunar dimension of character that casts a rainbow image. Your inborn sense of colour and appreciation of beauty has endowed you with a mystical quality. Both men and women alike have this affinity, but while it emphasizes a feminine principle it also underscores a harmonizing of the masculine and the feminine, which is associated with the Autumnal Equinox. In Druidic cosmology the equinoxes symbolized regenerating periods when light and darkness in equal measure promoted spiritual elevation as well as conscious self-growth. With 159, 166 or 179 you are charismatic and have a sexual magnetism. With 165 you have a pleasant voice and a graceful physical movement. With 160 you have a philosophical outlook, and with 162 you are a visionary with unusual concepts, which can be intriguing to others. With 163 you have a highly developed spirituality that requires tranquil retreats. With 164 or 167 your potential can be positively channelled into the arts or sciences. With 168 you are ambitious and prepared to bide your time until the right opportunities present themselves. With 169 you have original talents that are self-promoting, and with 170 your sensitivity is artistically directed and shows a spiritual nature. With 172 or 177 your sensitivity masks a real sense of personal inadequacy. With 161 or 175 your dreams can fail initially but you will find other avenues, though not so glamorous or exciting.

Hidden agenda

Your hidden agenda is to learn about the needs of others, which requires some self-sacrifices on your part. In past lives your strong sense of individualism became a weakness because you allowed it to interfere with your emotional and spiritual needs. During your current lifetime your karmic lesson indicates that you need to experience periods of loneliness in order that you may fully appreciate the love and support that comes with mutual commitments. Your psychological profile reveals deep-rooted frustrations, which may have originated from an initial lack of self-expression. However, deeply embedded in your psyche there is a compensating gift of natural eloquence, which emerges in due course. Your true potential as an Ash Tree character shows a natural peacemaker.

You have an enigmatic personality and character. Even your closest friends and family will find you difficult to know with any intimacy. You have, however, a great capacity to love and a primeval instinct to protect your partner and children. Your Shadow self dwells in your unconscious mind, a lunar dimension of character that still retains a powerful hold and influence on your behavioural pattern. You are therefore inclined to respond to current life situations with extraordinary insight by addressing the root causes rather than the resulting crises or surface debris. It is an excellent lunar position for a psychologist or holistic doctor; the downside can be an overwhelming desire to control or manipulate others. With 266 your emotions and personal desires are too intensely focused and require the constructive aspects of 264, 267, 270, 279 or 282 to fully direct your true potential. With 268 you must avoid recriminations linked to problems in the past, particularly where you feel you have been treated badly by certain individuals. With 204 you have a penetrating mind and intelligence that confounds critics. With 160 or 165 you have the capacity to love and forgive with true compassion. With 159 or 173 you have an unforgiving nature and a hot temper. With 161 you have a probing mind and a mentality ideal for a professional investigator or researcher. With 167 or 179 you are more sociable and communicative. With 170 you are a deeply spiritual person with a clear set of beliefs, but with 177 you may become a dabbler in the occult. The combination of your Celtic tree sign and lunar position reveals a fascination for the occult and unusual healing methods.

Hidden agenda

Your hidden agenda is one of the most difficult karmic lessons to fulfil. It requires a resolute will and blind faith in your ability to be able and willing to change your way of life. From a very early age you have been guided by your own instincts and emotive ideals, but this has often meant withdrawing into your own world of fantasy and self-illusion. Eventually you must venture out and soundly slam the door shut. The transformation will be astounding, and real self-growth will rapidly follow. Your psychological profile reveals an oppressive influence that has manifested on the very deepest levels of your unconscious and may require professional help or healing.

32

Ash
....
Moon in Scorpio

You are nomadic spirit who finds normal routine or permanent obligations extremely restrictive. You sail through life rarely dropping anchor – just long enough to take on board a few necessary supplies or relative information. While your curious mind and nature readily absorbs a vast amount of information, you are not always sure of your direction or purpose in life. Your Shadow self is a projection of your unconscious mind, a lunar dimension of character that has compounded your duality. Consequently, your ability to confuse people with what amounts to a

33

Ash
....
Moon in Sagittarius

change of identity is akin to the shape-changing skills attributed to the ancient Druids. The zoomorphic symbol of the Sea-horse is especially significant to you as it represents the evolving spirit of humanity, which summarizes your personal quest in life. With 171 your restless mind and spirit continually asks the wrong questions. With 217 you are more concerned with amorous affairs, while with 159 your interest lies in scoring points. With 160 you will take a moral stand and realize the strength of your convictions. With 161 you bore people with your knowledge, but with 162 you inspire people with your vision. With 163 you may find your own Shangri-La or Holy Grail, but few people will share your dream; with 266 your search may become an obsession, but with 267 you will touch upon some startling truths. With 167 and 168 you will evolve your knowledge into wise observations. With 171 or 174 your frustrations manifest with cynicism and extravagant claims. With 175 you will begin to see that honesty is your best salvation. Overall, your lunar position widens your whole perspective in life.

Hidden agenda

Your hidden agenda is concerned with de-programming or learning to think for yourself. In past lives your search for knowledge or higher-mind development accumulated too much irrelevant detail en route; this had the effect of imparting a superficial knowledge and distracted you from developing your true potential and anything of real worth. During your lifetime you will therefore journey on many foolish errands, but in the process you may discover the 'wisdom of fools' that has such profound meaning in esoteric teachings and in Druidry. Simple truths usually contain great enlightenment, and if you manage to discover them your karmic lesson is then fulfilled. Your psychological profile reveals a naivety or vulnerability towards people who call themselves masters and attract willing acolytes such as yourself. Though regarded as a weakness of character by others, your apparent willingness has most probably arisen through a lack of parental guidance during your childhood, or perhaps as a result of over-indulgent parents.

34

Ash
....
Moon in
Capricorn

You have an intuitive grasp of finances that helps to support your idealistic or self-creative projects – a rare combination of practical application and artistic merit. Your Shadow self is a projection of your unconscious mind, a lunar dimension of character that reveals a natural reserve and a more cautious approach generally. It also shows a deep sense of personal obligation, especially within your family circle. With your Celtic Moon sign relating strongly to vocational occupations, you may make it a professional choice and move into the administrative or management side at some stage. With regard to personal relationships you are inclined to put your career first, and marriage or parenthood is only likely to occur after your twenty-eighth birthday. Relationships in your book need time to mature. With 179 or 221 personal relationships are more contented and satisfying throughout your life. With 159 you may prefer to keep your independence, even when married or in a permanent relationship. With 160 or 167, though still totally committed to your career, you also manage to enjoy life to the full and people admire your boundless energy. With 161 you are prone to depressive moods and take life far too seriously. With 162 you have a rebellious streak that can suddenly take people by surprise; this aspect is also a sign of high intelligence and unusual talents. Overall, your lunar position emphasizes your strengths and weaknesses, which tend to alternate rather than counterbalance each other.

Hidden agenda

Your hidden agenda is to focus upon a clearer vision of the future. In past lives you were inclined to hold on to emotional ties that were spiritually redundant, in the sense that they had served their purpose. During your current lifetime you will gradually shed many layers of self-imposed restrictions if you learn to create your own future. You have the potential to become a leader or a teacher of the younger generation providing you overcome your inner feelings of initial rejection, and this is your karmic lesson to learn. Your psychological profile also reveals a dependency need where you have relied too much on your parents and on supportive friends. Your lunar position of Capricorn in the Celtic lunar zodiac marks the time of the Winter Solstice which, according to Druidic belief, marked a regeneration of spiritual and physical earthly existence – hence your need to transform your whole psyche and lifestyle.

You are a person who takes a rear-view seat in life and watches the world go by from a unique vantage point. Your Shadow self dwells in your unconscious mind, a lunar dimension of character that reveals an impersonal dedication to humanitarian causes. Your emotional nature is nevertheless extremely sensitive and compassionate, though intellectually controlled. With 157 or 171 you are highly expressive verbally but your mind lacks cohesive objectivity due to a superficial or imperfect knowledge. With 158 or 165 your social skills enable you to meet and mingle with influential people who are sympathetic to your ideals. With 159 you rely on surprise tactics, while with 160 you rely on luck rather than judgement. With 161 you are a secret planner and inclined to melodramatic outbursts. With 162 you are committed to highly controversial causes – in particular endangered wildlife species, which you identify with both psychologically and emotionally. With 163 your compassionate nature is deeply intensified, and with 169 or 267 your compelling arguments are powerfully directed. With 164 or 167 you are highly intelligent and idealistic, but you are also very practical and adaptable when it comes to achieving your objectives. Overall, your lunar placing denotes a great deal of mental and emotional objectivity, which leans towards scientific and artistic exploration.

Hidden agenda
Your hidden agenda is to fully develop your own unique potential. In past lives you were inclined to drift through life dreaming impossible dreams. Consequently, while there is a residual memory of freedom and inspired vision, it can easily end again with frustration or complacency.

During your lifetime you will, however, experience unique adventures that should help to activate your inner visionary and progressive mind. Your psychological profile suggests a need for supportive friends during emotional crises, even though you try to project self-reliant or indifferent attitudes. You have a strange tendency to wander away by yourself, lost in a crowd, and yet emotionally and spiritually you are a leader, and this is your karmic lesson to learn.

36

Ash
....
Moon in Pisces

You are a person who has one foot in the 'Otherworld' realm of consciousness, which – according to the Druids – provides access to a divine source of mystical inspiration. While associated with an artistic and gentle nature, it can be extremely destabilizing emotionally, and dissolve all reason or logic. Your Shadow self is a projection of your unconscious mind, a lunar dimension of character imbued with a double dose of Neptunian influences. You have a very different set of values compared to the rest of humanity; careful consideration must therefore be given to any aspects of Neptune. Generally speaking, any positive aspects will lessen the confusion and any positive aspects of Pluto will also syphon off a great deal of inner confusion. With 157 your mental abilities have a crafty cleverness, but with 167 or 168 your powers of reasoning are restored. With 158 you have considerable artistic skills and tend to be lucky in love and material assets. With 159 or 166 you are less inclined to drift aimlessly in life. With 160

or 161 your struggle with morality or value system finds positive influences. With 162 or 169 your unique philosophy of life has an intellectual bias. With 163, though you may choose to reside in a world of unreality, your compassion for humanity remains a source of light. With 170 your intuitive insight enables you to avoid anything too catastrophic. With 266 or 268 your escapist mentality can become paramount, but with 267 you will have the strength of mind to resist self-delusions and control your own destiny. Overall, your Moon probably conjuncts your Sun and this shows an imbalance operating within the psyche. Your hidden agenda should provide greater insight.

Hidden agenda
Your hidden agenda is a particularly difficult one to achieve. You have a highly sensitive psyche that recoils inwardly when confronted with painful experiences. During your current life you must therefore learn to walk softly without

disturbing any conscious or imaginary demons. In past lives you have witnessed many human atrocities that still haunt your dreams as a residual memory of fear and disgust. Psychologically speaking, you have to find your way across a mine-field of raw emotions. While other people need to confront such issues openly and honestly, with you it is rather a question of finding a new faith – not to mention faith in yourself – and this is your karmic lesson in life.

Celtic moon sign: Alder

Lunar Symbol: Hawk

The lunar symbol of the *Hawk* or hunting falcon was sacred to the Celtic Warrior-god Bran, who became identified with the alder-tree spirit or dryad. The alder was a symbol of fire, and the mythology associated with this tree is largely related to war and strife. The Celts regarded the hawk as a bird of omen and a circling hawk portended both victory and death – two aspects of destiny that had particular significance to a Warrior-god. According to Celtic legend, Bran was the ancient ruler of Britain and was depicted as a mighty giant armed with a spear and a sword at the time of the Vernal Equinox in order to push back the darkness of winter. The Druidic name for the Vernal Equinox was *Alban Eilir*, and the equinoxes were important dates in the Celtic seasonal and spiritual lunar calendar. They marked the time of the year when day and night were equally balanced, a brief interlude of spiritual harmony operating between Sun and Moon, but they also marked the dividing line when light would have dominion over darkness.

During the fourth lunar month of the year the Celts used the wood of the alder to make charcoal for their metalworking. It was a time to sharpen and forge new weapons for hunting and in preparation for any new battles in the coming months. The fiery red planet Mars, which the Druids called Merth, was identified with the Vernal Equinox and it marked a phase in the lunar calendar and zodiac denoting a time of crisis in action, a time when self-motivation was consciously activated to establish a new social order and to promote new spiritual awareness. King Arthur later became identified with the Alder Tree character, which is primarily an admixture of light and darkness, and therefore a combination of strength and vulnerability – a fabled Sun hero with an Achilles Heel.

Alder Tree character

You were born at the time of the year when light, your conscious self, begins to emerge as a self-reliant character, no longer bound by hidden fears but prepared to make its own way in the world.

The path ahead is still full of pitfalls, however, so the Moon, your unconscious self, has armed you with the virtue of courage. So eager are you to explore life that you often leave behind your friends and companions along the way. You are nevertheless a staunch ally should the occasion arise, but you really prefer to fight your own battles and set the pace for others to follow. Your final destination is always uncertain in life, and a restless spirit prevails as the Sun begins to cast its own shadow across the Earth.

Because your sign marks the first union and division in the lunar zodiac, personal relationships can provide either stability or instability. There is also the question of your vulnerability, which can manifest as a need for recognition, making you susceptible to flattery and false friends. Your vitality and enthusiasm for life are compensating factors and, psychologically speaking, you tend to have a very uncomplicated emotional life as you express your feelings and opinions openly and honestly.

With 159 you can become verbally aggressive, but with 158 you have the power to charm people like the Pied Piper of Hamelin, dancing to your tune and following you all the way – an excellent aspect, oddly enough, for finding a perfect love-match. With 180, while you have the courage of your convictions, your fiery temperament is extremely volatile and can lack compassion. With 181 you have a high degree of courage and vitality, well balanced with personal integrity and generosity. With 182 you are less competitive and inclined to be more self-centred. With 183 your physical and mental energy reaches a high pitch of nervous excitement, but with 184 your personal desires and ambitions can become submerged in impractical schemes. With 263 your reactions are extreme and obsessive, but with 264 you are able to make hard choices and rise above recriminations. With 185, 186 or 187 your physical stamina and clear objectives pave the way to successful achievements. With 190, 191 or 192, though you may struggle to reach your objectives in life, you have tremendous inner drive and belief in yourself. But the Moon's position holds the key to unlocking your true potential, and your Basic Paragraph is thus extended.

37

Alder
....
Moon in Aries

You are a moving force of energy that never concedes defeat. Even when you make mistakes or act irrationally, you know how to rapidly change course because you are an opportunist and a quick learner. Your Shadow self is a mirror image of your unconscious mind, a lunar dimension of character with the whole world in its sights when it comes to personal ambitions and desires. But you can become so intent on personal gain or making a quick profit that you can let something of infinitely more value slip through your fingers. You are basically a risk-taker, someone who doesn't play by the rules and yet you can win against all the odds. You have a natural spontaneity that attracts firm friendships, but your enthusiasm to change the world needs to be tempered with cold logic and more teamwork. With 217 you have highly erotic and passionate feelings. With 159 you have an explosive temper that can be unforgiving and cruel. With 160 your ambitions become less personal and directed towards helping others less fortunate. With 167 your abundant enthusiasm and energy can be scattered too widely, but you are more fair-minded, good-humoured and have the element of luck on your side. With 161 you are more conventional and less inclined to take risks, and with 168 you are a proud, self-reliant individual who takes life more seriously. With 162 your leadership qualities are pronounced, but your emotional nature is inclined to be erratic and unstable. With 166 your personal ambitions are intelligently directed and your passionate nature more controlled. With 172 or 173 personal relationships are difficult to maintain and can cause bitter frustrations. Overall, your fiery temperament needs to be moderated by more tolerant and mature thinking.

Hidden agenda
Your hidden agenda is to become less of an extremist and allow your self-growth more time to develop naturally. In past lives you were always in a hurry to finish things and never really saw the deeper issues involved or experienced the more fulfilling pleasure of personal achievement. During your current lifetime you may therefore frequently change direction, but there will come a time when you begin to realize that by staying put, the world will start to unfold around you. A different perspective is called for and this is your karmic lesson, which means being less self-centred and more emotionally attuned to the feelings of others. To achieve happiness in your current life it's really a question of controlling your inner urge to run away from situations that threaten your sense of freedom. Psychologically you have an inborn fear that provides an escape hatch when you are faced with the possibility of losing ground to others.

Y ou are a self-assured individual who is guaranteed to succeed through sheer persistent and practical application. While you have a less fiery temperament than attributed to your tree sign, your emotions run deep and you have highly sensual feelings as well as sexual allure. Your Shadow self dwells in your unconscious mind and projects a lunar dimension of character that responds primarily to the arts. You have a more refined outlook generally, and an inborn sense of being able to distinguish between

a fake and the genuine article. Material security is important to you, and therefore you are drawn to well-paid steady employment rather than pursuing fanciful ambitions. Personal relationships are also better managed, as you dislike upsets or emotional insecurity. With 178 you have a highly focused mind that can become too inward-looking or inflexible. With 167 or 168 your mind readily absorbs knowledge and you are a natural teacher or business administrator. With 158 your appreciation of the arts manifests as

38

Alder
∙ ∙ ∙ ∙ ∙ ∙ ∙ ∙ ∙ ∙ ∙
Moon in
Taurus

highly creative talents, and with 170 you may be drawn to a vocational career that is both emotionally and spiritually fulfilling. With 159 you are highly motivated in all your endeavours and this aspect also increases your sexual drive. With 160 you have a philosophical nature plus a built-in optimism that counters any setbacks or disappointments in life. With 161 there is a danger you can become too set in your ways and this can encourage self-doubt. Overall, your lunar position is a steadying influence and brings out some finer traits.

Hidden agenda

Your hidden agenda is to develop your creative talents, which are intrinsically linked to absorbing intuitive knowledge and reconstructing it in order to establish something of real worth. During your current lifetime you will experience a great deal of soul-searching when it comes to making important decisions, as you are disinclined to make any changes that might upset your domestic or working routine. In past lives you placed too much attachment on personal possessions as compensation for a lack of emotional security. Psychologically speaking, this can go right back to childhood, but with greater maturity you will discover that people love you for yourself, and you have much to give. Your karmic lesson is sharing your hopes and fears, and learning to put more back into life emotionally and materially rather than just taking what you feel you are owed.

39

Alder
••••••••••••
Moon in Gemini

You have a lively disposition and a vivacious personality. You also have a genuine duality of character that is subject to changeable mood swings, which denotes a hyperactive behavioural pattern. Basically, you have a low boredom threshold due to an insatiable curiosity for life. Your Shadow self is a mirror image of your unconscious mind, a lunar dimension of character that sleeps with one eye open. You have a high degree of emotional, physical and nervous energy all competing with each other rather than working towards a single purpose. In other words, your mind doesn't control your actions and your emotions can run riot. You are in fact operating at a kind of warp speed that few people manage to keep up with. With 159 you have a clever though mischievous mind, but with 166 you have the ability to grasp the basic facts and transform them into a convincing argument. With 165 you are inclined to fall in love too quickly, but this aspect helps to harmonize all personal skills and action. With 167 your impulsive desires are also more controlled, but you have expensive tastes. With 159 or 160 you require mental and physical stimulation at all times; failure is detrimental to your health and well-being. With 168 it encourages a more practical outlook and generally strengthens your personal resolve. With 162 it endorses any writing skills and indicates a brilliant intellect. With 163 or 170 you have a highly perceptive mind, but you must be wary of self-deception. Your lunar placing requires as many stable aspects as possible if you are to succeed in any of your endeavours in life. But you have such extraordinary ingenuity that nothing will interfere with your enjoyment of life.

Hidden agenda

Your hidden agenda is to learn to consolidate your energies and tie up the loose ends scattered behind you. During your current life you will accumulate an encyclopedia of useful and specific information – needless to say your own life is equally interesting. In past lives you were

inclined to gossip, which aroused unnecessary hostility from others. Your psychological profile is complex, with your duality of character transmitting differing messages or signals. Ultimately you must elevate your conscious mind to the highest possible level in order to transform your duality into a third dimension, which the Druids referred to as the spiritual inspiration of *Awen* – the higher reasoning faculty. This is your karmic lesson, and it is one of the most fundamental but profound spiritual experiences to learn.

You have a shrewd character with an instinct for making money. Although your tree sign is associated with risk-taking and a 'devil may care' attitude, your lunar placing holds the crucial key to your innermost thoughts. Your Shadow self dwells in your unconscious mind, a lunar dimension of character that reveals a highly psychic nature. As an Alder Tree character you are therefore more cautious generally, and inclined to trust your intuition or gut feeling. The fiery aspect of your character may be diluted as a result, but when you have to stand your ground you are a formidable adversary – though this may seldom occur, as you plan your moves in such a way as to avoid head-on collisions or confrontations. Family businesses and obligations are also associated with the position of your Moon and, while you may have been a headstrong child, you have learned many important lessons early in life as a result. With 161 you have an excellent memory which facilitates scholarly interests. With 167 you are

less inhibited, and inclined to speak your mind – particularly on emotive issues. With 160 you have a seductive charm and social poise that can be directly linked to inherited traits of character. With 159 your financial skills are impressive, and with 166 your highly competitive nature is more aggressive and used to good advantage. With 168 you are a person of principle and your family influence has instilled a sense of duty and traditional values. With 162 you are a family rebel, and with 171 or 177 you are too easily influenced by dishonest people. Overall, your lunar position shows an emotive character rather than rational thinker.

Hidden agenda

Your hidden agenda is to learn new emotions and attitudes, as you have inherited powerful memories that are either backward-looking or deeply rooted in the past. In past lives you experienced a lack of appreciation within your family circle and close contacts in general. A residual

40

Alder
··············
Moon in
Cancer

memory of this remains in your current life, but eventually you will discover that you have been acting as an emotional blotting paper, absorbing the fears or apprehensions of others. When this day dawns you will then begin a transformation that frees your trapped spirit, and this is your karmic lesson to learn. In psychological terms you should experience a great moral victory and feel as if the weight of the world has been lifted from your shoulders.

41

Alder
....
Moon in
Leo

You have supreme style and social skills that are perfectly tailored to your ambitious plans in life. Your natural eloquence denotes a fine public speaker, actor or politician, though in any chosen profession you will rise to the challenge and make your mark. Your Shadow self is a mirror image of your unconscious mind, a lunar dimension of character that reveals an inborn sense of self-power and authority. Your generosity and kindness to friends or even total strangers is commendable, but your egotistical nature can too easily become deflated if subject to criticism or public censure. In your case, wounded pride can become a source of great heartache that can affect your health or well-being. Overall, however, you have tremendous vitality and courage that sustains you through any personal crises. With 159 or 176 you have a quick temper and will follow it up with aggressive countermeasures. With 160 or 167 your great sense of humour disarms friend and foe alike. With 161 you are less likely to attract personal criticism but people are generally wary of your motives. With 162, while some people applaud your unconventional methods, others take the view that you are a dangerous extremist. With 163 you must beware of self-deceit, and with 266 your ruthless tactics can make dangerous enemies. With 169 your powers of persuasion or influence are less selfishly applied and your creative skills have great potential if also with 168. With 175 or 267 you can rise above any setbacks or personal scandals and rebuild a new life.

Hidden agenda

Your hidden agenda is to realize your dreams rather than acting them out. Your self-indulgent nature is to blame, and yet you are not a selfish individual – quite the contrary when it comes to helping others less fortunate in life. During your current life you will come into contact with famous and glamorous people and may very well become a leading figure yourself. The measure of your success depends on learning greater self-discipline, but major turning points in your life revolve around your own children or young people with whom you can identify. Your psychological profile indicates a fear of being alone or unloved, which can be linked to your overly generous and affectionate nature. Provided you do not put a price on love as being reciprocated in terms of expensive gifts or generally giving way to ulterior motives, you have the capacity to make a loving partner and parent. This is your karmic lesson to learn.

You set great store by knowing the facts and figures before committing yourself to any enterprising scheme or opportunity. You tend to do this intuitively, but there is an underlying need to quietly assess and analyse anything that affects your emotional security, which in turn can affect your health and peace of mind. Your Shadow self dwells in your unconscious mind, a lunar dimension of character that has a latent form of low self-esteem. As a result your tendency to worry can generate a jaundiced view of life. Alder Tree people are generally self-confident, but your lunar placing is at best a discriminating influence that provides a good business sense with a practical approach. With 183 you are a brilliant researcher with an analytical mind, though inclined to be a loner. With 166 you learn very quickly and have greater adaptability. With 159 you are a hard worker in your chosen field, and though highly ambitious you do not like too much responsibility. With 160 you are kind and thoughtful, and technical and scientific skills are emphasized. With 161 you are prudent and methodical, totally dedicated to your career and inclined to moralize. With 162 you have a brilliant mind, but are inclined to eccentric behaviour. With 266 you have a probing mind that delves deeply into the sources rather than the apparent effects – an excellent aspect for an analyst, surgeon or a psychiatrist. With 167, 169 or 267 you should be able to fully utilize your precise skills. With 171, 172 or 177 you may at times retreat inwardly, and this can become a highly stressful experience. Overall, on a more positive note your lunar position shows that painful self-appraisal can yield outstanding work.

Hidden agenda

Your hidden agenda is to sift through your innermost thoughts and bring them to the surface; by exposing them to the light of day, so to speak, you can then begin to find yourself. In past lives you spent a great deal of time deep in thought, and in doing so you became oblivious to the needs of others as well as yourself. Your psychological profile indicates too much self-absorption, which can become an unhealthy obsession. But what you have to offer in terms of serving humanity is, or can be, extremely beneficial all round. Your karmic lesson is to pioneer projects that can bring about changes for the greater good of humankind.

42

Alder

·············

Moon in
Virgo

You are a person at ease with yourself and with the world in general. Although you show plenty of initiative and enthusiasm for new projects or ideas, you also prefer to do things at your own steady and relaxed pace. This is important to you as there are times when you find decision-making a divisive intrusion. Your Shadow self is a mirror image of your unconscious mind, a lunar dimension of character that is well integrated with your conscious self. As an Alder Tree character your lunar position occupies the sign marking the Autumnal Equinox, and the position of your Sun occupies the sign marking the Vernal Equinox. The

43

Alder

·············

Moon in
Libra

equinoxes were important dates in the seasonal and spiritual calendar of the Celts. They marked a brief interlude when the Sun and Moon formed a divine union. In personal terms it focuses upon individual qualities that are regenerated and fully integrated. With 159 you prefer to take the initiative in all relationships, but your enthusiasm is liable to wax and wane with the lunar cycle. With 160 expansion in life is directly linked to working partnerships, and it also indicates artistic and writing skills. With 168 you have greater patience and impartial judgement – an excellent aspect for lawyers and politicians. With 162 you have marked humanitarian traits, and with 163 your easygoing nature is inclined to be non-materialistic. With 266 you are a high-flyer with the Midas touch in business. With 167 personal and working partnerships can be highly successful, but with 172 or 173 you find compromises very difficult. Overall, your lunar placing reveals

a natural charm and courtesy, but self-reliance may have to be consciously developed. Read the Vine-sign mythology for greater insight.

Hidden agenda
Your hidden agenda is to make others aware of their own self-worth. In past lives you were more concerned with establishing your own credentials or pandering to your ego. During your current life you may therefore have to make a few personal sacrifices for the good of a partner or others. Providing you don't regard this as a personal loss of freedom or choice you will remain in harmony with your whole psyche, and this is your karmic lesson. Your psychological profile reveals an awareness of your own unique individualism that can become frustrated if your partner doesn't provide equal support. It is therefore imperative that you do not marry or form partnerships too early in life or too hastily.

44

Alder
....
Moon in
Scorpio

You know how to work hard and play hard – there are no half measures in your life: people will either be drawn to your intense magnetism or avoid your company altogether. Your Shadow self is a mirror image of your unconscious mind, a lunar dimension of character that reveals a high level of smouldering emotion that can suddenly explode like a volcano. You are also subject to moodiness and, sometimes, a kind of immorality that can become self-destructive. In a more positive light your self-determination can overcome severe setbacks that would

quite literally destroy weaker mortals. With 266 you can become sarcastic and resentful, even mentally cruel if unchecked with more constructive aspects. With 264, 273, 279 or 282 these aspects will direct your energy and ambitions in greater harmony with self and others. With 159 you are a deeply passionate individual and all personal relationships will run at a high emotional level, jealousy being a common factor. With 166 your emotions are more controlled, and with 167 you have an altruistic nature. These two aspects also emphasize the accumulation of wealth. With 160 moderation in all things must be consciously developed, as your intense desire for life can encourage extreme self-indulgence. With 161 you have executive business ability, and though you are somewhat inflexible you have strong inner resources. With 176 your explosive temperament is activated. Overall, your lunar position reveals a powerful attraction to the occult or the mysteries of life, and you may become either a professional or amateur investigator.

Hidden agenda

Your hidden agenda is to overcome your extreme desires and covetous nature. In past lives these two character traits became your greatest weaknesses, and undermined your real sense of purpose. If you fail to overcome them in your current life it may encourage criminal tendencies or sexual harassment of others. During your lifetime you will therefore be confronted with moral dilemmas that have a direct bearing on learning your karmic lesson of self-control and moderation. Your psychological profile reveals a self-destruct button, which is deeply symbolic in terms of analysing your behavioural pattern. You are an instinctive survivor nevertheless, and this symbol demonstrates your ability to plot your own destiny, both a blessing and curse.

45

Alder

· · · · · · · · · · · ·

Moon in Sagittarius

You have a constant need for challenge, both mentally and physically. While you can readily grasp a situation and quickly turn it to your advantage, your actions are tempered with a sense of fair play and good humour. Your Shadow self dwells in your unconscious mind, a lunar dimension of character that reveals 'the eternal student' with a natural curiosity of life. Your true potential is, however, not always shown during school years, but will shine with greater maturity either at university or adult training colleges. You also have a natural flair for writing, which should be encouraged. With 160 or 167 this writing skill will flourish, but if with 161, 174 or 177 your creative ideas can flounder for a variety of reasons. With 175, though an ongoing struggle, you will achieve your objectives in life through sheer will-power and self-tuition. With 163, 165 or 170 your creative thoughts and ideas turn to poetry, romance, spiritual matters and the arts, while with 159 they will be directed towards public acclaim and financial rewards and with 162 or 169 towards modern technology, computers or scientific inventions. With 266 or 267 you could become an investigative journalist or financial adviser. Overall, a general restlessness prevails which must find positive or creative outlets in order to disperse a high level of energy.

Hidden agenda

Your hidden agenda is to always be conscious of your actions and words. This is because you have a tendency towards indiscretion, and you can so easily be misunderstood despite your sincerity and honesty. It is basically a lack of tact or diplomacy on your part that can cause unnecessary conflicts. In past lives you conducted your affairs in very much the same manner, but your karmic lesson is to develop a more discriminating perspective in order to absorb greater life experience, which provides an inner depth of wisdom. During your lifetime you will travel widely, and the great outdoors is where you prefer to be rather than in the stifling atmosphere of suburbia or city life. Your psychological profile indicates an inborn need for space and personal freedom. It is also an indication of a unique potential for enormous spiritual and intellectual growth.

46

Alder
....
Moon in Capricorn

You have a conflicting set of values that can undermine your ambitious strategy in life. Your instinctively cautious nature and emotions can suddenly give way to impulsive words and actions. Your Shadow self is a mirror image of your unconscious mind, a lunar dimension of character that acts as a sombre voice of conscience. As an Alder Tree character it is a restrictive influence, but your natural enthusiasm and enterprise are powerfully harnessed and directed. Conflict arises because you sometimes feel you are missing out in life when it comes to simply enjoying what you have worked so hard to achieve. Your lunar placing also indicates family burdens or a physical handicap that may have limited your full participation in sport or in life generally. But with 160 or 167 you have excellent communication skills and an expansive outlook on life. With 166 your energy and time are constructively deployed and you should enjoy positions of power and authority. With 161 you have tremendous self-discipline, but the high altar of success is achieved through personal sacrifice. With 168 your emotions are controlled to the extent of lacking real warmth or demonstrative expression. It is an excellent aspect, however, for reaping high financial rewards. With 169 you have mathematical and scientific ability. With 172 or 173 your heart is not always in your career, and personal relationships suffer through a lack of thought or spontaneity. Your lunar position overall indicates sudden bouts of depressions or a pessimistic nature which requires the uplifting positive aspects of Jupiter, Venus and Mars.

Hidden agenda

Your hidden agenda is to raise your general expectations to a higher level than others expect from you. In past lives you experienced powerful family ties and obligations, but this time round you have to break free from those self-enforced chains in order to develop greater consciousness or self-awareness. During your lifetime you may be faced with situations that undermine your sense of self-worth, which can be attributed to family disharmony. If you can rise above it you will experience a dramatic transformation of personality and attitudes, and this is your karmic lesson to learn. In psychological terms it's a question of reaching a mature level of both thinking and feeling without relinquishing your innate sense of innocence or trust.

You are an unconventional and original thinker who values personal freedom and free speech above all else. At the same time you are a humanitarian, and show great kindness and loyalty to friends and family. Although you can be obstinate and cranky at times, this doesn't outweigh your positive character traits. Your Shadow self is a projection of your unconscious mind, a lunar dimension that reveals an inborn ingenuity and a natural aptitude for modern sciences. There is also usually a flair for astrology and astronomy. Emotionally you can be somewhat aloof or undemonstrative at times, and this is linked to your need for independence and a high degree of nervous energy which requires conscious control if relationships are to succeed. With 164 this nervous tension is positively channelled through excellent reasoning and logic. With 165 or 179 you have charm and personal magnetism, and your feelings are warmly expressed. With 159 this reveals emotional discord that heightens tension, but in emergencies your reactions are quick and helpful. With 162 or 169 you are an outstanding student or scholar in your chosen field, but your erratic behavioural pattern can cause a few social problems. With 168 you are more predictable and your perspective is more focused, but your emotions are less affectionate. Overall, your lunar position in relation to your tree sign reveals an overwhelming need for personal independence that can prevent any intimate or emotional relationships from forming lasting ties or bonds.

Hidden agenda

Your hidden agenda is to share your dreams and ideas with others in a less impersonal manner, and this is your important karmic lesson to learn. You may then discover that your indifferent attitudes, which have arisen through inner discontent, will quickly evolve into a genuine knowledge or understanding of your unique talents. In past lives you experienced periods of great inner loneliness or isolation which, though self-imposed, were linked to self-growth and spiritual awareness. Your psychological profile actually reveals a powerful ego, which can disguise itself through dispassionate emotions or feelings. Your sense of 'difference' is really a form of elitism only exhibited as indifference. You are, however, a powerful agent for expressing new concepts of universal humanity that require a radical approach – in short, a New Age pioneer.

47

Alder
. . . .
Moon in
Aquarius

You are an intriguing individual. While you have a gentle and amicable nature, you are also a passionate activist when it comes to championing worthy causes, especially animal rights or victim support groups. Your Shadow self is a mirror image of your unconscious mind, a lunar dimension of character that is highly sensitive and at times gullible or naive. You are also inclined to change your mind at critical periods in your life, which adds to the confusion or compounds incoherent thinking. Your imagination is well developed and you

48

Alder
. . . .
Moon in
Pisces

are likely to have good artistic ability. Providing your energy and motivation are flowing, you may pioneer exciting new and highly creative work. With 163, while there is a strong emotional desire to help others, energy can be easily drained and misdirected. With 160 or 167 you show great compassion for the suffering or afflicted – excellent aspects for medical or healing professions. With 166 you show more initiative, and with 168 you have enough self-determination and integrity to fulfil your hopes and dreams. With 170 you are a charismatic individual and a highly evolved soul. With 162 or 169 you are a true visionary and idealist. With 177 you can easily dream your life away unless more stabilizing aspects are in place. Your lunar position certainly requires strengthening in order for you to be able to harness your potential constructively. Look for the more self-assertive aspects of Mars and the more supportive aspects of Saturn and Jupiter.

Hidden agenda

Your hidden agenda is to wake up to all the possibilities in life instead of selecting a few that won't take up too much of your time. In past lives it appears that you were locked into your own kind of reality and morality that was not conducive to self-growth. During your lifetime you will therefore find it hard to get off the starting line, but once you begin to realize you are a worthy competitor you will intuitively find your way. Your psychological profile indicates a great deal of soul-searching or a tendency to withdraw into your own world. It may be that you find the physical world too exhausting. But you have the ability to transcend it through passive contemplation without relinquishing your grasp of reality, and this is your karmic lesson.

Celtic moon sign: Willow

Lunar Symbol: Sea-serpent

The Celtic lunar symbol of the *Sea-serpent* personified the serpentine dance of the Celts' Moon-goddess, who controlled the oceans and the fate of humankind. The sacred symbol of the Serpent has always been linked with wisdom and prophecy according to many ancient myths. The Celts and the ancient Greeks associated the willow tree with a triple-headed Moon-goddess whom the Greeks referred to as Hecate and the Celts collectively referred to as the 'Old Veiled One'. She was associated with the dark phase of the Moon – a time when the Moon becomes invisible in the night sky – which occurs approximately four days before the shining crescent of the New Moon appears. While this archetypal goddess represents the darker aspects of the psyche, she primarily symbolizes the necessity of confronting the reality of evil or the negative thoughts and fears that hinder human development.

Deeply embedded in our unconscious mind there exists a perennial wisdom, and during the fifth lunar month of the willow the Druids performed sacred rites at the Beltane Fire Festival in order to draw upon this spiritual source. Beltane was one of the great Spirit Nights of the year, the other being Samhain (Halloween). It was a time for prophecy and divination, but more importantly a time when all Celts regenerated their spiritual and physical vitality – hence the fertility rites celebrated at Beltane were symbolic of birth and the rites celebrated at Samhain honoured the dead. The archetypal Arthurian Moon-goddess 'Morgan Le Fay' is identified with this sign.

Willow Tree character

You were born at the time of the year when new life was stirring across the land, a dynamic earth energy that stimulates plant, animal and human growth. This invigorating influence in human terms, however, has deep psychological significance. It arouses our sensual nature and activates our innermost desires. In terms of character analysis, because you were born under one of the most mysterious and elusive signs in the Celtic lunar zodiac, it has quite literally drawn a veil over your true potential. You are therefore extremely difficult to understand or get to know in any great depth or detail. You have also inherited a number of powerful family traits and, perhaps more significantly, psychic ability that can lie dormant for many years. Women will always exert great influence in your life, particularly grandmothers or great-aunts. Any daughters or grand-daughters will be a stimulating challenge and, for you, they represent the missing part of your developing self-awareness.

Your ruling planet, the Moon, has always been considered a symbol of illusion, as nothing born under the Moon's influence endures; she is constantly changing and reshaping everything in her path. How it manifests will depend on your ability to balance or integrate your highly intuitive nature with reason and practical application. Combined with the conjunctions 163 or 184, your psychic abilities are powerfully activated and can encourage attachments to strange religious sects or secretive societies. Generally speaking, you tend to rely on your intuitive nature, which stems from a rich vein of shrewdness and resourcefulness. You are also inclined to hold strong opinions and have powerful emotional feelings. This can be either your greatest strength or your greatest weakness, depending on just how tolerant you are. With 167 or 186 you have a healthy tolerance level, and with 204 you have good reasoning ability that can be constructively critical without ignoring any potential merit. With 180 your time and energy is aggressively channelled to self-improvement and ambitious objectives.

With 181 you are a natural healer with a profound philosophy of life. The extreme nature of this conjunction can also encourage an extravagant lifestyle and permissive behaviour. With 184 you tend to lead a secretive life, but with aspects 159, 166 or 185 you will lead an eventful life – albeit an exercise in physical and mental endurance. With 188 your psychic abilities lean towards paranormal activities, while with 189 or 200 you are a born poet and mystic. With 158, 165 or 179 your feelings are affectionately expressed and your charm and personal magnetism attracts many friends and admirers. These aspects also show artistic ability and a love of nature. With 190, 191 or 192 your energy and vitality can wax and wane with the lunar cycles, which are primarily controlled on the subconscious level. With 257 this conjunction creates an imbalance operating within the whole psyche which can emphasize all the negative traits of character. But with 258 it shows a positive integration of the unconscious and conscious mind that manifests as a harmonious blend of personality and character. Your lunar position is, however, the key to your unique potential and destiny. Your Basic Paragraph is thus extended.

49

Willow
....
Moon in Aries

The integrating combination of your Sun and Moon positions endorses all the restless and emotional traits of character associated with your sign. From a very early age you have learned to be emotionally independent and self-sufficient. You are a forceful individual who speaks your mind quite freely in everyday matters, but when it comes to controversial subjects you are more hesitant as you are inclined to hold many strange and passionate opinions. If drawn, however, you will make your position clear regardless of the consequences. Your Shadow self is a mirror image of your unconscious mind, a lunar dimension of character that quickly responds to challenges and situations requiring immediate action. This lunar energy can be positively channelled into the arts or careers requiring a 'hands-on' approach, for you are above all else a person whose personal growth revolves around first-hand experience. With 162 or 176, while tact is not your strongest asset, you will steadfastly defend free speech or the underdog. With 158 or 170 your feelings are warmly expressed and personal relationships can be very fulfilling. Artistic ability is also emphasized. With 159 or 166 your ambitions are positively activated. Look for further positive aspects of Jupiter and Saturn to provide the necessary self-motivation and stability that can lead to personal achievement. With 161, 173, 174, 177, 236, 237 or with any other negative aspects between the Sun and Moon, your true potential can remain locked within. But overall your lunar position reveals a strong-minded individual who can retrieve a situation by sheer will-power and original thinking.

Hidden agenda

Your hidden agenda is learning to contain your initial impulsiveness and to develop your original thinking into a constructive plan of action that yields solid results. In past lives you frequently changed direction in order to find complete personal fulfilment, but it always eluded you. In your current life you may have to make many compromises, which usually means periods of adjustment. But you are well qualified when it comes to moving forwards and, psychologically speaking, you have very little emotional baggage to slow you down. You may also experience periods when you require time to yourself and at such times it is essential that you respond to your inner self. This will enable you to understand that personal isolation is a cleansing process, which leads to self-discovery and unites the whole psyche – a karmic lesson that promotes rapid self-growth.

Y ou have a highly evocative sensual nature that attracts you to the arts and the pleasures in life. With the Moon in its most stable position you are also extremely practical, and you therefore place your emotional and financial security at the top of your personal agenda. Your Shadow self dwells in your unconscious mind, a lunar dimension of character that curbs impulsive behaviour and provides a persistent and determined outlook. It also emphasizes a sociable nature and artistic potential. While it may encourage a certain possessiveness in personal relationships and a need to own beautiful objects generally, overall your lunar position provides a steadying influence that counterbalances extremes of any kind. However, the aspects will confirm the true extent of this harmonious lunar energy. With 158, 179, 218 or 221 you have considerable charm and all the social graces. Artistic talents are also well channelled and form an integral part of your personality and character. With 172, 214, 222 or 224 your sensual nature and sensitive emotions have been suppressed early on in life, which usually occurs as a result of unsympathetic parents or social conditions. If with other aspects such as 166, 167, 181, 186 or 204 you will overcome any setbacks through good humour, optimism, vitality and tenacity. With 163 or 184 the mystical side of your nature is powerfully activated, but mental and emotional confusion can occur. With 170, 189, 206 or 244 your mystical nature provides inspiration and practical guidance into spiritual matters and artistic abilities. Overall, the stabilizing position of your Moon emphasizes a positive outlook and a shrewd head for business.

Hidden agenda

Your hidden agenda is to develop a more versatile strategy and personal initiative. The combined lunar dynamics of your tree sign and lunar position reveals an important phase of transformation which requires careful examination of your real motives. In your current life your survival instinct is strong and comes from residual memories of persecution, which can be linked to your psychic abilities, as well as from your powerful family ties and influence. During your lifetime you will therefore experience a series of personal crises as a result of an inability to change your value system, which is fundamentally out of date and *time*. Your psychological profile indicates a powerful sex drive and deeply rooted emotions that can be counterproductive with regard to promoting loving relationships by encouraging lustful desires. Your karmic lesson is to understand the difference between needs and desires.

51

Willow
....
Moon in Gemini

You have a high degree of nervous energy and changeable ideas, and this stems from an extremely restless mind, body and spirit. It is also linked to an unsettled early education and family background. Your Shadow self is a mirror image of your unconscious mind, a lunar dimension of character that can don many disguises in order to blend into any niche in society – or simply for the sheer delight of watching the reaction of others. You are basically a 'people watcher', fascinated by human behaviour. Your ability to communicate your ideas and life experiences is drawn from the combined energies of the Sun and Moon, which promote writers and skilful negotiators as well as occupations that require keeping abreast of new ideas and techniques. Because of your need for self-expression, if any aspects create mental or psychological blockages your nervous and emotional energy will build up to such a degree that your only course of action is demonstrated in explosive outbursts; alternatively you may employ crafty measures to achieve your ambitions. With 160, 167, 181, 186, 188, 197, 203, 204 or 205 you will develop your communicative skills to a high level and absorb a great deal of knowledge through your varied interests and studies. With 177, 194, 209 or 211 your psychic abilities tend to lack focus and reliability. Overall, your lunar placing reveals a curious mind that will delve into the mysteries of life or any unresolved problems. You are perhaps the best qualified Willow character to explain the Moon's intricate nature.

Hidden agenda

Your hidden agenda is to become adept at all levels of communication, which will enable you to form a powerful connection with your higher self. But first you must develop a neutral standpoint in order to integrate your own opinions with those of others. While this is part of your karmic lesson, your elusive type of mentality – having originated from an eternal restlessness or the mystical process of creative thought – requires greater self-discipline. If this can be achieved in your lifetime your karma is also fulfilled. In past lives you became involved in numerous intrigues that diverted your attention away from your true potential or personal goals. During your current life you will experience some profound influences of a philosophical nature that will greatly change your lifestyle for the better. Your psychological profile reveals a need for social activity and acceptance by others, which, if achieved, should synchronize with higher-mind development.

52

Willow
....
Moon in Cancer

You have a powerful imagination and a high emotional level that requires positive channelling. You are probably a natural clairvoyant or medium who experiences dramatic premonitions or a pronounced sense of déjà vu. Your Shadow self is a projection of your unconscious mind, a lunar dimension of character that is greatly affected by the changing phases of the Moon. How it manifests will depend on the lunar aspects but, generally speaking, you follow a behavioural pattern of mood swings that begins with the New Moon and reaches a climax around the

Full Moon, only to reach subliminal depths during the dark phase just before the New Moon. In personal analysis the lunar cycle usually begins with a renewal of emotional energy and enterprise, with the Full Moon marking a culminating point of realization. The waning period is not necessarily a depleting cycle of energy, as it also marks a time to quietly recharge your emotional batteries, but it is not the best time to take on too many commitments. The dark phase is a period of inner illumination which provides the spark of an idea that suddenly manifests with the New Moon. With conjunctions 163 or 266 the depth of your emotions can become incomprehensible on a conscious level, but can be reached through the symbolism of dreams. With 167 or 168 you have moral integrity which provides a working frame of reference and strengthens your powers of concentration. With 184 the mystical element associated with your tree sign can be both inspirational and negatively seductive. With planetary conjunctions such as 239, 240, 241, 248, or 249 you have the ability to influence public opinion or people in authority, and these aspects provide great inspiration as well as great inner strength and luck in life. Overall, your lunar position reveals a highly charged emotional and psychic nature which requires quite a few stable aspects. Look for positive aspects between and the Sun and Moon, and the Moon with Mercury, Saturn and Pluto.

Hidden agenda
Your hidden agenda is to come to terms with your emotional nature – or, in other words, to understand the feminine principle of unconditional love in its highest form. In past lives you had to cope with many family responsibilities and obligations that drained your emotions and inner reserves of compassion. During your current life, it's a question of history repeating itself, but this time you will begin to shed layer upon layer of emotional guilt, which can dramatically change your mental attitudes and physical appearance. Such transformations inevitably create a younger image all round, and also fulfil your karmic lesson of a spiritual and physical rebirth. Your psychological profile, however, indicates a powerful resistance to change that stems from a fear of failure, and yet you are an accomplished participant in life with everything to play for, so do try to bear this in mind in order to overcome your fears.

You have sophisticated tastes, passionate emotions and an affectionate nature. You are also highly competitive and well organized in both your social life and your career objectives. Your Shadow self is a mirror image of your unconscious mind, a lunar dimension of character that has an inborn sense of pride and showmanship. Life is always full of dramas, which can be largely of your own making. You are basically a colourful character who has actually 'invented' yourself – a consummate actor or actress of many parts, but always taking a leading role.

53

Willow
....
Moon in
Leo

While you will cultivate friendships from a wide circle of acquaintances, they in fact represent a selected 'mini-audience' so that you can enact your personal dramas. This is not to say that you are lacking warmth and sincerity; it is rather that deep down you are a highly sensitive person who can initially lack self-confidence. With 165, 166, 167, 181, 186, 188, 227 or 258, however, self-confidence has never been a problem and you have all the best qualities imaginable to succeed in all your endeavours, with the proviso that you avoid the pitfalls of self-indulgence. With 172, 174, 191 or 213 your love of luxury can become a vice and serve to weaken your vitality and moral fibre. With 163 your psychic abilities can yield false illusions of grandeur, but with 170, 189, 241, 244, 249 or 250 your artistic and spiritual nature is highly advanced and you will fully utilize your psychic and artistic abilities. Overall, your lunar position provides an inner vitality that is most uplifting.

Hidden agenda

Your hidden agenda revolves around building upon your individual confidence and integrity in order to create an example for others to follow. This is your karmic lesson to learn, which is by no means an easy task. But you have inherent qualities of leadership that people admire, and this factor alone should attract a number of followers in your wake, as your influence is not for personal glory. In past lives you experienced moments of weakness and false pride; if the saying 'he who hesitates is lost' means anything to you, then these words will ring true and should remain uppermost in your mind. Your psychological profile indicates a difficulty in finding the core of your true self. You are therefore drawn to measuring your achievements from how you are seen by others in order to gauge your true worth. If you are prepared to spend some time on your own you may discover that self-criticism is the best method of self-recognition, warts and all.

54

Willow
....
Moon in Virgo

Your perception of life is meticulously monitored by your ability to switch off the emotional button. While this leaves you in a unique position to interpret and analyse precisely what you are feeling, it also places you inside a vacuum of emotion. Your Shadow self dwells in your unconscious mind, a lunar dimension of character that can easily become a separate state of being instead of an integral part of your self. However, your ultimate goal of striving for self-perfection is an act of purification, which is the fundamental

origin and purpose of the Beltane Fire Festival. You are therefore working in close harmony with the lunar energies of your tree sign. With 164, 166, 167, 185, 186, 197 or 203 your range of ideas is extended and your intellectual capacity is finely attuned to your psychic abilities. With 171, 208, 245 or 271 your mind lacks cohesive direction and though you may appear well informed you have a number of misconceived ideas. With 169, 188, 205, 240 or 250 you have a progressive and visionary mind, which identifies the humanitarian principles of New Age thinking. Overall, your lunar position promotes a discriminating type of intelligence and passive emotions.

Hidden agenda
Your hidden agenda is to develop and perfect your intuitive knowledge of nature and use it to help others in the field of research, medicine and healing – the latter being of the utmost importance if we are to evolve in harmony with our environment. This is your karmic lesson and it means considerable dedication. In past lives you tended to lead a very solitary existence due to your highly developed spiritual nature. During your current life you may therefore experience considerable doubt as to the purpose of your objectives, or become dismayed with the destruction of the environment, nature's child that you are. Your psychological profile indicates that you are prone to bouts of anxiety and nervous disorders, which can be linked to subjective or introspective thinking. This is not an easy thing to remedy as it forms part of your personal make-up, but awareness can become a mitigating factor.

Y ou have an artistic temperament that can be at odds with your intellectual abilities. It's a question of your emotions influencing your decisions at crucial periods in your life. Your Shadow self is a mirror image of your unconscious mind, a lunar dimension of character that can either act in a contrary manner or find an ideal compromise. You have natural charm and charisma that people find difficult to resist, and yet in personal relationships it can become a distraction or a highly manipulative subtle manoeuvre. With 165, 179, 217, 221 or 273 you have an irresistible and engaging manner which makes you extremely popular socially, and you are likely to be lucky both in love and in financial matters. With 172, 222, 224 or 274, while you are a passionate lover, a note of disharmony impairs your chances of finding a permanent or loving relationship. With 216, 225 or 226 you have a magnetic charm and artistic skills but are vulnerable to self-delusion and deceitful partners. As you may have gathered, partnerships play an important part in your life. Your lunar energy works best through close or direct partnerships where decision-making can be shared. If you read the character analysis for the Vine sign marking the Autumnal Equinox, the importance of this statement is more clearly defined.

Hidden agenda
Your hidden agenda revolves around self-esteem and guarding against a strong ego influencing your current life. Ultimately you must learn the very subtle lesson that your individual qualities have equipped you for a harmonious role or relationship rather than a solo lifestyle, and this is central to achieving your karmic lesson. In past lives your ambitious objectives were completely ruled by self-interests. During your current lifetime you may indeed find yourself playing a solo part, but this should ensure that you

55

Willow
. . . .
Moon in
Libra

reconsider your goals and objectives. Your psychological profile indicates a tendency to change your mind and your allegiances when the going gets tough. But if you can learn to evaluate the painful lessons you will soon realize that winning or losing is less important than actually taking part.

56

Willow
....
Moon in Scorpio

You are undoubtedly one of the most enigmatic Willow Tree characters. Everything about you is mysterious and elusive, and yet people are never left in any doubt as to your true feelings and passionate desires. Your Shadow self is a mirror image of your unconscious mind, a lunar dimension of character that responds to the dark phase of the Moon. You have always moved in magical circles and have the psychic faculties of an adept. How you live your life is another matter; on the surface it can seem quite ordinary, but sensitive people will always regard you as someone not quite 'of this world'. If this sounds overly dramatic, perhaps your psychic abilities have not yet been activated, but it's only a question of time. With 167, 169, 186, 188, 189, 197, 203, 204, 264, 267 or 279 your psychic ability is positively channelled and you will use it to help others. With 159, 166, 185 or 231 your penetrating insight will be directed to high finance, and though you are into power games you will make firm but fair judgements. With 179, 217, 272 or 273 your powerful sex drive is balanced with a romantic and loving nature. With 172, 190, 194, 209, 237, 263, 265, 268, 277 or 289 any one of these aspects can lead you in the wrong direction regarding your psychic gifts, your powerful emotions and your sense of purpose. Overall, your lunar position is precariously poised as a source of either healing and regeneration or ruthless exploitation and degeneration. Study all aspects well.

Hidden agenda

Your hidden agenda is to develop your inner strengths for future transformations. You appear to be at the 'crossroads' in your current life, which can mean retracing your steps rather than moving off in another wrong direction. In past lives your single-mindedness became entrenched in power-games. As a result, during your current lifetime you will probably become involved in numerous disputes over ownership of property or things of material value. Psychologically speaking, this represents an accumulation of excess emotional baggage which needs to be swept away. Subconsciously you know that drastic action is called for, and your ability to make ruthless decisions can appear to others as mindlessly self-destructive. But your ability to rebuild your life is intrinsically linked to future transformations or enlightenment, and this is your karmic goal.

You are a seeker of truth, and thus you will explore endless possibilities and philosophies in your search for ideal solutions. Your inborn sense of optimism and cheerful nature makes you a popular friend or companion. Your Shadow self is a mirror image of your unconscious mind, a lunar dimension of character that provides an uplifting sense of purpose and inner confidence. Your psychic abilities or intuitive insights are drawn towards religious or moral issues, but your curious nature and need for independence ensures an unbiased approach. You may therefore discover many hidden secrets relating to human psychology and the mysterious elements in nature. With 160, 167, 181, 186, 197, 203, 205, 230, 234, 241 or 244 you have marked personal qualities and the courage of your convictions. With 174, 177, 191, 194, 208, 211, 223 or 245 your restless nature and lack of discretion can take the upper hand, and if this occurs you will squander both material and spiritual inheritances unless other aspects provide a counter-weight. If also with 175, 192, 238, 239 or 278 your tremendous inner drive and inborn sense of justice will prevail. While every aspect reveals unique influences and needs to be read in its entirety, your lunar placing remains a source of inspiration and a magnanimous disposition. So despite a few wayward exploits, and with greater maturity, your self-knowledge becomes your strongest asset.

Hidden agenda

Your hidden agenda is to remain steady on your course, though direction early on in life is not easy to find. It usually comes through the help of an older person, or sometimes parental guidance. But your need for independence can blight your perceptions; in past lives it encouraged a nomadic existence. During your current life you will therefore initially avoid making any kind of commitment, which in turn can make other people less likely to take you seriously. Your psychological profile reveals a duality of polarized traits of character rather than complementary attributes. Your search for truth is actually a search for your real identity, and the elusive nature of your tree sign symbolizes your karmic quest.

57

Willow

. . . .

Moon in
Sagittarius

You are a serious student when it comes to spiritual or esoteric matters. Your own psychic abilities and intuitive knowledge may also be regarded with some unease or caution. Your Shadow self is a mirror image of your unconscious mind, a lunar dimension of character that is both a stabilizing influence and, at times, a restrictive or limiting influence. It's a question of alternating mood swings and an inborn sense of self-discipline which can be harshly applied. In short, you tend to make life difficult for yourself by doing things the hard way rather than seeking easier options. While this can result in hard-earned fame or fortune, it seldom brings inner contentment or happiness. But the planetary aspects are often mitigating influences and can also reveal another hidden dimension of character.

58

Willow

. . . .

Moon in
Capricorn

With any of the following aspects – 160, 167, 169, 179, 181, 185, 185, 187, 188, 203, 204, 232 or 242 – the more sombre side of your nature is effectively neutralized, and your powers of endurance become a lesson in positive objectivity. If you have more than two of these aspects you are indeed a strong character who can rise above any early setbacks and conquer you inherent inhibitions. With 161, 182, 198, 209, 245 or 283 your mood swings frequently dip into depression and acute melancholia, and this can sap your energy and motivation. With 165, 217 or 273 personal relationships are better managed and you should find an ideal partner. Overall, your lunar position at best endorses virtuous traits of character and increases your intellectual abilities.

Hidden agenda

Your hidden agenda is to achieve spiritual and emotional maturity. In the Celtic lunar zodiac your lunar placing marks the turning of a new solar year at the Winter Solstice. During your lifetime you will therefore experience a major shift of awareness or self-growth. But having arrived at the gateway, you are not sure about having to sacrifice your ego, hence your current karmic lesson in learning to make sacrifices for others. In past lives you remained a law unto yourself and held positions to this effect, administering a very one-sided justice. In psychological terms you are being confronted with having to let go of your prejudices in order to be reborn with a clean slate or a clear conscience.

59

Willow
·············
Moon in Aquarius

You have the power of prophecy and vision. While your emotional nature can appear quite dispassionate on occasions, you have strong humanitarian feelings which respond to injustices. Your Shadow self dwells in the unconscious mind, and this lunar dimension of character in your chart is highly ingenious; many astrologers are born under your lunar placing, the emphasis being on scientific skills of an abstract nature. Generally speaking, you are inclined to hold controversial opinions and behave in an erratic or eccentric manner from time to time. Just how pronounced these traits are will be shown with the planetary aspects, but the way it manifests in psychic ability can be extremely unnerving for others, as it strikes at the heart of orthodox belief systems by shattering false illusions that have been manufactured rather than drawn from a mystical spirituality. With 162 or 169 your psychic nature is brilliantly deployed with intellectual prowess and intuitive knowledge. With 183 or 188 you are a progressive thinker who can inspire others with your amazing insights, but there is a high degree of nervous tension that requires creative outlets and self-discipline in order to avoid bizarre behaviour. If supported with 205 or 250 you are able to put your views across through constructive dialogue and sound arguments. Any planetary aspect involving Uranus needs to be carefully examined, but if with 167, 168, 181, 186, 187, 197, 204 or 232 your humanitarian nature is well activated and you are able to develop some remarkable psychic powers. Overall, your lunar position reveals an individualistic perception of life that provides unique insights into a number of perplexing issues.

Hidden agenda

Your hidden agenda is to elevate your feelings and emotions from a position where they are artificially contrived in order to fit in with your intellectual ideals. In past lives you were inclined to let your head rule your emotions with disastrous consequences. It not only isolated you from people for whom you cared deeply, but their rejection left a lasting impression of pain as well as feelings of guilt. During your current life you must therefore learn to shed a few superficial masks that have created a false image which can preclude any real intimacy with others – including your partner. This is your karmic lesson. Your psychological profile indicates a powerful will, which can become extremely overbearing, but your sense of fair play provides a form of self-regulation that is a significant strength in achieving your karmic goal.

Y ou are a born artist and mystic. You see the world from a unique vantage point of spiritual purity, or what some cynics would call lack of reality or naivety. Your Shadow self is a mirror image of your unconscious mind, a lunar dimension of character that is highly receptive to the thoughts and emotions of others. This can make you extremely vulnerable to negative energies as well as to the positive or constructive forces that are at work. Psychologically this can have the effect of creating a need for solitude and inner contemplation. The difficulty that arises on a psychic level is learning to distinguish between negative external influences and your inner source of vision and wisdom. Your ability to serve as a channel for healing energies will at some stage compel you to be of service to humanity in a practical and meaningful way. But as your weaknesses stem from the same source as your strengths, you can all too easily lose your way and turn to drugs or alcohol as a temporary relief. Any planetary aspects to Neptune must therefore be carefully examined. With 163 or 184 your vision and compassionate nature requires more coherent direction, but with 170 or 189 your artistic temperament and spiritual nature is well balanced and intelligently handled. With 164, 167, 168, 186, 187, 197, 206, 244 or 251 these aspects are supportive and practical influences, which can strengthen your mind and your emotions. With 174, 177, 194, 208, 211, 247 or 289 your tendency towards escapism can be destructively employed, causing you to become trapped in a world of fantasy and chaos. If also with conjunctions 160, 162, 180, 196, 199, 227, 229, 230 or 240 you will experience sudden bursts of energy and become highly motivated at critical periods in your life. Overall, your lunar position reveals an artistic temperament and a spiritual source of strength that can overcome any weak traits.

60

Willow
....
Moon in
Pisces

Hidden agenda

Your hidden agenda is to learn to protect yourself from energies that are mentally and emotionally disturbing without shutting out those which are uplifting. In past lives you spent a great deal of your time on your own in search of spiritual enlightenment. While you developed your spiritual strength, you remained extremely vulnerable to people of ill intent. During your current lifetime you may therefore experience many odd encounters with people and places that will have a strange effect on you, but providing it doesn't threaten your hold upon reality or become psychologically paralysing you should evolve even greater insight. Your karmic lesson, therefore, is learning to come to terms with the darker side of humankind. Your psychological profile is a fascinating example of fifth-dimensional thinking, which redefines both time and space. On a spiritual level it reveals prophetic vision.

Celtic moon sign: Hawthorn
Lunar Symbol: Silver Chalice

The lunar symbol of the *Silver Chalice* represents the magical 'Cauldron of Ceridwen', a divine source of immortality in Celtic myth. It was one of the four treasures brought to Ireland by the Danaans, a mysterious race of 'radiant people' who became the gods and goddesses of the Celts. Ceridwen was a powerful Moon-goddess who had learned the magical arts from the 'Books of Feryllt' (ancient alchemical formulae). She knew the secrets of Creation, everlasting life and the power to heal and restore the dead back to life. The Cauldron later became identified with the Silver Chalice in the Arthurian 'Quest of the Holy Grail', which begins with the story of the 'Glastonbury Thorn' that recounts the tale of Joseph of Arimathea. He was believed to have visited Glastonbury and planted a hawthorn staff that grew into a tree, which still flowers today out of season at Christmas. It symbolizes Christ's birth and the founding of the first Celtic Christian church in England. Joseph was also said to have buried a silver cup or chalice, used by Christ at the Last Supper, in the Chalice Well at Glastonbury Tor.

During the sixth lunar month, Celtic knights and Sun-kings drew closer to their quest so their spiritual self could be reborn at the Winter Solstice. The symbol of the Cauldron or Chalice also relates to the metal craftsmanship of the Celts and their Smith-gods, who were custodians of *Celestial Fire*, which directs the higher powers of the mind. The mythology of Vulcan, a Smith-god, is particularly relevant, for there is a close connection between metalworking that links smithcraft to ancient initiations associated with the evolving soul. Vulcan and his Celtic counterpart, Govannan, both represent invisible deities situated in a place next to the Sun that is too intense to gaze upon or fully comprehend.

Hawthorn Tree character

You were born at the time of the year when the radiance of the Sun and nature were in harmony, and the Hawthorn character was thus forged from a dazzling form of light and energy which created a multi-talented individual who adapts easily to any situation.

In personal terminology your great strength is knowing the weaknesses of your adversaries or any opposing forces, but you are not a ruthless person, merely a clever strategist. People born under this sign generally have charismatic personalities, stemming from a glowing inner self-confidence that in turn produces great leaders and people who inspire others. What, then, are your weak points? You invariably have a volatile temperament that is likely to explode every so often with bursts of anger directed verbally with the cutting edge of steel. However, you also have a sympathetic nature, and are a good listener as well as a natural communicator. Your sense of humour can at times be sharp and full of innuendo – the type often missed by less quick-witted people – and is a talent that attracts you to writing and journalism. Because you can adapt very quickly to circumstances, you will redefine your personal skills to a fine art. Your youthful appearance has a kind of freshness that appears to last even

into old age, the secret being your agile mind and willingness to experiment with new ideas. This Mercurial-Vulcan quality has all the alchemy and ingredients of life in a flux, ever changing, never still. When you do relax, the whole earth appears momentarily on hold.

With 157 you are inclined to live on your wits, but you also have a high degree of intelligence and many versatile talents. With 158, 165, 179, 217 or 234 your charisma is extremely magnetic and you are drawn to the performing arts. With 160, 167, 181, 186, 227 or 244 you tend to adopt a philosophical and moral outlook and you are capable of influencing people on a wide scale. These aspects also emphasize your sympathetic nature. With 176, 190, 235 or 268 your volatile temper can cause havoc in your personal life, and if not brought under control can overturn your very existence or position in life. With 164, 168, 187 or 242 you are more controlled in all your actions and these aspects add a stabilizing feature of good common sense and careful management of finances. Hawthorn characters are also thought to have highly psychic mental abilities associated with telepathy and telekinesis – the ability to move objects by the power of thought. Your powers will be especially pronounced if with any of the following aspects: 170, 183, 184, 188, 189, 199, 205, 255, 258 or 285. The position of your Moon will also clarify many aspects of your lunar character. Your Basic Paragraph is thus extended.

61

Hawthorn
·············
Moon in
Aries

You have a quick but changeable mind and you find discipline hard to accept. You are, however, extremely adaptable and a first-class competitor in any chosen field or sporting interest. Your Shadow self dwells in the unconscious mind, a lunar dimension of character that prefers action not words. While you are a headstrong character, you also have a strong survival instinct, which provides ingenious escape routes at a moment's notice. You are basically an unconventional person with a strong sense of individualism. You also prefer to keep your options open and, though you can act on impulse and verbally commit yourself, you are inclined to change the goalposts to suit yourself. Personal relationships are therefore difficult to maintain, since personal freedom is an emotional issue. You are an adventurer and opportunist first and foremost. Your ability to charm the opposite sex is powerfully activated with your lunar position, but the aspects will help to clarify your true motives. With 158, 170, 179, 189, 195, 201 or 273 your motives are inclined to be honourable and you have a natural charm and sensitivity to the feelings of others; you also have artistic skills. With 190, 214, 222, 263, 265, 268 or 274 your motives are questionable and you are inclined to manipulate people. With 162, 169, 183, 185, 188, 199, 205 or 233 your telepathic powers are activated. Overall, your lunar position reveals a high level of physical, mental and emotional energy, which can prematurely burn out if not capped and used more sparingly.

Hidden agenda
Your hidden agenda is making a conscious decision about your true direction in life and sticking with it – a karmic lesson that, for you, is not any easy task, and you will probably waste a great deal of time at the beginning. In past lives you were easily bored with dull or routine work that interfered with your social life and ambitious strategy. In your current life this residual memory remains a restless influence, and it is still very difficult for you take anything too seriously, although your attitude can suddenly change given your volatile nature. A carefree lifestyle, however, has to be consciously worked at, and your psychological profile suggests a need to establish your own personal mark in life.

62

Hawthorn
·············
Moon in
Taurus

You have a calming influence on others and a balanced outlook on life. Your emotions run deep, but are very stable when it comes to personal relationships. Your Shadow self is a mirror image of your unconscious mind, a lunar dimension of character that provides a measure of common sense and artistic potential. You also have a very sensual nature, which is attractive without overstating your obvious interest or desires. Your main aim in life is to enjoy a comfortable lifestyle without too much effort or hardship. Nevertheless you are a reliable worker or employee, and financial security is important to you. It is a question of finding the right career, which is likely to be one where you feel you are doing something worthwhile. The theatre or the arts and educational services may attract, all being spheres of influence that suit your basic nature and satisfy your high standards. You are a perfectionist when it comes to any work or performance. With 158, 159, 170, 179, 189, 195, 201, 216 or 221 your artistic temperament is fully engaged and you will lead a very glamorous life. You will also attract many admirers, but you must be wary of false flattery. With 177, 194, 211, 214, 224, 226, 253 or 274 your true potential is more difficult to realize and you can too easily become discontented and disillusioned. Personal relationships are also very difficult to maintain. If with 166, 167, 169, 181, 185, 188, 202, 203 or 205 your whole persona has a vibrant quality and your focus on life is greatly expanded. All these aspects will improve the mind and increase the likelihood of telepathic or psychic powers. Overall, your lunar position is consolidating factor of influence and a source of inner strength.

Hidden agenda

Your hidden agenda is to learn to spread your wings and broaden your horizons. In doing so you will discover that there is so much more to life than mere existence. You have a lot of ground to make up if you are to find real peace of mind or inner contentment. While you may have built a comfortable niche for yourself, you are just as vulnerable as the rest of society to a rapidly changing world. In past lives you reached positions of authority, but your views were rather dogmatic and self-indulgent. During your current life you will have the chance to greatly influence others, but you must be prepared to listen to their own ideas and expectations. Your psychological profile reveals a deep-rooted fear of the unknown, which actually symbolizes a need to evolve and transmute your energies in order that you can experience a new rebirth during your life. This, therefore, is your karmic lesson to learn.

Y ou enjoy playing the 'Fool' in life. If you know about tarot symbolism you will know that this role has profound meaning that summarizes the soul's quest for wisdom and perfection. It also symbolizes an unconfined energy that permeates all things, and on a psychic level becomes highly charged. Your Shadow self is a lunar dimension of character, a projection of your unconscious mind that reveals a sense of awe and boundless curiosity. To others it may appear that you are at times extremely naive, almost childlike in your ability to speak the truth regardless of the consequences. But children see the world without the blinkered sight of bigotry and cynicism. You are therefore in a position to learn a great deal of knowledge which has a simple but profound message for those prepared to listen. However, it does depend on your ability to grasp the deeper meanings, as your lunar influence can also promote a superficial or shallow mind. Generally speaking, you have the ability to see both sides of the coin, but because of the volatile temperament associated with your tree sign you can suddenly change your mind and

63

Hawthorn
. . . .
Moon in
Gemini

make your views known with great force and impact. With 157, 171 or 208 you will indeed only grasp the essential details, albeit a good working knowledge that enables you to appear more informed than you really are. With 167, 169, 181, 185, 188, 197, 199, 203 or 205 you have an excellent mind, great personal integrity and a natural flair for writing and lecturing on your subject. With 158, 170, 189, 195, 201 or 206 you have strong artistic leanings which may attract you to the limelight of acting, and this is where you could score as a comedian or a clown, as you are a natural mimic. Your lunar position overall shows a need for self-discipline, so if with 168, 187 or 204 you have good reasoning powers and self-control that modifies your flash-point temper. Look for positive aspects between the Sun, Moon and Venus for inner harmony and tolerance.

Hidden agenda

Your hidden agenda is not to step off the edge of the world like the Fool. In other words, don't try to be too clever, as the real Fool is only making the gesture whereas you could easily fall into strange company and be led astray. During your current life you will meet all kinds of people on your travels, but you must remain true to yourself if you are to achieve your goals. Psychologically speaking, you are an enigmatic character who is extremely difficult to analyse, as you tend to strike different chords with different people. In spiritual terms you have retained an elusive spirit over the centuries. Your karmic lesson, not surprisingly, is consciously to establish your true identity or quite simply *be yourself*, rather than creating false images that can distort the truth that lies within.

64

Hawthorn

·············

Moon in Cancer

You are shrewd tactician who is always ahead of the game when it comes to investing for the future or securing a safe position in life. You have an uncanny knack of being in the right place at the right time. Your Shadow self is a projection of your unconscious mind, a lunar dimension of character that is highly attuned psychically to the changing cycles of life – hence your ability to move with the prevailing tide rather than against it. It must be said, however, that you can become too entrenched in your attitude or actions, and this can impede your sense of reason. At heart you are a traditionalist and a conservative rather than a trend-setter. Personal

relationships are inclined to be intense affairs, and you can become an overly protective parent or partner. With 160, 165, 167, 179, 181 or 186 your caring nature is endorsed and your tendency to worry inwardly is greatly reduced. Both your love life and finances should flourish. With 161, 182 or 209 you are prone to bouts of depression and too much inward-thinking, and this can mar relationships. With 170, 184, 189, 287 or 288 your psychic abilities indicate a natural medium. With 177, 194, 211 or 289 you are vulnerable to picking up the 'wrong wavelength' – channels of chaos which could be dangerous to your health. If also with 242, 250 or 282 your endurance and stamina will keep you on track, despite any adverse influences. Overall, your lunar position reveals a hypersensitive nature that requires positive aspects to promote less inward-thinking generally.

Hidden agenda
Your hidden agenda is to value things which money can't buy and to value your emotions and feelings more than power; these are your karmic lessons to learn. In past lives you tended to take advantage of the weaknesses in others, but during your current life there may come a time when this is reversed. Your psychological profile shows a complex behavioural pattern. It also reveals an old-fashioned morality, while your abiding sentiment appears to be 'all is fair in love and war'. It's a question of fair to whom? Residual memories of past lives usually provide instinctive reactions that manifest as a 'twinge of conscience', which serves as a guide in achieving your karma.

Y ou appear to know exactly where you are going in life and you will also organize everyone else around you. Your Shadow self is a projection of your unconscious mind, a lunar dimension of character that is determined not to wait in the wings. How it works is quite simple: you know how to make things happen without any hassle or hardship. The only difficulties that may arise are when other people don't cooperate, but even that will not slow you down. You then resort to 'Plan B' where you can act the injured party and gain support from your many friends in high places. But you do have a number of admirable qualities, including your style and imagination and the fact that there isn't a malicious bone in your body. In a grey world you are a colourful character with a great deal of warmth and personal integrity. However, your ability to influence people must always be tempered with sincerity and humility, otherwise you are in danger of becoming arrogant and dogmatic. With 160, 165, 167, 179 or 186 you have the right balance of charm without appearing patronizing, and your organizational skills will be greatly appreciated. With 161, 173 or 182 your natural vitality is difficult to sustain and your objectives can fail through sheer bad luck. With 162, 169, 183 or 188 you have a dynamic personality, a brilliant intellect and original style. Overall, your lunar position does require more tolerance and less pomposity. If also with 204, 219, 232, 239 or 279 your positive lunar traits will triumph, despite any initial self-doubts or lack of modesty.

Hidden agenda
Your hidden agenda is to be careful what you wish for, as you have creative powers that can actually make it happen. This ability stems from a residual memory relating to past lives, when you were an accomplished alchemist. In your current life more thought and less egotism is required in your everyday strategy. You need to mix freely with all levels of society, and your greatest asset is your magnanimity and broad-mindedness. Your karmic

65

Hawthorn
· · · · · · · · · · · ·
Moon in
Leo

lesson is to consciously develop these traits to the highest possible level, which should then exclude any feelings of superiority or elitism. Your psychological profile reveals a gregarious individual who enjoys sociable company and constant attention. You also tend to idealize your partner or put them on a pedestal. This can result in greater disillusionment than is reasonable, which again is due to your tendency to fantasize.

66

Hawthorn
··············
Moon in
Virgo

You are a master planner when it comes to organizing your life, with every detail carefully worked out. Basically you have the mind of a computer programmer. Your Shadow self is a projection of your unconscious mind, a lunar dimension of character that takes nothing for granted and is inclined to worry about everything, including health matters. Your perception, though inclined to be narrowly focused, does produce some remarkable insights into the working mechanics of any system or subject material. You literally have your finger on the pulse of life. Your emotional nature is also finely honed and controlled, which appears to neutralize the volatile temperament associated with your tree sign. However, it must manifest somewhere, and it is most likely to produce a slightly fanatical zeal or passion for your work and objectives in life. You are therefore a latter-day crusader who may become involved in setting the world to rights. With 163, 177, 194 or 211 you think in abstract terms which can become totally divorced from reality. But if with 164, 167, 181, 186, 197 or 203 you have access to a wider vision and your tendency to worry unduly is largely mitigated. With 165, 179 or 189 your cool emotional nature is softened and more expressive. Also, you are more sociable and gracious in your manner due to a positive blend of emotions and intellect. With 162, 169, 183, 188, 199 or 205 your mental application, though erratic, shows a mind bordering on genius that can produce some startling facts and figures. Overall, your lunar position reveals a discriminating outlook and a disinclination to accept the possibility of influences that are beyond your control.

Hidden agenda

Your hidden agenda is to combine your logical deductions with more subtlety of thought. In past lives you adopted a critical approach and eventually lost sight of the wider picture or implications because you were inclined to prejudge people and issues. During your current life this residual memory remains a negative influence, and as a result you will continue to follow a few dead-ends. But you have the ability to consciously reprogram your own mind and senses, and this is your karmic lesson. Your psychological profile is fascinatingly complex and full of contradictions, but you also have a greater understanding of humanity than you perhaps realize.

You could certainly write a book on good manners and how to impress your boss or anyone else, for that matter. Your Shadow self is a projection of your unconscious mind, a lunar dimension of character that is finely balanced between self-interests and a genuine concern for the welfare of others. You are basically a person who dislikes confrontations or discord of any kind, so you will try to maintain a diplomatic approach. However, this can sometimes have the effect of perpetuating a state of pointless compromise – a situation where nothing is really achieved unless you are prepared to act decisively and not backtrack or take the easy option when the going gets tough. This is even more apparent with regard to personal relationships, as your feelings can become fickle and your indecision can actually cause more conflict. Your volatile temperament is also inclined to swing between two extremes when your diplomacy fails. With 160, 164, 167, 179, 186 or 197 all these aspects are favourable for making fair judgements and for pursuing a worthwhile career. With 159, 162, 166, 180 or 185 you will pursue your objectives more aggressively and independently as an advocate of free speech and the rights of the individual.

With 163, 177, 194, 200 or 211 you are easily distracted and can be manipulated by others; these are difficult aspects generally for making decisions, and there is a tendency to pursue unrealistic projects. Overall, your lunar position activates your psychic powers linked to telepathy, and this can be particularly effective in business dealings or partnerships.

Hidden agenda

Your hidden agenda is to develop an inner harmony and ultimately extend this to your relationship with a partner. You have reached the point of individualism which cannot evolve without the input of another soul. During your current life you may find yourself in isolated positions in order to prove your self-sufficiency or self-worth. But the warmth and affection provided in a stable relationship is paramount to your spiritual and emotional survival, and this is your karmic lesson to learn. A residual memory of past-life experience can make you very hesitant, because in the past you felt betrayed by those closest to you. In your current life, as a result, you tend to act on the premise of no regrets, despite your feelings of guilt. Psychologically speaking, you are a loner who yearns to come in from the cold.

67

Hawthorn
....
Moon in
Libra

Your penetrating insights and highly psychic nature automatically place you in a position to influence people, regardless of which tree sign you were born under. Your Shadow self is a projection of your unconscious mind, a lunar dimension of character that reveals a powerful inner battle for supremacy on the most basic levels of human nature. While it largely entails coming to terms with your sexuality, it also hovers around your sense of morality. You are a person who has effectively created your own value system without reference to external

68

Hawthorn
....
Moon in
Scorpio

principles. Generally speaking, you have a dynamic energy and will-power that can lead to high achievement, but because you do nothing in half measures, once committed to a course of action you will pursue it whatever the risks may be. This single-mindedness can be your greatest strength but also your greatest weakness. The volatile temperament associated with this tree sign can become extremely explosive and unforgiving. It can cause great damage in personal relationships, but it may also manifest in work situations, where you will be inclined to make dramatic exits. With 167, 181, 186, 195, 197, 203, 273 or 279, any of these aspects will help to 'lighten up' your whole psyche, and your single-mindedness becomes more focused on helping others. Scorpio lunar positions always have powerful residual influences that can become constructive or destructive; either way, they are extremely difficult to disperse or resolve. With 163, 177, 184, 211, 263, 268 or 289 these aspects are negative influences, which can evoke the darker elements of your psyche. Overall, your lunar position shows great inner turbulence due to repressed emotions, but you also have sufficient inner strength to overcome any emotional upsets.

Hidden agenda

Your hidden agenda is to attune yourself to a simple ethical code without becoming a fanatic. Your repressed emotions are a residual memory of past lives when you belonged to austere religious sects. During your current life you will be confronted with critical choices that you have subconsciously invoked, and you also know the answers. Your psychological profile reveals strength of character and a set mentality that pushes everything to the limit, including painful self-assessments. Your self-imposed ordeals relate to the initiation rites of Celtic Smith-gods, who symbolically represent the need to reduce a basic substance back to its original core, thus exposing its most precious quality – an ordeal that reveals your karmic lesson in life.

69

Hawthorn
· · · · · · · · · · · · ·
Moon in
Sagittarius

You have the ability to raise people's spirits merely by your presence. Your sense of humour and self-confidence are extremely infectious. Your Shadow self is a projection of your unconscious mind, a lunar dimension of character that springs from an eternal source of optimism or hope. You are therefore a person who can influence others for the greater good. You are also aware that others will try and interpret your actions and words, and you have a conscious fear of being misunderstood. As a result you may initially opt out of society or refuse to make personal commitments of any kind. Eventually, however, you will feel compelled to take life more seriously, as your lunar position has long been associated with eternal students who accumulate a wealth of worldly and philosophical knowledge. But such a process demands greater self-discipline. With 160, 167, 186 or 197 your word is your bond and you have a deeply philosophical mind, but your sense of humour remains undiluted. Laughter is a great healing mechanism, and your concern for the welfare of others may direct you into the caring professions or the ministry. You also have the capacity for writing or journalism. With 161, 168, 175, 192 or 198 you take life far too seriously and are inclined to preach or take the high moral ground rather then help others. With 162, 169, 183, 188, 199 or 205 you are highly intelligent – a revolutionary thinker who can upset people in authority with your uncompromising stand on humanitarian issues. Overall, your lunar position shows your volatile temperament is directed towards addressing injustices inflicted on others.

Hidden agenda

Your hidden agenda is to steer clear of becoming entangled in too many causes or vast projects that have no clear mandate. In past lives you were inclined to waste your time and energy chasing rainbows rather than following a detailed map listing your priorities. In your current life it is essential that you broaden your horizons and, while a few diversions may provide useful notes for future reference, your karmic lesson is learning how to use your highly developed intuitive powers more wisely. You will also meet many people with differing viewpoints, but you remain a likely candidate for finding a source of truth that relates to the spiritual quest of the Holy Grail, which requires asking the right questions. Your psychological profile reveals a deep sense of expectation in your current life, and this type of residual memory usually confirms a belief in reincarnation.

Y ou are a person who learns the hard way rather than taking advice or going for the easy option. You are also a reliable and conscientious individual with a great deal of common sense. Your Shadow self is a projection of your unconscious mind, a lunar dimension of character that is forced into taking a dominating role as a natural response to the needs of others. Your personal life is therefore limited as you struggle to sort out the problems of others. Generally speaking, you have a dignity that people admire. But underneath that tough exterior you are extremely sensitive and easily hurt, and you can then become depressed and feel insecure. Your volatile temperament has been suppressed early on in life, but if you feel that others are taking advantage of your good nature, you will speak your mind and deliver a chilling rebuke. With 159, 162, 166, 180 or 185 you are unlikely to be taken advantage of, and though you will help others, it will be strictly on your own terms. With regard to financial matters you should soon become a person of independent means. With 160, 164, 167, 169, 181 or 186, any of these aspects add depth and breadth of character. You have powerful individual traits and talents that have the hallmark of an entrepreneur. With 161, 175, 182, 192, 198 or 209 you are a profound thinker who feels as if the weight of the world is on your shoulders. Nevertheless you will struggle on to achieve your objectives and eventually succeed where

70

Hawthorn
. . . .
Moon in Capricorn

even the most resolute people have failed. Overall, your lunar position is a stabilizing influence for realizing your potential.

Hidden agenda
Your hidden agenda is to break free from a behavioural pattern that you have inherited from past lives, and which has also manifested itself in your parents. Family karma is extremely complex and you have been forced to replay your role many times. During your lifetime, however, you will sooner or later discover that you have been duped. In other words, you will suddenly realize that you have been a willing participant in your own downfall. Your psychological profile reveals an alternating strength and weakness of character, which needs adjusting so you can begin to develop your true self. When you can rise above your family disharmony you have taken the first step in the right direction and will begin to fulfil your own karmic lesson.

71

Hawthorn
....
Moon in Aquarius

You have a unique vision of the world and humanity generally. You are, as a result, inclined to become involved with unconventional or controversial issues, which it appears that only you understand. Your Shadow self is a projection of your unconscious mind, a lunar dimension of character that has access to an advanced human consciousness not yet in operation. You are not alone, however, as you will begin to discover when New Age thinking starts to become a reality. How you handle it depends on a great deal of self-discipline and being able to convey your ideas to others in a simple, practical manner rather than through convoluted rhetoric. Because you are a strong-willed individualist you tend to have dogmatic opinions, even though much of your thinking is highly original and progressive. You are also intellectually inclined and emotionally contained regarding your expression of feelings. Basically, you are a kind and thoughtful person who prefers expressing your emotions on an impersonal and humanitarian level. With 162, 169, 183, 188, 199 or 205 you have a brilliant intellect and, while it requires firm control, you are a person destined to make a name for yourself in the New Age movement. With 160, 164, 167, 181, 186, 197 or 203 you have a more balanced mind and a personal integrity which earns respect. You are essentially a broad-minded individual who abides by an honourable code of conduct. With 176 or 210 your vision and intellectual potential lacks stability and can become extremely reactionary if left unchecked. Overall, your lunar position reveals a high degree of emotional tension which requires more conscious control.

Hidden agenda
Your hidden agenda is to learn the value of friendship and the value of your dreams or vision. In your current life you will receive telepathic guidance or messages in your dreams that should help you to understand the reason for your actions. In past lives you were discontent with society and emotional relationships,

hence this residual memory encourages you to constantly change course or seek greener pastures, only to find that you have become more entangled both emotionally and financially. Your psychological profile reveals a powerful ego that operates through a destructive form of self-pride. Once you relinquish this grip of self-importance you should then be able to see yourself through the unclouded mirror of your mind, a spiritual experience and karmic lesson to learn.

Y ou are a person who can be greatly troubled by dreams. As a result you will spend a great deal of your life avoiding people or situations that instinctively make you feel ill at ease or intimidated. Your Shadow self is a projection of your unconscious mind, a lunar dimension of character that is highly receptive and, at times, highly vulnerable to negative influences. Your greatest asset is, however, a perfected sense of idealism, which the rest of humanity could learn from. You have a gentle, amicable nature and, though you can be extremely gullible, you have the ability to rise above the darker aspects in the human psyche: power and avarice. You also have the ability to influence people through compassionate deeds and creative artistic talents. The latter can take many forms, but there is a mystical alchemy associated with your tree sign which promotes magicians and illusionists. Your compassionate and non-materialist nature also leans towards vocational caring careers. With 167, 170 or 189 you are more likely to become involved with charitable or aid work and groups concerned with healing on a spiritual level. You have a quiet serenity that provides a calming influence. With 163, 177, 184 or 194, though you have artistic and healing abilities they can lack cohesion and encourage unrealistic goals. With 168, 187 or 204 you have a greater concentration all round and your self-discipline enables you to perfect your true potential. Overall, your lunar position reveals a spiritual nature and artistic abilities.

Hidden agenda
Your hidden agenda is to transcend your unconscious fears, which have become incompatible with self-growth. In past lives you worked closely with people who suffered greatly from painful illnesses or social deprivation. In your current life you should be able to re-channel this residual memory and energies into a constructive programme of self-development. Your compassionate nature will be tested many times and these experiences can become quite exhausting, both spiritually and physically, but can also banish any false illusions or fears. This is your karmic lesson to achieve. Your psychological profile reveals feelings of anxiety, which can initially stem from low self-esteem. As a result you tend to hide behind a stronger partner or make excuses for your non-attendance.

72

Hawthorn
. . . .
Moon in Pisces

Celtic moon sign: Oak

Lunar Symbol: White Mare

The lunar symbol of a horse, associated with the time of the solstices, had a sacred origin for the Celts. Its association with their Horse-goddess, Rhiannon, as the *White Mare* at the Summer Solstice, represented their ancient matriarchal culture. The symbolic rebirth of her son, Pryderi, as the *Black Horse* at the Winter Solstice, acknowledges the primeval power of their Moon-goddess, whose battle for supremacy with solar deities eventually reached a compromise. In Celtic myth, Pryderi was stolen at birth and his mother was falsely accused of his death and forced to undertake a humiliating and unjust penance. Pryderi's timely return in Celtic myth restored the ancient autocracy of their matriarchal Moon-goddess and confirms the authenticity of an ancient Celtic lunar zodiac. The symbol of a horse or mare was a favourite totem or tribal god of the Celts, and horses were depicted on the earliest Celtic coins.

The oak tree in Irish Celtic myth was associated with the 'Good God' or the 'Dagda', who was akin to the ancient Greek god, Jupiter, being synonymous with the planet Jupiter. Both were Thunder-gods and the oak, like the ash, was said to court the lightning flash which, according to the Druids, symbolized divine inspiration. During the seventh lunar month the oak tree marked a turning point of earthly existence when the soul was raised to the heights of Gwynved (Celtic Heaven) in order to be reminded of its purpose or trial on Earth. The Summer Solstice marks the time when the Sun (light) is at its zenith, and Jupiter in the Celtic lunar zodiac represents the expanding consciousness of humankind.

Oak Tree character

You were born at the time of the year when the radiance of summer light reaches its apex. Your notable characteristics are therefore associated with an enlightened mind that has great depth, breadth and vision. Oak Tree characters, not surprisingly, personify all the very best human qualities imaginable. You are, as a result, naturally drawn to demanding professions and responsible positions in life. You are inclined to adopt a strong moral code and this, combined with the ability to speak the truth no matter what the consequences may be, relates to the sacrificial nature of the Oak-king who symbolically dies at the Summer Solstice. In Druidry it represents the sacrificial ego of the Sun-king, who then journeys through the Underworld kingdom during the second half of the year. Psychologically speaking, it can make you a willing victim or a 'devil may care' character who lives life to the full.

Your inherited traits of character come from your father's side of the family, but your mother was most probably the strongest parental influence during your youth, as father figures or male influence tend to be missing at this time. It can be as a result of a divorce or your father pursuing a career which took him away from home for long periods. With regard to your own personal relationships, you have a generosity of spirit that can make you an ideal parent or partner. But because you are inclined to set high standards of personal behaviour, it is sometimes difficult for others to live up to, and if you feel that you are being undermined at home or in your marriage, a great deal of your motivation will be temporarily drained or misdirected. You are more vulnerable than any other sign regarding the affairs of the heart, as your trusting nature tends to make you a victim rather than a perpetrator of discord. But generally speaking, Oak Tree people appear to sail through life with great style and self-confidence and they attract powerful friends.

With 160, 167, 181, 186, 197 or 203 all the positive traits of character are activated and your keen sense of fair play and personal integrity is never in doubt. Your abundant vitality and personal enterprise will always open doors with uncanny timing, as you have what appear to be the 'keys to the kingdom'. There is, however, always a price to pay, and with such fortunate influences surrounding you it can also create complacency, extreme self-indulgence and ostentatious behaviour. If also with 161, 175, 187 or 204 you are less inclined to take things for granted and you are a more profound philosopher of life. With 164 you have great oratorical skills, and with 165, 170, 179 or 189 your charming manner and social background should ensure a high position in life. There is also a strong association with the arts and glamorous friendships. Generally speaking, you will always attract people to your side as there is a radiance or magnetic aura surrounding you. Your lunar position will clarify just how finely attuned it is, and your Basic Paragraph is thus extended to provide another hidden dimension.

You have what it takes to set a course through life and follow your own objectives to the letter. While at times it may appear that you are acting out of self-interests, you are determined to set in motion changes that will ultimately be beneficial to others. Your Shadow self is a projection of your unconscious mind, a lunar dimension of character that reacts strongly to adversity. Though you are inclined to be tactless and intolerant, you are capable of striking a few blows for individual freedom and justice that help to create a more level playing field for everyone. Whatever your motives, no one can accuse you of lacking the courage of your convictions. You make a strong ally but a dangerous foe, as you tend to operate on the premise that people are either for you or against you. With 159, 166, 180, 185, 196 or 202 you are a human dynamo who is able to out-perform all competitors. Your audacity and sharp wit is a marked character trait, but you must learn to curb your impulsive and aggressive behaviour. With 170, 179 or

73

Oak
....
Moon in
Aries

189 you have a romantic nature and a generally more sensitive and affectionate disposition. Overall, your lunar position reveals ardent passions and a fiery temperament.

Hidden agenda

Your hidden agenda is to develop your skills as an independent referee or agent. While you make a worthy opponent, your real strength of character lies in your ability to speak the truth or make fair assessments. In past lives you were inclined to act on impulse and then bitterly regret the consequences. During your current life you will therefore find it extremely difficult at times to make firm commitments, but you are also able to learn from your mistakes and revise your game plan. Your psychological profile reveals a headstrong individual who finds it hard to accept advice or help from others. You prefer to do things your own way because you fervently believe in yourself. Personal relationships will always figure strongly in your life as the means of learning how to integrate your head with your heart or with unconditional love, which is your karmic lesson to learn.

74

Oak
....
Moon in Taurus

You are person of impeccable taste – a refined attribute which enables you to invest shrewdly in antiques or art. You are adept in business and highly proficient in handling finances. Your Shadow self is a projection of your unconscious mind, a lunar dimension of character that provides an inner sense of harmony and grace. You will move through the charmed circles of society, and though you are not a pretentious person you have natural poise and self-assurance. You are warm-hearted, affectionate and have a firm set of values. Just as the oak tree is deeply rooted in the earth, so you too want to set down roots and achieve solid or lasting results. But you may also become rooted in your opinions and too obsessed with routines. A feeling of security is obviously important to you, and this can be transferred to your partner, manifesting as either jealousy or possessiveness. With 165, 170, 179, 189, 195 or 201 your refined tastes and artistic leanings are fully engaged and you will be fortunate in love and financially secure. With 177, 182, 194 or 211, all these aspects have the effect of undermining your true potential. With 272 or 274 your possessive and jealous streak will result in painful separations and inner torment. Aspects 164, 167, 181 or 186 will increase your mental flexibility and generally help to broaden your viewpoint. Overall, your lunar position reveals strong powers of endurance.

Hidden agenda

Your hidden agenda is to learn to distinguish the difference between your own desires and the needs of others. In past lives you were a highly sensual individual who appreciated the finer things in life, although this became an obsession. During your current life your karmic lesson is to evolve an inner sense of contentment to a new level of consciousness or enlightenment. Your psychological profile reveals a certain intensity of feelings which can be difficult to express openly. You are perhaps wary of sharing your dreams, as there is a residual fear or memory that you have been deeply wounded in the past. While this sense of insecurity can manifest early in your current life, it also relates to past lives and represents an ongoing conflict or battle of wills with a partner or children. Because you are a strong-willed character it can leave little room for compromise in any family disputes, and usually manifests as personality clashes. As an Oak Tree character you will, however, make personal sacrifices for your family.

Y ou know how to communicate your ideas with superb artistry. You are witty, highly adaptable and have a flair for writing and languages. Your Shadow self is a mirror image of your unconscious mind, a lunar dimension of character that interacts with your conscious self on an intellectual and emotional level. Consequently, your imagination is highly developed and soundly based on logic and intuition – a rare combination. You are, however, emotionally still inclined to be fancy-free or very flirtatious. Generally speaking, you have a restless curiosity that acts as a prime directive in acquiring knowledge and insights into a vast range of information. As an Oak Tree character you have an inborn sense of right and wrong, which enables you to be extremely influential with regard to moral issues. As a journalist or a commentator you rank highly as an informed source. But whatever your chosen profession, you know how to impress people with your versatile skills. With 157, while you are extremely witty and intellectually inclined, you can lack sincerity. With 160, 164, 167, 186 or 197 your code of ethics is enforced and your search for knowledge delves deeply into many profound philosophies. With 162, 169, 183, 188, 199 or 205 you operate from a higher mind level that enables you to glimpse the future. Overall, your lunar position reveals a fluidity of thought and feelings that requires creative channelling, otherwise it is too easily dissipated.

Hidden agenda
Your hidden agenda is to learn what the world looks like through the differing perspectives of others. You should discover that all the negative qualities of others mirror your own lack of understanding of self. In past lives you were very clever at projecting your thoughts on to others, and therefore during your current lifetime your karmic lesson is to learn by merely looking and listening. Your psychological profile reveals a multi-faceted personality who lives in a two-dimensional world of reality and illusion. The trouble is you are such a good 'double-act' that it is difficult for others to fully comprehend who you really are. But perhaps that is part of your contribution to society – being able to stimulate other people's imagination and curiosity.

75

Oak
....
Moon in
Gemini

76

Oak
·············
Moon in
Cancer

You are a kind and sympathetic person with strong maternal or paternal instincts. You have a clannish-type mentality, which is highly protective to all family members and close friends. Your Shadow self is a projection of your unconscious mind, a lunar dimension of character that is highly psychic. Because you are an extremely sensitive individual you can easily become upset emotionally, and over-sensitive to criticism. The sacrificial nature of your tree sign can also be negatively engaged, which can make you either a willing martyr or inclined to talk excessively about your own tales of woe. Generally speaking, the lunar cycles have a tremendous impact on your emotional behaviour, and your mood swings – like a pendulum – can rise and fall between the two extremes. If your Moon has positive aspects, your caring and charitable nature has all the hallmarks of a patron or benefactor to worthy causes. With 160, 167, 186 or 197 you are a truly enlightened individual who will devote a great deal of time to helping and caring for others whom society has rejected. With 161, 175 or 182, while you have great inner strengths and well-defined ambitions, you are inclined to sombre moods and lack a sense of humour. With 170, 184 or 206 your psychic ability is highly advanced and you are a true mystic and natural healer. Overall, your lunar position denotes a resourceful and enterprising individual.

Hidden agenda

Your hidden agenda is to learn to tolerate failure in yourself. In past lives your feelings of inadequacy became physically debilitating and encouraged a potent form of hypochondria. During your current life you will experience strong family burdens and thus you may learn the emotional needs of others. Your psychological profile reveals a tendency to dwell in the past or, by focusing upon past events, relive painful memories in the form of a retrograde emotional cycle. When you are finally able to reach a stage of validating your current life experience, you should then be able to make a karmic transition of self-renewal; thus your karmic lesson is to accept who you are and only *then* decide whether to make any necessary changes. In the Celtic lunar zodiac it symbolizes moving from winter cold and darkness to summer light and warmth: a path of the reborn soul.

77

Oak
·············
Moon in
Leo

You are an extremely straightforward character. There is nothing complex or difficult to understand about you or your objectives in life. You have an inner glow of self-confidence that also promotes enthusiasm and expectation in others. Your Shadow self is a projection of your unconscious mind, a lunar dimension of character that manifests in your sense of dignity and social skills. You have powerful emotions and express your feelings forcefully, but always with great affection and loyalty. Indeed, as an Oak Tree character, affairs of the heart take precedence over everything else in your life. However, because you are also extremely vulnerable to false friends and flattery, you need to approach all personal relationships with more caution and care. But this can be a difficult lesson to learn, as your natural instinctive behaviour is one of magnanimity and trust. On the other hand you do court mutinous or underhand behaviour from others, as you are inclined to want to dominate or organize their lives in line with your own plans. With 165, 170, 179 or 189 you are more sensitive to the feelings of others, and are likely to find great contentment and happiness in romantic relationships. Artistic talents are also emphasized. With 190, 194, 196, 207 or 222 you are likely to experience discord and discontent in most personal relationships as a result of being extremely demanding or completely insensitive. Overall, your lunar position reveals a high level of emotional and physical energy, which can be positively channelled into the arts and sport.

Hidden agenda

Your hidden agenda is to harness your enormous energy and will-power for a team effort rather than a solo path to glory. While initially you need to strive for excellence on a personal level, your greatest period of self-growth will come with sharing your good fortune and expertise with others. In past lives you achieved personal recognition through taking the initiative in critical situations. During your current lifetime you will certainly be called upon to use your leadership qualities and, if necessary, make some personal sacrifices. The symbolism of the 'sacrificial ego' as the pathway to spiritual expansion and growth, associated with your tree sign, is the most difficult task for people with Leo Moons, but it is part of your karmic lesson to learn. Your psychological profile reveals a great inner pride in being free to make your choices rather than be counted among the 'common herd'. When you begin to realize that any form of elitism is contrary to the freedom of the individual, you may then fulfil your karma.

Y ou are a person who strives to build a core of self-confidence by analysing your ideas and objectives to a perfect ideal, which can compromise your emotional needs. Your Shadow self is a projection of your unconscious mind, a lunar dimension of character that initially refuses to be influenced by the heart or conscience. You prefer instead to work from the intellectual argument of scepticism and logic – only then to discover that your conclusions have a hollow ring of superficiality. You

are basically a person at odds with nature and your own spirituality. You will, however, unconsciously absorb a great deal of knowledge or enlightenment that inevitably draws you towards the self-sacrificing virtues of your tree sign. The negative aspect attached to your lunar position is the tendency to worry inwardly; this can become a debilitating feature since it can, in turn, affect your physical and mental vitality. With 164, 166, 167, 185, 188, 196, 197 or 204 your mind is greatly

78

Oak
•••••••••••
Moon in Virgo

strengthened and you have a broader out-look and physical vitality. With 161,182 or 209 your tendency to worry can become a major factor of under-achievement and low self-esteem. Vitality and motivation are also difficult to maintain. Overall, your lunar position shows a keen business acumen and cool emotions that can be extremely difficult for others to respond to or fully comprehend, so try not to appear too aloof or alienate others in the process.

Hidden agenda

Your hidden agenda is to use your analyt-ical powers with humility and overcome your inherent fear of becoming a victim of persecution or deceit. This fear is a residual

memory of past-life experience and has a complex nature. Your refusal to be overly influenced by your emotions is the mani-festation of your instinctive need to resist being manipulated by others, which is the prime reason for your natural sense of reserve. During your current lifetime your ability to recognize the root cause of pain in others can become a source of healing for your own wounds. Your psychological profile reveals a highly sensitive and empathetic nature underneath layers of restrained emotions. Your head may rule your heart, but you are vulnerable never-theless to external forces that may gradu-ally change your attitudes, and this is your karmic lesson to learn.

79

Oak
·············
Moon in
Libra

You have an extremely friendly and easy-going nature on the surface, but deep down you are carefully weighing up the odds in your favour. This seemingly calculating form of behaviour is, however, designed to provide the best means of leading a carefree lifestyle. Your Shadow self is a projection of your unconscious mind, a lunar dimension of character that knows the advantage of compromise and diplomacy. But, though you have a strong ego, self-reliance needs to be consciously developed if you are to achieve any objec-tives in life. You are nevertheless a natu-rally charming and refined individual who epitomises some of the best Oak Tree characteristics. Your weak point is your tendency to vacillate, which is due to your fluctuating emotions and physical energy. With regard to personal relationships, especially partnerships, you strive to find

harmony to such an extent that you can unwittingly create a false illusion of hap-piness. In other words, you will find it hard to admit that your changeable behaviour and indecisiveness is in any way respon-sible for domestic upsets. With 165, 179, 201 or 217 you are fortunate in love and in securing a profitable income. Your appre-ciation of the arts is also actively pursued. With 172, 190 or 222 these aspects denote disharmony and turbulent emotions which stem from a self-indulgent nature. Over-all, your lunar position reveals a genuine sense of fair play and courteous manners, if somewhat fickle emotions.

Hidden agenda

Your hidden agenda is to balance your own expectations and needs with those of others. It is perhaps one of the most diffi-cult karmic lessons to learn, as your lunar position marks the polarizing energy of the equinoxes, which can either create a schism within your psyche or unite your heart and mind. In past lives you were inclined to compromise your position through taking the easy options. During your current lifetime you will be drawn into acting as a referee or neutral adviser in all kinds of disputes. This experience should help you to become more objective or decisive, but most of all it will remind you of the consequences of your own actions. Your psychological profile reveals an inner sense of loneliness that impels you to seek the company of others from an early age. But while you will quickly learn the art of socializing, you also need to learn to love with equal sensitivity.

80

Oak
....
Moon in
Scorpio

You are a great survivor and this is largely due to your ability to make fresh beginnings without regrets of any kind. Your Shadow self is a mirror image of your unconscious mind, a lunar dimension of character that can rise above the yoke of an earthbound spirit. The only thing you need to watch out for is your tendency to over-dramatize situations, which can result in burning too many bridges, making you an exile rather than a full participant of life. You have powerful emotions and passionate desires that can also overwhelm others. As you do nothing in a half-hearted manner, you are inclined to over-indulge in the pleasures in life, which can weaken your spiritual self. Your penetrating insight into human nature can make you a perceptive analyst. As an Oak Tree character your self-sacrificing nature can take an ironic twist. Being armed with the fatal sting of the scorpion you are not a passive victim; you will stand your ground and force others to capitulate. With 159, 166, 180, 185, 196, 267 or 276 you are a force to be reckoned with, but while people may not warm to you, they will respect your courage and honesty. With 190, 207, 268, 271 or 277 all the destructive traits are activated and you can become totally ruled by your turbulent emotions and succumb to self-indulgence. Look for more stabilizing aspects of Saturn. Overall, your lunar position reveals powerful undercurrents of emotion and psychic energy, which require all your strength of character to control.

Hidden agenda
Your hidden agenda is to transform your old behavioural patterns of past lives, which have resurfaced in your current life, manifesting as a smouldering intensity. You can also activate karmic energy in others, and this is why some people feel uneasy in your presence. During your lifetime you will have to realign your tremendous inner strength and redefine your sense of purpose. While much needs to be discarded, you have an inherent sense of right and wrong, or black and white, but it's time to explore the rainbow colours of your higher mind. Your psychological profile reveals a secretive nature, difficult even for analysts to come close to understanding. But while you are inclined to keep certain thoughts to yourself, one by one they should suddenly crystallize into a formula for self-growth.

81

Oak

....

Moon in
Sagittarius

You are the archetypal Oak Tree character. People love you for your generosity of spirit and jovial nature. You are extremely adaptable and broad-minded, and though you are a free-loving individual you are also very dependable in times of crisis. Your Shadow self is a mirror image of your unconscious mind, a lunar dimension of character that provides an eternal source of optimism and good will. While your lunar position confirms the positive aspects of your tree sign, the negative aspects can take the form of the extreme or the outrageous rather than an actual limiting force. In other words, you tend to become blindly optimistic rather than pessimistic. In your early years you are inclined to be unconventional for the sheer hell of it, but as a mature adult you will suddenly change and become a leading member of the community. There is also a restless energy permeating your whole psyche which requires creative channelling. With 160, 167, 181, 186 or 197 you are true to form, being generous, sincere, philosophical and high-minded, but never with a sense of superiority. Generally these are fortunate aspects that provide an element of luck throughout your life. With 174, 191 or 208 you will squander any inheritances and waste your energy and talents on frivolous escapades. Overall, your lunar position endorses your tremendous potential, but you will also have to develop an equal amount of self-discipline in order to utilize it fully.

Hidden agenda
Your hidden agenda is to put your own affairs in order before you begin philosophizing on what is wrong with the world and society in general, otherwise you will leave yourself open to ridicule by operating double standards. In past lives you were inclined to undertake reckless pleasures and pursuits. During your lifetime you will certainly make a few errors of judgement that could threaten your lifestyle or financial security. But the 'Dragon's Eye', a Celtic karmic symbol of continuous soul-growth, has dealt you such a fortunate hand that you are able to survive the blows of fate. Your psychological profile reveals a robust physical and mental constitution, which prescribes to a healthy state of mind and body.

82

Oak

....

Moon in
Capricorn

You are a person who gains ground by sheer persistence and self-discipline. Nothing falls easily into your lap, but you have the inner strength of the Oak Tree character and the concentrated energy of your lunar position. Your Shadow self is a projection of your unconscious mind, a lunar dimension of character that has all the strengths and weaknesses associated with the Moon. On the one hand you have a great deal of common sense and tenacity, and a resourceful nature. On the other hand you are prone to depressive moods and can harbour resentments. With regard to affairs of the heart you are less likely to let people get close enough to hurt you, but your lack of warmth can have a rather chilling effect on others. You are a very sober edition of your tree sign and yet there is a virtuous side to your nature that is less flamboyant but extremely praiseworthy. Your dry sense of humour can also be exceedingly funny, relying on a few well-chosen words. With 160, 167, 179, 181, 186 or 197 these aspects will boost your spirits and generally fire your imagination. Also, personal relationships are more likely to succeed. With 161, 172, 182, 192, 198 or 209, while you may have a profound mind and tremendous inner drive, you lack physical and spiritual vitality and can become too materialistic. Overall, your lunar position errs on the side of caution and self-reliance, but as a stabilizing influence it has a great deal to offer.

Hidden agenda

Your hidden agenda is to break out of the self-imposed prison you have created for yourself. You have a highly sensitive and compassionate nature that has been buried under tons of karmic rubble accumulated over centuries – hence your current trait of collecting junk. Karmic rubble is just as worthless, and yet you feel that you might find something of value. During your lifetime your finer qualities will gradually begin to surface and you should find something of immeasurable value that you have overlooked – namely your self-respect. This is your karmic lesson, which paves the way for future growth. Your psychological profile reveals a strong conscious need to take control of your own life, which may be due to a domineering or emotionally demanding parent. This may have contributed to your inability to express your feelings more openly, but it can also stem from a physical handicap. Either way you need to assert yourself more effectively.

You are a child of the New Age. Whether you are now old or young, you are naturally attuned to the future rather than the past. Your Shadow self is a projection of your unconscious mind, a lunar dimension of character that has a unique insight into the changing face of humanity. Just as an astronomer watches the unfolding spectacle of our universe and far beyond, you can plot humankind's destiny as a social reformer or an astrologer. You have the essential qualifications or mind-set to expand human knowledge to the outermost limits of comprehension, but yours is not an easy task. You will find bigotry and closed minds everywhere, and this can be most daunting.

Your unconventional lifestyle and lack of respect for authority can also create a few social problems. Your independent stance is admirable, but it can manifest as an emotional barrier that keeps even loved ones at bay. With 162, 169, 183, 188, 199 or 205 you are an outstanding individualist who will make radical policy changes from the shop floor to top management. With 176, 193 or 210, while you have intellectual prowess, your unpredictable mood swings and eccentric behaviour can invalidate your credentials. You also need to go back to basics and train your mind accordingly. Your lunar position overall shows a genuine humanitarian who believes the best in

83

Oak
. . . .
Moon in
Aquarius

people until proved otherwise, especially in affairs of the heart.

Hidden agenda

Your hidden agenda is to remind others that life is a unique adventure. Though you may find yourself quite literally out in the cold, you are no stranger to adversity. You have been pursuing your current dreams for many incarnations, and now you are about to realize their true potential. During your lifetime you will, however, have to move away from an egotistical perception of the world and replace it with your new-found humanitarian outlook, and this is your karmic lesson to learn. Your psychological profile reveals an inner need to dominate those close to you, but for some strange reason you tend to become the victim or the underdog. And for that reason alone, or the fear of it happening, you will beat a hasty retreat. Your unique characteristics can seem rather odd and quite bewildering for others to understand or accept, but your kindness to friends and strangers alike will, however, engender loyalty and affection.

84

Oak
· · · · · · · · · · · ·
Moon in Pisces

You have what appears to be an unworldly perception of life, but you are actually touching upon the essential spirit of goodness, which can empower humanity. Your Shadow self is a projection of your unconscious mind, a lunar dimension of character that fosters compassion and humility. You are highly intuitive and super-sensitive to the feelings of others, especially if they are suffering pain or stress. You can, however, become overloaded, both emotionally and physically. There is a certain frailty about you, but as an Oak Tree character you have great inner vitality and endurance. Your compassionate nature is bound to attract you towards the caring professions, but you also have an artistic temperament that is apparent in your dress and sense of colour. Combined with your ability to step into the world of illusion, it is ideal for acting, writing and photography. With 170, 189, 200 or 206 your artistic skills are activated and so are your healing skills. You have a natural serenity and personal magnetism. With 163, 177, 184, 194 or 211 you are too susceptible to negative influences and you will tend to drift through life in a haze of confusion and unreality. Look for positive aspects of Jupiter and Saturn as counterbalances. Overall, your lunar position reveals a nebulous type of Oak Tree character that is more mystical than practical; consequently affairs of the heart can be either extremely romantic and fulfilling or disastrous interludes of deceitful partnerships.

Hidden agenda

Your hidden agenda is to integrate your intuitive or abstract mind with your rational and analytical mind. You are currently operating only one dual lever, which creates an imbalance. A residual karmic influence is apparent and is the source of nervous tensions as you try to make this adjustment. In past lives you felt more secure in using your left-hand brain, or rational thinking, but this has brought you to the brink of spiritual decline. During your current lifetime you therefore tend to overcompensate in your desire to show compassion and humility. Your psychological profile shows that you are capable of immense clarity of thought but not complete peace of mind. You will, however, make great progress by nurturing your spiritual self and helping others along the way, and this is your karmic lesson to learn. Psychology provides a discerning insight into human behaviour, but the spiritual nature of humankind is more like a butterfly – a Celtic symbol of reincarnation and of the ancestral spirits that challenge rational thinking and the material world.

Celtic moon sign: Holly

Lunar Symbol: Unicorn

The lunar symbol of the *Unicorn* represented a five-season solar year in the ancient Celtic Boibel-Loth alphabet, and its horn, a symbol of solar power, was centred in the dog-days of mid-summer, which corresponds with the lunar month of the holly. Though today the unicorn is regarded as a mythical beast, in medieval Europe its spiral horn was believed to protect kings from being poisoned. As a heraldic beast it has figured in the English Royal Arms since around that period, and a spiral horn reputedly belonging to a unicorn is in King Edward's collection of artefacts in Buckingham Palace. In the mystical world of legends, unicorns once roamed Earth and were said to have a purity of spirit that cast a light around the world. Only virgin maidens could touch or tame them, and only then if their own hearts were pure. While the human spirit can flicker in the winds of darkness, the spirit of the unicorn has become a mysterious source of lunar light.

In the ritual lunar calendar and zodiac of the Druids, the Holly-king was referred to as the 'Dark Tanist', who represented the dark-twin (Avagddu) of Taliesen, an Oak-king and a Sun god. The holly tree represents the evergreen aspect of the soul, and the oak, the sacrificial ego. Hence the White Mare, symbolizing the oak month, transforms into the fabulous unicorn at the turning of the year when the solar spirit was confined to the Earth plane. During the eighth lunar month the unicorn, a symbol of undiminished light, acted as a guide through the Underworld realm of the Earth Mother Goddess, Danu, ruler of this sign.

Holly Tree character

You were born at the time of year which marked the waning light of the Sun. Days, however, are still longer than nights until the Autumnal Equinox. Your notable characteristics are influenced by a conscious need to establish a firm set of values. You are therefore an enterprising individual who may become a founding member of societies or institutions. You have a practical, down-to-earth outlook on life, and though you can also become involved with grandiose schemes, you are not a risk-taker. Generally speaking, you have a strong blend of personal qualities and, while you are hospitable and supportive, you will expect everyone to work as hard as you do for a living. You have a loving and affectionate nature and might well marry a childhood sweetheart. However, you can become prickly or irritable if people do not respect your feelings or ideas.

You have inherited some powerful traits of character from your mother's side of the family, which relates to your autocratic bearing. Your mother's ancestors were 'empire builders' in the sense of constructing things that would endure or last. You may still be involved in running a family business or using skills that have been passed down through generations. You can, as a result, become a dogmatic and pompous individual who is inclined to interfere in your children's lives or those of close family members. Providing you allow them to pursue their own interests and ambitions, you will make an ideal parent and partner. Psychologically speaking, you are a strange mixture of tough talking and highly emotional behaviour. You have a very serious side to your nature and a personal integrity that can be lost on people who have no scruples or moral fibre. But it is your strongest personal asset.

With 160, 164, 167, 187, 197 or 204 your positive traits of character are activated and you have the ability to rise above any initial setbacks and build a prosperous life for you and your family. If with 161, 182, 192, 198 or 209 the serious side of your nature can become extremely boring and austere. You will also probably dislike competition of any kind, and will play the martyr by winning sympathy rather than respect. With 168 or 175, while you are a trifle too serious and prone to moody behaviour, your inherited traits are powerfully activated and you will achieve your objectives, albeit a hard-won victory. Your tree sign is also associated with strong religious feelings or beliefs, which again relates to powerful ancestral influences. While they are likely to be orthodox beliefs, you have inherited a deep interest in the spiritual nature of humankind. Your lunar position will clarify this interest and other aspects. Your Basic Paragraph is thus extended.

85

Holly
....
Moon in Aries

You dislike any kind of restrictions, and this includes family pressures. You will therefore come into conflict with your parents at an early age. While you may still respect their ideas, you have a different set of values that can cause a few upsets, with neither side giving way.

Your Shadow self is a projection of your unconscious mind, a lunar dimension of character that reveals an adventurous spirit and a highly enterprising nature. You will always take a direct approach in life, and what you lack in diplomacy you will make up for in honesty and loyalty.

You are able to grasp the essential issues and move quickly in order to gain an advantage. This can work amazingly well most of the time, but there is a danger that you can too easily overlook important details in the process, and this can undermine exciting new projects. You need a good partner – in business and in marriage – who can provide the necessary anchor. Your emotions run at an uneven level and you will have to learn to control your temper. With 165, 166, 179 or 217 you have a positive blend of characteristics which are attractive to others and less likely to cause friction within your family circle. With 159, 172, 173 or 222 your rather aggressive tactics and self-interests will make you an unpopular figure in society and love is never really able to blossom under these aspects. Look for positive aspects between the Sun and the Moon, and between Jupiter and Venus. Overall, your lunar position requires greater self-discipline and staying power.

Hidden agenda

Your hidden agenda is to learn cooperation rather than confrontation. Not an easy task when you have a rather short temper. But as a Holly Tree character you know when to move to the high ground if a situation becomes untenable. That doesn't mean you will make insincere compromises, but you are smart enough to know when to move with the times. During your lifetime few people will get close enough to know you well, as you are constantly on the move and changing your views. Your psychological profile reveals a secret fear of failure or not having enough time to fulfil all your dreams and desires – hence you are always rushing to complete things. But it has another context if you believe in reincarnation. You have a residual memory of having to fight for all the things you needed or things you had to protect, which makes you a natural fighter or competitor; your karmic lesson is, however, to positively activate your inborn sense of honour and integrity.

You have plenty of charm and appreciate the finer things in life. You will endeavour to create a comfortable home for your family, and because you need to feel secure financially and emotionally you will work hard to achieve permanent success. Your Shadow self is a projection of your unconscious mind, a lunar dimension of character that reveals a strong set of values and a practical outlook. You are therefore a very positive type of Holly Tree character who will uphold traditional family values. While you are a very patient and reliable individual, you have a highly sensual and possessive nature that is easily sparked by jealousy. In turn it can provoke a furious temper. You are, however, slow to respond initially, but once roused you find it hard to forgive, as your emotional feelings are difficult to shut off. With 165, 170, 179, 195, 201 or 217 your sensual nature is intense but emotionally stable, and your affectionate nature is warmly expressed. You should therefore find an ideal partner and achieve financial security. Your artistic

86

Holly
. . . .
Moon in
Taurus

talents are also activated. With 177, 190, 194 or 222 these aspects weaken any creative skills and personal relationships. Your passionate nature can also become extremely self-indulgent and generally destructive. Look for positive aspects between Jupiter and Saturn, and the Sun and Moon with Venus. Overall, your lunar position reveals a strong-willed individual with good business skills, who will always succeed against the odds.

Hidden agenda

Your hidden agenda is to broaden your mind and your interests so that you can learn about the ideas and needs of others. You have adopted a very compact lifestyle, which can become extremely claustrophobic emotionally and spiritually. In order to achieve self-growth during your lifetime you must therefore acquaint yourself with other methods of doing things. Your potential is not in doubt regarding personal achievement, but it can isolate you from experiencing a real sense of awareness. In past lives you pursued material goals to the extent of losing your spiritual identity. Your psychological profile reveals a highly sexual content that you tend to associate with personal power, and this in turn reinforces your powerful ego. When you are able to willingly transform this energy into creative outlets it should release those feelings of insecurity. It should also raise your base instincts to a higher level of the mind. It is really a question of looking within, to your inner self, in order to achieve this state, and this is your karmic lesson to learn.

87

Holly
....
Moon in
Gemini

You have the habit of infuriating people with your quick wit and clever answers. Verbally you are a tour de force, and while this can get you out of difficult situations, the truth is that you have unwittingly engineered these situations in the first place. Your Shadow self is a mirror image of your unconscious mind, a lunar dimension that knows how to project different images at will. You are also a natural mimic, and are inclined to use this ability to undermine people you see as boring individuals. To others you have a childlike nature bordering on precociousness. As a Holly Tree character with one foot in the Otherworld, you personify a fairy-like creature that can become a mischievous sprite. Generally speaking, you have your own set of values that are amoral rather than immoral, but few people will understand the difference. However, you are a sympathetic and spontaneous individual with an amusing line in conversation that makes people laugh, despite their misgivings – a precious gift in a world that can become dark when the light of laughter begins to fail. With 164, 167, 186 or 203 there is nothing superficial about your mind or your strength of intellect. You also have strong morals and highly versatile skills, especially as a writer or actor. With 194 or 208 you are indeed a mischievous sprite who can weave a few spells of discord or discontent among society in general. While not usually malicious, it can be extremely disconcerting to others. Your lunar position overall reveals a high level of emotional tension and a tendency to avoid family commitments.

Hidden agenda

Your hidden agenda is to learn how to interact with others and with society in general. Though you are an excellent communicator, you tend to pass through people's lives like a nomadic traveller, never settling permanently in one place. While this is a learning curve initially, when your direction in life become less vague the knowledge that you have learned through your travels will provide a noteworthy record book. In past lives you worked from the premise that the journey itself was more exciting than arriving at the destination. But your karmic lesson in your current life is to consolidate your position and contribute something of real worth. Psychologically speaking, you need a great deal of personal freedom in order to mature at your own speed.

You are a person who is likely to face conflicting needs involving family demands and your career responsibilities. Difficult choices therefore have to be made, but a satisfactory compromise is seldom achieved. Your Shadow self is a projection of your unconscious mind, a lunar dimension of character that responds to the Moon's cycles with extraordinary precision. As a result your emotional behaviour can change from being reasonably stable to harbouring high expectations, and then breaking down into troughs of depression, even melancholy. As a Holly Tree character you will always have your family interests at heart and you also abide by family traditions and values. The conflict mentioned earlier is deeply psychological. You are inclined to place yourself at the centre of your family life, and consequently you enjoy the role as chief provider and protector. With 158, 160, 167, 181 or 197 your tendency to worry is lifted and you are a more sociable and broad-minded individual.

With 161, 182, 198 or 209 your changing moods can undermine any constructive achievement and family burdens take a toll, both emotionally and financially. With 170, 184 or 200 your highly sensitive nature and religious interests are drawn towards spiritualism or strange sects. Overall, your lunar position denotes a shrewd and resourceful person with highly charged feelings that require constant affection from others.

Hidden agenda

Your hidden agenda is to learn humility, as you have an innate sense of self-importance, and this is your karmic lesson to learn. It is also time to recognize that your values need updating. There is a tendency to cling to past memories that have become a source of fantasy rather than reality. During your lifetime you may therefore experience a few rude awakenings in having to confront family karma. Psychologically speaking, this entails coming to terms with family relationships

88

Holly
·············
Moon in
Cancer

that continue to cause disharmony, despite your attempts at placation or compromise. On the other hand your own behaviour can be a contributory factor that requires a great deal of soul-searching. The main source of your discontent is a feeling of being unappreciated, though once again this charge could be levelled at you; the truth lies somewhere in between.

89

Holly
··············
Moon in
Leo

You are top-management material and keen to reorganize any family business or investments. You have a brand of self-confidence that is a commercial winner. Your Shadow self is a projection of your unconscious mind, a lunar dimension of character that provides a constant source of energy and enthusiasm. You are an affectionate and warm person who shows great loyalty to family and friends. You have sophisticated tastes and a love of luxury. You are also extremely sensitive, and take to heart any slights or unfair criticism. You will form strong opinions early on in life, which stems from a stubborn nature or a need to do things your way. But generally speaking you have many creative ideas and you know how to promote them. You can also inspire others with your natural enthusiasm and robust manner. Though you are highly ambitious you are not a ruthless person, and you have considerable charm and generosity of spirit. However, you can appear rather arrogant at times, which other people can find tedious. With 158, 170, 179 or 189 you have magnetic charm, and though you are inclined to vanity, you are a popular figure and your creative talents are artistically channelled. With 174, 191, 194 or 208 you are a spendthrift and are apt to exaggerate your achievements. You are basically lazy and tend to hold snobbish opinions. Overall, your lunar placing adds a great deal of style and panache to your basic tree sign character, which can otherwise become a little austere or autocratic.

Hidden agenda

Your hidden agenda is to act out your dreams, which can then become a reality. This will help you to develop an inner strength that enables you to become a leader rather than a follower of current trends. While you can take pride in being an individualist, you must also learn teamwork, which helps you to overcome any self-doubts, and this is your karmic lesson to learn. In past lives you were fortunate in inheriting wealth, and this weakened your own merits or potential achievements. During your current lifetime you will meet a variety of people who will increase your sense of awareness, but they can also weaken your resolve or knock your self-confidence. It is, however, not always apparent, as it can be conducted with great subtlety. Fortunately, you are a strong-willed individual who seldom takes advice, which is perhaps an intuitive response to people who say that they have your best interests at heart. Your psychological profile reveals a flamboyant personality with an unpredictable behavioural pattern that stems from a need for originality and freedom of expression.

You have an astute business sense with the mentality of an accountant, always checking the details of financial expenditure. You are therefore a valuable member of a business team or a family firm. Your Shadow self is a projection of your unconscious mind, a lunar dimension of character that finds it difficult to relax, as you have a lot of nervous energy to burn off. You have rather puritanical emotions and feelings that can be off-putting to more demonstrative people, and though you have a high degree of intelligence, it can lack breadth and vision. As a Holly Tree character with a propensity to worry, your lunar position increases this trait and emphasizes psychological inhibitions that can, in turn, affect your health and well-being. As a result you probably have a great interest in health and diet, and hypochondria can all too easily manifest. It is basically a question of natural vitality that can be diverted solely to mental activity. Physical activity is therefore essential, as is the liberation of your mind from an accumulation of irrelevant detail. With 166, 167, 185, 188, 196 or 197 these aspects will free your mind of clutter and increase your mental and physical vitality by helping to disperse nervous tension. With 158, 165 or 217 your cool emotions give way to more passionate responses and you will find time to socialize more freely. With conjunctions 161, 182, or 198, while you may develop profound knowledge, you can lead a very singular and empty life. Overall, your lunar position reveals a cool temperament and a quest for perfection.

Hidden agenda
Your hidden agenda is to develop the ability to say what you really feel, rather than always saying what you think you should say. In learning this karmic lesson you should discover that your natural instincts are strong and likely to be more accurate than simply relying on your ability to analyse feelings and thoughts to such minute detail as to obscure their true meaning. In past lives you were both persecuted and admired for your religious and political persuasion. During your lifetime people will begin to lean on you, as you appear to have the answers. However, this in effect makes you reliant on them, and this type of interaction can cloud your vision. While you have a strong compassion for humanity and a set of perfect ideals, in reality they represent a lack of self-confidence. Your psychological profile reveals that you are inwardly highly critical of others – a reflection of your own perceived weaknesses.

90

Holly
....
Moon in
Virgo

You appear to be a fairly cheerful and optimistic person, but underneath you are more complex and therefore more interesting. Your ability to make light of a difficult situation is an accomplishment, and not just an easy way out. Your Shadow self is a projection of your unconscious mind, a lunar dimension of character that has a strong sense of justice and diplomacy. You are certainly qualified to settle family disputes, and this is where you can be most decisive and effective. But with regard to personal relationships, however, especially partners, this is where you

91

Holly
....
Moon in
Libra

may experience a few problems. Apart from having a highly flirtatious nature, there is a tendency to fall in love too quickly and perhaps too early on in life, before you have properly learned the art of compromise. You are, however, more likely to find a difficult partner, as you are always intrigued to find someone who will not be swayed by your ready wit and charm. In effect, this actually amounts to more of a challenge rather than a romantic liaison. With 165, 179, 201 or 217 you will most probably find the ideal partner and be lucky both in love and in securing a comfortable income. These aspects also emphasize artistic talents and a fine appreciation of arts in general. With 177, 190, 214 or 222 your social attributes are impaired and your charm can turn into a cynical exercise of manipulation and subterfuge. Overall, your lunar position reveals a refined nature and personable attributes that outweigh any faults.

Hidden agenda

Your hidden agenda is to develop and harness your inner resources more effectively. As a result you should find that your relationship with a partner is more harmonious and less stressful. It is a question of dependency, as you are inclined to rely too much on your partner's support when you should be sharing responsibilities, particularly where children are concerned. In past lives you were often indecisive at critical periods and lost sight of your main objectives. During your current lifetime you may be pushed in new directions in order to find one central goal. This will have the effect of focusing your energy and making decisions relatively easy. Your psychological profile reveals a fairly well-balanced behavioural pattern and no major weaknesses of character, other than a need to re-evaluate your motives in life. Karma prescribes unselfish love, which can only be reached through self-sacrifice – your karmic lesson to learn.

92

Holly
. . . .
Moon in
Scorpio

You are totally ruled by your powerful emotions, which have a depth and intensity that permeates your whole psyche. But you also have a perceptive and analytical mind that can penetrate the root cause of any problems. Your Shadow self is a projection of your unconscious mind, a lunar dimension of character that is dynamic and intriguing. As a Holly Tree character your lunar position endorses family loyalties, but you are inclined to be a demanding parent and child. While you have a strong set of values, you must not try to force them on to others. Your single-minded sense of purpose in life can become an overbearing trait of character that wins few friends, and it can even divide family loyalties. Your greatest strength is being able to adjust rapidly to critical turning points in your life, which involve having to make tough decisions. Your greatest weakness, however, is an inner urge to destroy what you have created, which can make your family or business associates very reluctant to support you financially. With 166, 185, 217, 267 or 276 you are more controlled in your actions and emotions, and while you are extremely ambitious and materialistic, you show great loyalty to friends and family. You are an ardent lover rather than a romantic one. With 190, 265, 271 or 277 your relentless pursuit of power and wealth can eventually sap your energy and cause hardship in later life. Look for positive aspects between Mars and Jupiter, and also Saturn with Mars and the Sun. Overall, your lunar position reveals tremendous stamina and passionate desires.

Hidden agenda

Your hidden agenda is to shake off the negative and oppressive influences that form a kind of barrier against developing new self-awareness. While it is necessary to delve deeply into your unconscious mind, you can become submerged or entrapped by an accumulation of past-life karma. Your lunar position marks the Celtic Festival of Samhain, a time in the ritual Druidic calendar and zodiac when the boundaries of the natural and supernatural worlds were dissolved. It was a time for divination, but more significantly a time when the soul could descend into the Underworld region of Annwn, which has been referred to by qabalists as the 'Dark Night of the Soul'. Dwyll (Celtic Pluto), God of the Underworld, guarded the source or germinal seed of life, which represents the 'dark seed' aspect of transformation buried deeply within the psyche. In psychological terms it means a complete transformation of your behavioural pattern, thus achieving new spiritual direction, and this is your karmic lesson.

Y ou have a restless nature, but your intuitive powers are highly developed. They encourage philosophical studies that give the impression of a well-educated individual. Your Shadow self is a mirror image of your unconscious mind, a lunar dimension of character that reveals prophetic vision and a need for freedom of expression. You have tremendous intellectual potential, although this is not easily developed in your youth, as you need to explore all the avenues or paths to knowledge. You are also too easily distracted by the pleasures in life. Though you need to expend a great deal of physical energy, you also seek constant intellectual challenges or rapport in personal relationships. If you find yourself in the situation of having to defend your need for freedom in any relationship, you will make a rapid exit. As a Holly Tree character you may therefore find family obligations difficult to fulfil, and you will also make an early exit from your parental home. With 160, 167, 181, 186, 197 or 203 your intellectual potential is activated, and though you still need room to manoeuvre, you have strong moral principles and values that will endear you to older members of your family. With 174, 191 or 208, while you have a generous spirit and sparkling vitality, you are inclined to exaggerate your case and waste time, money and energy on ill-conceived ventures. Overall, your lunar position reveals frequent changes of residence and a tendency to speak your mind too freely, which stems from a lack of thought or tact. Try

93

Holly
. . . .
Moon in Sagittarius

to rationalize your thoughts before you speak, and generally modify your lifestyle.

Hidden agenda

Your hidden agenda is to learn to discriminate between fact and fiction. Because you enjoy expressing your ideas and philosophies to anyone who cares to listen, you have developed the art of becoming an excellent storyteller. In past lives you were also inclined to exaggerate your achievements. But in your current life, if you wish to be taken more seriously, you will have to cast a more critical eye over your store of information or repertoire. With regard to karmic lessons, it is a question of seeking the truth, which is initially obscured as you have difficulty recognizing the light or truth within. Psychologically speaking, you are an attention-seeker, and though this can be conducted with good humour and spontaneity, it can become exhausting for friends and family alike. You nevertheless have an underlying strength of character that shows great fortitude against corruption or injustices – a higher-mind level of truth.

94

Holly
....
Moon in
Capricorn

You are a serious-minded individual with a natural self-dignity that other people admire. Your Shadow self is a projection of your unconscious mind, a lunar dimension of character that has conventional values and self-discipline. As a Holly Tree character you will respond to family obligations to the letter because of your sense of duty and morality. You do, however, find all personal relationships very difficult to handle on any intimate level. You are also a born worrier, and prone to depression. Having said that, you do have the ability to surmount all problems with patience and perseverance. While some may think you lack a sense of humour, this is not wholly true as you have a knack for defusing difficult situations with a few well-chosen words. People will also know exactly where they stand with you, as you are a plain speaker and a reliable friend. With 160, 167, 181, 186 or 197 your serious nature is uplifted with optimism and greater warmth of feelings.

Though you will still remain a serious thinker, your subject matter is more varied and you possess more vitality, both physically and mentality. With 161, 182, 198, 209 or 217 your sombre moods and lack of demonstrative feelings are inherited family traits which can be difficult to overcome. If also with 223, 242 or 258 these aspects will improve your chances of success and generally mitigate negative aspects. Your lunar position overall reveals a hypersensitive nature, which explains your reluctance to expose your true feelings.

Hidden agenda

Your hidden agenda is to release your feelings of guilt, which can accumulate in your current life as a residual memory of many past incarnations where you exerted power or control over others. So while you are currently experiencing heavy family responsibilities, the underlying message is one of showing greater compassion and understanding, and this is your karmic lesson to learn. You can then cherish your own sense of self-worth. Failure to do so can make you a family martyr or a tyrant. During your current lifetime as you move towards greater understanding of your own needs as well as those of others, you will begin to grow remarkably younger in appearance. Your lunar position marks the Winter Solstice, a time when your spiritual vitality is low but on the verge of being regenerated with the turning of the solar year. In psychological terms it means planning ahead with greater confidence and imagination.

Y ou are a person with a vision. It forms a large part of your perception and your attitudes, and is focused upon the future or things to come. Your Shadow self is a projection of your unconscious mind, a lunar dimension of character that is the source of your reforming spirit and ideology. Though your ideas are often beyond the comprehension of others, in time your vision can suddenly become the driving force behind the changing opinions in society. You are in effect a trendsetter. As a Holly Tree character you will find it difficult to uphold family traditions and values if you feel they represent outdated and therefore obsolete directives. But you are also intelligent enough to realize what is worth saving in order to be recycled or marginally updated. Emotionally, however, you are inclined to be indifferent to sentimental ideals, and your need for independence can create a few upsets in family expectations. Your strong points of kindness, sympathy and humanitarian values can be undermined with unpredictable action or rebellious behaviour. With 162, 169, 183, 188, 199 or 205 your vision and humanitarian beliefs are fully activated, and you are a brilliant student of modern technology and the sciences. As a unique individualist you have the potential to make a difference. With 176, 193, 210 or 252 your eccentric behaviour and rebellious nature are tools of self-destruction. Look to Saturn for positive aspects for more stability in general. Overall, your lunar position reveals a New Age student.

Hidden agenda

Your hidden agenda is to curb your egocentric behaviour and acquire more self-discipline. A budding genius can be extremely wearisome, and you can all too easily waste your time and energy on displays of intense pride that fail to impress. Though you adopt a cool manner bordering on indifference, you are making a statement that implies superiority or elitism. During your lifetime you are likely to spend a great deal of time on your own, which can become counter-productive in realizing your full potential. If you can respond with the humility associated with your tree sign you can become a guiding influence for generations to come, and this is your karmic lesson to achieve in your lifetime. Your psychological profile reveals a need to identify with radical causes as the means of justifying your own beliefs. You are, however, a sincere supporter of personal liberty and free speech. In short, you are an activist.

95

Holly
. . . .
Moon in
Aquarius

96

Holly

. . . .

Moon in Pisces

You have a very gentle and compassionate nature. You are also highly intuitive and sensitive to energies that surround people and places. Your Shadow self is a mirror image of your unconscious mind, a lunar dimension of character attuned to the beauty of nature and the elementals or fairy people. As a Holly Tree character the mystical unicorn represents your spiritual guide who can take you safely through the Otherworld. You can intuitively identify with the true concept of the lunar dimension, which opens up another world of myth and legend that exists in the abstract or imaginative mind. Some of the world's most inspired artists draw upon this source, and you also have the potential to do so as an artist or a musician. With regard to family influences, you can be easily dominated by an overbearing parent, or your good nature may be taken advantage of – hence you find the world of fantasy and dreams an escape route. But you must avoid irrational behaviour or confusing unreality with reality. With 170, 184, 189, 200 or 206 you are a true mystic and inspired artist, a time-traveller into the mysteries. Because these aspects powerfully activate your lunar self, you will need at least one of the following aspects to provide stability and positive integration of the abstract and rational mind: 164, 178, 204 or 258. With 163, 177, 194, 211 or 259 you are locked into an unreal world, which can affect your mental and physical health. Look to Jupiter for positive aspects, and also to Saturn, Mercury and the Sun in relationship to the Moon. Overall, you lunar position is a mystical influence that needs practical application.

Hidden agenda

Your hidden agenda is to crystallize your thinking. Assuming that the world you live in is a separate world to the Otherworld of dreams and fantasies is to divide your conscious and unconscious selves into separate compartments. There is an interaction operating between these two mind-levels that draws upon the universal consciousness that is at one with nature and the higher intelligence of enlightened thinking. In past lives you led a very reclusive existence in order to achieve 'unity' or 'oneness' with nature and its creator. During your lifetime you will experience this unity or the mysterious essence of life. Your karmic lesson is to use your remarkable intuition for that purpose and to make the necessary transition. Your psychological profile reveals a nervous irritability that is difficult to explain, but can be linked to natural allergies; in your mind you are like a fish swimming in polluted streams, but this ordeal, however, is largely self-imposed and can be rectified through a belief that nothing is impossible or beyond your means.

Celtic moon sign: Hazel

Lunar Symbol: Salmon

The lunar symbol of the *Salmon* represents the oracular powers of the hazel tree dryad or spirit. In the Irish legend of Finn, the nuts of the hazel tree dropped into Conla's Well and fed the rainbow salmon swimming in it. The hazelnut was an emblem of concentrated wisdom, and all the knowledge of the arts and sciences was to be found by eating it – hence the expression 'in a nutshell'. When Finn caught one of the salmon and ate it, he was instantly endowed with wisdom and prophetic vision. The salmon is regarded as the king of all river fish, and the mystical element of water is relevant to Celtic ancestral knowledge. The source of Conla's Well is the River Boyne, named after the goddess Boann, whom Irish poets believed was the source of artistic inspiration, and the Celts have been known from antiquity as the 'People of the Sea'.

In Celtic mythology the hazel tree was known as the Bile Ratha or the venerated tree of the 'rath' in which the poetic Aes Sidhe (Fairy spirit) lived. It also gave its name to Mac Coll, or Mac Cool, 'Son of the Hazel', an Irish god who was one of the three ancient rulers of Ireland. According to the Irish Celts, their love of poetry and rhetoric originated through the inventive nature of their ancient god Ogma, who is akin to Hermes or Mercury, ruler of this sign. He was known as the God of Eloquence who had devised the first means of writing. During the ninth lunar month of the year the Druids used hazel wands for divination and to locate secret wells. They also carried white hazel wands as a symbol of arbitration when they were called upon to settle disputes and administer Celtic Law.

Hazel Tree character

You were born at the time of the year when daylight is beginning to fade at late summer. But it is the time when hazelnuts begin to ripen, and thus light is symbolically condensed into tiny particles of pure light. You therefore have tremendous personal potential that is highly focused, and your inner urge to acquire knowledge can make you a scholar or an expert in your field. You are highly perceptive and endowed with good reasoning powers or logic. You are basically a clever individual with potential abilities for the arts and sciences that could make you a fine craftsperson, tutor or writer. Emotionally, you are a rather cool customer who appears to be completely in control of any situation. But nervous tension can make you prone to severe headaches, and usually your body is physically not as robust as your mental stamina.

While your artistic temperament comes from your mother's side of the family, your intellectual or practical abilities come from your father's side. This relates to your duality of character, which tends to paint a black-and-white portrait of characteristics that appear contradictory. However, people born under the sign of the hazel are the most rational people in the Celtic lunar zodiac. You are above all else a clever strategist who always organizes a set of contingency plans just in case things go wrong. It's not that you are overly pessimistic, but rather that experience has taught you to be prepared for anything. Your keen insight into human nature can make you highly critical or cynical on occasions. Your inquisitive mind generally can also become prying or underhand. Although you are not a demonstrative person, you are inclined to indulge your partner and children, which can be detrimental to your financial security – a compensating trait that balances your unease at not always being able to express your feelings openly.

With 157 or 171 you will tend to live on your wits. But with 164, 167, 186, 197, 203 or 258 you have a more expansive and philosophical attitude and a curious but practical mind that can absorb a great deal of knowledge. You generally have a more rounded character and personality with a more optimistic outlook. With 172, 178, 198 or 259 your inability to express your feelings is emphasized and you are inclined to hold fixed opinions. A discordant note is operating between your conscious and unconscious mind, which can frustrate your true potential. With 169, 188, 199 or 205 your scientific ability is pronounced, and with 170, 184, 189 or 206 your artistic abilities, especially poetry, are activated and you are also a more romantic soul all round. Generally speaking, your dual character requires careful analysis, and the planetary aspects should provide more conclusive information. However, your lunar position will clarify the hidden dimension of your unconscious mind, which can reveal a depth of character not yet apparent. Your Basic Paragraph is thus extended.

97

Hazel
············
Moon in
Aries

You are a person who enjoys intelligent debate or arguments. You have sharp reflexes physically and mentally. While you are inclined to be impetuous and temperamental, you are a great competitor when there are accolades to be won. Your Shadow self is a projection of your unconscious mind, a lunar dimension of character that responds with sincere enthusiasm, although patience needs to be more consciously developed. You have a very unconventional approach to life in general and you dislike taking advice. But it is precisely this type of attitude that brings out the unique potential associated with your tree sign. You have new ideas that may ultimately challenge and overturn conventional wisdom that has become too entrenched. You must, however, learn to be more tactful if you are to succeed in influencing people who hold powerful positions – people who could become staunch allies rather than dangerous adversaries. With 165, 170, 179, 189, 195 or 201 you have charm, finesse and a personal magnetism that attracts powerful friends. There is also a strong association with the arts, and though you are an idealist your intuitive mind has practical application. With 159, 166, 180, 185, 196 or 202 you have persistence and determination that will make you a force to be reckoned with. But you need positive challenges and direction in life. Overall, your lunar position breeds champions.

Hidden agenda

Your hidden agenda is to achieve your potential in life without demanding what you consider to be its just rewards. In other words your achievements will merit their own rewards of rapid self-growth and the satisfaction of knowing that you have made a difference, which is the highest level of karma and your karmic lesson to learn. During your lifetime you must learn to refocus your attention on the needs of others who mirror your own weaknesses or traits of character. In past lives you were inclined to be overly aggressive and blamed others for your shortcomings. Your psychological profile reveals alternating behavioural patterns that can be overly assertive as a response to feeling inadequate or highly indecisive at critical periods in your life. It's a question of integrating your dual character into a single identity. While self-examination can provide the key, you are basically a unique individualist who should not apologise for asserting your rights, providing they represent fairness and honesty.

You have a positive outlook on life since you are a self-reliant and ambitious person. This is because your objectives are carefully planned and worked out to the finest detail. Your Shadow self is a projection of your unconscious mind, a lunar dimension of character that provides great stability and reinforces your powers of reason and logic. You are a very warm and affectionate person, which countermands the cool nature associated with your tree sign. You are also more drawn towards the arts than the sciences, but you do have the potential to be an architect or engineer. You have an eye for design and enjoy constructing things that have a practical use as well as aesthetic appeal. With regard to any intellectual ability, you are a particularly thoughtful person, not overly impressed with academic qualifications but rather inclined to respect practical experience. With 164, 165, 179, 195 or 201, while your artistic potential is activated, you also have a high degree of intelligence and can master most subjects with technical efficiency. With 172 or 211 you are easily discouraged and lack social graces. With conjunctions 161, 182 or 198, while you have a serious and rational mind, you can lack imagination. With 167, 181, 186, 197 or 203 your ideas and potential are considerably broadened and you will always have an element of luck on your side. Overall, your lunar position provides positive direction.

Hidden agenda

Your hidden agenda is to go on the offensive and become less intense about your objectives. Most of your actions are still controlled from your unconscious mind,

98

Hazel
∙∙∙∙∙∙∙∙∙∙∙∙∙∙
Moon in Taurus

which contains a powerful residual memory of insecurity. Hence in your current life you avoid taking any risks, and your ambitions are inclined to be low-key. During your lifetime you may therefore experience a rude awakening that comes with having your head buried a book. Your psychological profile reveals great inner calm that is a positive indication of a well-balanced individual. In fact you are not in any need of psychological counselling unless the planetary aspects say

otherwise. The Druids believed in reincarnation and referred to it as the 'unbroken thread', while Eastern astrologers refer to it as an unbroken chain of soul existence with karma providing a time link. While you may not believe in reincarnation, your lunar position symbolizes many experiences of déjà vu. You have a highly intuitive mind that should also provide clear insights. Your karmic lesson is to evolve this ability to a higher level of consciousness in order to realize your true potential.

99

Hazel
....
Moon in
Gemini

You have a pronounced duality of character, which manifests as physical and mental restlessness, indecision and changeable opinions. Your need to do several things at once, however, is vital to your psychological well-being. Your Shadow self is a mirror image of your unconscious mind, a lunar dimension of character that lives in the head or mind. In other words you tend to intellectualize your feelings. But far from being unemotional, you have a volatile temperament akin to the hawthorn character. It is a question of trying to come to terms with unstable emotions, and this is why you try to justify your actions. As a Hazel Tree character you are inclined to let your head rule your heart, and this becomes intensified by your lunar position. But while your mind is therefore extremely complex, you are highly articulate and intelligent with an aptitude for learning difficult subjects. You also know how to use a little knowledge so skilfully that people think you are more intelligent than you really are. With 164, 197 or 203

your mental faculties are impressive and stable. You can set your sights very high. With 171 or 208 you have superficial values and attitudes and prefer gossip to serious conversation. With 168, 187 or 204 these aspects provide a great deal of stability which adds to your perceptive mind, and while it encourages a more serious outlook you will learn all subjects in greater depth. Overall, your lunar position can make permanent relationships less likely, but this is largely of your own choosing, as you have your own set of goals to achieve.

Hidden agenda

Your hidden agenda is not to lose sight of your main objectives and to focus your multi-talented gifts where they are needed most. You are a natural agent or emissary with a mission in life to make people fully aware of the facts, but you must make sure that your information is soundly based. During your lifetime you may find it difficult to settle in one place, but this is part of your learning process. Your psychological profile is intriguing in the sense that you have not yet formed a single identity. It is symbolic of a karmic transformation still in the initial stages of a new-life experience. It manifests as a desire to remain free from the pressures of society and personal obligations. When you do decide to join the rest of humanity you will experience a dramatic shift of consciousness, due to your ability to make informed judgements rather than obscure hypotheses. This is your current karmic lesson to learn, since in past incarnations you were inclined to voice popular prejudices.

You are a highly emotive person who acts on instinct rather than on rational thought. While you have a powerful imagination, you are also a shrewd and tenacious individual. Your Shadow self is a projection of your unconscious mind, a lunar dimension of character that is highly sensitive and sympathetic to the feelings of others. You have a clannish mentality and your family hold the central position and greatest influence in your life. You have an inner need to cherish and protect them, but you can also draw strength from them psychologically. This is something you may have watch, as it can make them feel too dependent on your good will. You are also inclined to overstress your authority. Nevertheless you are a loving partner and parent who will work hard to provide a comfortable home life. But because you are greatly influenced by the lunar cycles and aspects, you are prone to mood swings. With 160 or 167 you are less inclined to worry unduly about your family and you have a wider range of interests. With 161, 175, 182 or 198 you can take life far too seriously, and family obligations can become heavy burdens. But while these aspects have a sombre quality, they also provide great inner strength that enables you to overcome any setbacks or psychological blockages. With 158 or 165 you are a kind and charitable person, fortunate in love and in finances. Overall, your lunar position reveals a high level of emotions that can undermine your mental faculties if you are not careful.

Hidden agenda
Your hidden agenda is to build up your self-esteem so that you are not so reliant on your family or the sympathy of others. While you may appear extremely self-confident in public, how you behave at home can be a different matter entirely. The home is where you can become dictatorial and emotionally unstable. During your lifetime you will experience emotional traumas, but in due course they will prove very instructive regarding self-development. Your psychological profile reveals a need for recognition or social status. Basically you are a materialist, or inclined to judge people on their material success. This is why you work so hard to achieve a comfortable lifestyle when you should be concentrating on your own emotional welfare and that of your family. You need to overcome a residual memory of self-created anxieties, and this is your karmic lesson to learn.

100

Hazel
. . . .
Moon in
Cancer

101

Hazel

· · · · · · · · · · · ·

Moon in
Leo

You have a powerful presence and enjoy a certain popularity among your friends and work colleagues. This is because you have a generous nature and the courage of your convictions. Your Shadow self is a projection of your unconscious mind, a lunar dimension of character imbued with the spirit of creativity and enterprise. Basically you have the ability to inspire others, and this in turn can make you a great leader. Alternatively, if your Moon is badly aspected you can become patronizing or dictatorial. However, you do have a sense of showmanship and drama that draws people to your side. You are a very demonstrative person generally and will openly express your feelings with passion and grand gestures. As a Hazel Tree character this will dramatically change the way you think and behave. Your intellectual capacity will be drawn to the arts, and you would make an excellent scriptwriter or theatre producer. You are also a natural performer who could become an actor or politician. With 158, 167, 170, 179, 189, 195 or 201 your artistic abilities are activated and you will attract many admirers, and your love-life mirrors a very romantic lifestyle. With 177, 194 or 211 your artistic abilities and mental capacity lack concentration or discipline. Feelings are also inclined to be frivolous and insincere. With 157 your intellectual ability is emphasized, but it lacks flexibility. With 204 you have a good blend of artistic talent and intellectual prowess. Overall, your lunar position reveals passionate ideals and a strong will-power.

Hidden agenda

Your hidden agenda is to learn self-discipline – a basic karmic lesson to learn – but you have a strong and wayward ego. Though you have a great deal of self-confidence, you can become lackadaisical if not fully stretched. Life can become one long pleasure trip, as you have a self-indulgent nature that goes with expensive tastes. While you have great potential for earning money, you can also quickly spend it on a lavish lifestyle. This relates to a residual memory of past glories and social status. During your current life you are likely to experience both wealth and relative poverty unless you learn to manage your finances more effectively. Your psychological profile reveals a complex mind and behavioural pattern. It's as if you can't make up your mind what you really want in life. Sometimes you feel on top of the world and then you start to worry about your extravagant lifestyle and have periods of moderation that can become an extreme form of self-denial. The key to finding contentment lies with making firm decisions and becoming less susceptible to flattery.

You personify all the discriminating mental faculties and emotions of the Hazel Tree character. Everything you do follows a meticulous system with a keen eye for detail and precision. Your Shadow self is a mirror image of your unconscious mind, a lunar dimension of character that is highly focused. Emotions are therefore controlled to such an extent that you seldom display any feelings that could compromise your sense of reserve and modesty. Your chaste demeanour certainly conjures up visions of wishing to belong to religious orders or retreating from the world in order to serve humanity behind closed doors. But you are nevertheless a disciplined thinker and analyst. You are drawn to the sciences, and as a researcher or lecturer you could make your mark. While your private life is kept strictly private, you are exceptionally gifted in the role of arbitrator or adviser. With 166, 167, 185, 188, 196, 197 or 204 your mind has breadth as well as depth, and you have greater vitality all round which will counterbalance your reclusive tendencies. With 157 you are highly intelligent, but can lack depth of thought. With conjunctions 161, 182 or 198, while you have a deep and precise mind, you have limited experience of life and are subject to depression. Overall, your lunar position reveals an aptitude for the sciences and restrained emotions that can become a source of ill health unless you find more time for friends and family.

Hidden agenda

Your hidden agenda is to make the transition from having vast knowledge to simple wisdom. By shutting off your emotional needs you are in danger of becoming a human robot rather than a humane individual. Though you have an inner need to serve humanity, you also need to experience both pain and joy, and this is your karmic lesson to learn during your current lifetime. As a natural sceptic you probably regard karmic philosophy, reincarnation and even astrology as superstitious nonsense. But you may find a suitable analogue in psychological analysis. Your psychological profile reveals a great sensitivity to pain in others, which stems from carrying great pains or scars within. Your belief in healthy diet and natural medicine is proof of a residual past-life memory when you were a healer.

You have a romantic nature and a charming manner that people find extremely attractive. Underneath your apparent easy-going disposition, however, you know how to subtly manipulate people to your advantage. Your Shadow self is a projection of your unconscious mind, a lunar dimension of character that dislikes disharmony or arguments, but is at the same time responsible for changeable emotions, thus creating uncertainty for yourself and others. People are never quite sure exactly how you will react emotionally, even though you are inclined to talk them round to your way of thinking. Your analytical mind can be very persuasive, and you tend to rely on your ability for smooth talking to promote what can often be unpalatable facts. While you are a fine arbitrator in business, in your personal life things can be in reverse. Because your emotional nature tends to swing between two extremes of behaviour, you will find it difficult to keep a domestic situation from getting out of hand. With 158, 165, 179, 201 or 217 you are an extremely persuasive lover and financial adviser, and your interests are more arts-orientated. Although these aspects emphasize your personal magnetism, you are given to self-indulgent luxuries that can cause weight or health problems. With 172, 173, 190, 214 or 222 these aspects denote complex emotional problems and your mental and physical energy can be impaired. Look for positive aspects between Mercury and Jupiter, and also Venus with Mars. Your lunar position overall reveals an uneven temperament but a genuine desire to promote harmony and compromise.

Hidden agenda
Your hidden agenda is to reconsider your objectives in life so that your time and energy is more focused. It is a question of subjecting your desire for harmonious relationships to the ultimate test of rejecting your own egotistical motives, and this is your karmic lesson to learn. This is when you will find greater harmony within, which is then projected outwards in your emotional behaviour. During your lifetime you will meet many people who have similar personalities or problems that mirror your own. This is a karmic regrouping of individuals who represent a soul-group that can only evolve through finding the other part of their selves. Marriage or business partnerships will often provide the most vital contacts. Your psychological profile reveals a difficulty in recognizing your own weaknesses or shortcomings; confronting your own ego will always be difficult.

104

Hazel
. . . .
Moon in
Scorpio

You are a highly imaginative but discerning individual, and you are both subtle and persistent in your efforts to succeed in life. Your Shadow self dwells in your unconscious mind, a lunar dimension of character that has an intense personal magnetism which other people can find intimidating. You have enormously powerful energies and hidden depths of emotion that few people can really appreciate or understand. You tend to keep your thoughts and deeper emotions to yourself, largely because you mistrust other people's motives. While this may sound like paranoia, it is true to say that you have some psychological blockages which can suddenly surface with explosive anger or feeling – a necessary safety valve for such powerful emotions. As a Hazel Tree character you have a very penetrating mind that can dig up facts and information that may have been deliberately hidden for criminal or highly questionable motives – facts that can discredit others. With 159, 166, 267 or 276 you have the instincts of a bloodhound when it comes to persistence in pursuing your quarry. Your passionate nature is also more controlled and your analytical mind is razor sharp. Though you will attract dangerous adversaries, you are equally feared. With 190, 265, 271 or 277 you are inclined to use force and ruthless tactics to succeed. Overall, your lunar position reveals a sense of purpose, which can drive you to the brink of self-destruction if not kept in check.

Hidden agenda

Your hidden agenda is to win respect rather than fear. While you may not intentionally set out to make people wary of your own motives, your inner need for power can become a form of megalomania. Although this only occurs in rare cases, you will have to tread more softly and avoid dramatic displays of emotions. During your lifetime you will experience periods of feeling completely alone, even alienated from those closest to you. These periods are karmic lessons, which are painful reminders of where you have gone wrong in the past – and which are now being repeated in your current life. Your psychological profile is worthy of deeper analysis than we have time for here. Suffice to say that you are experiencing a critical transformation of consciousness, which is essential for a healthy state of mind – a cleansing process that will banish the old ghosts that haunt your dreams.

You have a philosophical turn of mind, which greatly expands and refocuses your Hazel Tree characteristics. You are certainly not a prude or in any way drawn to self-denial. Your Shadow self is a projection of your unconscious mind, a lunar dimension of character that is determined to disturb your thoughts with outrageous ideas and restless emotions. As a result your behaviour is highly contradictory in the sense that you may say one thing and do something quite different – a form of acting out of character every so often, as a kind of protest at being stereotyped. It will also prompt more frank exchanges and improve your judgement. If negatively aspected it may, however, adversely affect your concentration. Your restless emotions require positive aspects in order to be channelled creatively; most of all they need to be channelled physically, as they represent abundant energy.

You also require a great deal of personal freedom. With 160, 167, 181, 186, 197 or 203, while you have high morals or ethics, you are also good-natured, openly affectionate, optimistic and good-humoured – a handful of personal assets which promote a humanitarian approach rather than an impersonal analytical response. With 174, 191 or 208 you still retain humanitarian principles but tend to throw away your chances to improve your education or waste time generally on useless qualifications. Look for positive aspects between Jupiter and Saturn, and Mercury with Jupiter and Saturn. Overall, your lunar position enhances your mental faculties with broader knowledge and vision.

Hidden agenda

Your hidden agenda is to disperse your highly nervous and restless energy. Though

105

Hazel
....
Moon in
Sagittarius

it is a ready source of mental as well as physical energy, there is a danger it can become counter-productive to steady self-growth and development. As a Hazel Tree character you are now more aware than most of the importance of moderation. In past lives you became entangled in complicated relationships that depleted your physical, mental and emotional energy. During your current life you will constantly change direction, but at some stage you should find a niche and settle down. You will, however, always remain a restless spirit at heart. Your psychological profile reveals a diverging duality of character that explains your contrary nature or behaviour. It could even be described as a psychological contest between a superficial personality and a high-minded intellectual; then again, the reverse may be true. Your karmic lesson is to integrate both.

106

Hazel
·············
Moon in
Capricorn

You have prudence and perseverance, and a great deal of self-discipline and ambition. Emotional feelings are difficult to express due to a shy nature or inability to communicate. Your Shadow self is a projection of your unconscious mind, a lunar dimension of character that has a natural reserve, which can be mistaken for a lack of warmth or affection. Basically you need time to get to know people. As a Hazel Tree character you have a most rational and serious mind, which could be described as cool and calculating. Your ideas are always constructive and you will plan ahead in detail, in the knowledge that you have done your homework. While you are not a quick learner, you will gradually overtake cleverer people with your determination to succeed. You may lack creative imagination but you do have a mathematical mind and a talent for construction work, which requires structure and balance. With 160, 167, 181, 186 or 197 you have a more vibrant nature and imagination. You are also more outgoing and inclined to have idealistic views and less materialistic values. With 161, 182, 198 or 209, however, you are prone to depressive moods and may result in a serious social problem. This in turn brings out all the negative qualities that are associated with your tree sign. Look for positive aspects to Mars and Venus. Overall, your lunar position reveals an inner depth of character that could propel you straight to top of your profession.

Hidden agenda
Your hidden agenda is to focus upon your potential for achievement. Though you have more than your fair share of family responsibilities, which can become emotionally draining, you also need to experience the freedom of having your own career. In past lives you have been a willing workhorse or doormat for your family. Hence in your current life you are still acting out the same role, but this time round you are forced to assume a more dominant position. You may feel that you are at last fulfilling a need to provide support and security for others, but it stems from a residual memory of feeling

insecure and unloved. Your lunar position marks the Winter Solstice, a time when the Druids believed that the soul must await judgement in order to be regenerated for another journey on the Golden Wheel of Life. Psychologically it represents a need to assume responsibility in all areas of life.

Y ou have a friendly disposition towards everyone and a genuine belief in humanitarian principles. You are also inclined to eccentric behaviour, but people do not usually find this disagreeable as you are an exceptionally interesting character. Your Shadow self is a projection of your unconscious mind, a lunar dimension of character attuned to progressive academic and social development. Although you are an idealist you are also intellectually orientated and drawn towards modern sciences. Your lunar position is associated with astrology, astronomy and original concepts or inventions. Emotionally you can appear rather detached, and therefore you have difficulty forming intimate relationships. You are basically a very independent person, a complete individualist who needs personal space in order to work and live without restrictions of any kind. This is why you have an unpredictable behaviour pattern; time means very little to you, and normal routines represent restrictive programmes. With 162, 169, 183, 188, 199 or 205 your humanitarian principles are emphasized and you have brilliant potential in the sciences. You have a high intelligence which requires positive direction, otherwise it becomes extremely erratic and unstable. With 176, 193 or 210 you have highly radical opinions that can get you into trouble with the authorities because of their revolutionary nature. Overall, your lunar position reveals unconventional behaviour, but loyalty to friends is paramount.

Hidden agenda

Your hidden agenda is to constantly revise your attitudes and feelings as you have a great deal of self-pride. In trying to be too unconventional, you can unwittingly upset those closest to you with tactless remarks and cool indifference. In past lives your irrational behaviour caused discord in personal relationships. As a result you will spend part of your life alone, which may help you to come to terms with your unique potential. Your Moon is positioned in the degrees marking the Celtic Festival of Brigantia – a significant influence that strikes like a lightning flash of inspiration that germinates an idea. Hence your unique potential for original thinking and vision can help all of humanity, providing you can handle it with the discriminatory nature of your tree sign, and this is your karmic lesson to learn. Your psychological profile reveals an erratic behavioural pattern, which stems from a high degree of nervous energy and tension. Your need for personal independence can also become cranky, but your self-containment shows a formidable strength of character with a will to overcome bigotry and ignorance.

107

Hazel
....
Moon in
Aquarius

108

Hazel
∙∙∙∙∙∙∙∙∙∙∙
Moon in
Pisces

You are emotional and sentimental, and extremely impressionable or vulnerable to outside influences. While you have a compassionate nature and powerful ideals, you also have an unworldly perspective that rejects materialism. Your Shadow self is a projection of your unconscious mind, a lunar dimension of character that provides a source of highly intuitive knowledge and insight. As a Hazel Tree character you have a special blend of qualities that can give form to your artistic potential and strengthen your resistance to negative influences. As a result you can become an inspired writer of fact or fiction. You will also be drawn to marine biology or subjects relating to marine life or laboratory research. In addition, there is an attraction to photography or film-making. Your compassionate nature and interest in health can also become a compelling influence in becoming involved with community welfare. With 170, 189, 200 or 206 you are more likely to be involved with the arts, but you are also something of a mystic, and this could attract you towards the realms of spiritual healing. With 163, 177, 184, 194 or 211 your highly abstract mind and your sensitivity can create confusion and an overwhelming sense of unreality unless combined with 164, 187 or 204. Overall, your lunar position reveals a highly psychic Hazel Tree character whose perception is greatly enhanced with humility and foresight.

Hidden agenda

Your hidden agenda is to adjust your perspective and thus advance your idealist thinking. Your karmic lesson, however, is to refrain from passing judgement on others. This will rapidly evolve your self-development, otherwise you are swimming against the current tide of New Age thinking. Your lunar position in Pisces can form an exact polarity with your Celtic Moon sign in the degrees of Leo and Virgo. This will be shown on the Lunar Zodiac Wheel as a Sun/Moon polarity or 'square aspect' when you begin noting the planetary aspects. Such a polarity reveals a conflict in the personality that relates to past lives and can re-emerge in your current life as being tied to a career or way of life in which you are not suited or really interested. Your tree sign also forms a polarity with the rowan and ash, which shows a conflict of values between materialistic and non-materialistic rewards. Your psychological profile reveals a behavioural pattern that has a basic duality. While you can surmount or solve difficult problems in life with mental agility, any emotional problems can remain a source of worry or nervous anxiety if you feel that you are being manipulated by others. Your best defence is in expressing your feelings more openly.

Celtic moon sign: Vine

Lunar Symbol: White Swan

The lunar symbol of the *White Swan* personifies the radiant divinity of ancient Celtic gods, the Tuatha Danaans, who disappeared into the Otherworld during the month of the vine at the time of the Autumnal Equinox. In the Irish myth of Lir, a great Sea-god, his four beautiful children were the last and the most gifted children of the gods in the arts and music, but they were turned into white swans by a wicked stepmother. By the time the spell was broken, Christianity had displaced the old gods of Ireland and they died of a broken heart. The haunting cry of a swan's lament at the death of their lifelong partner is still associated in Ireland today with the lament of their long-lost gods.

In Druidic cosmology the Autumnal Equinox is represented by Queen Guinevere, a name derived from the Celtic Brythonic word Gwenhwyvar, meaning white ghost or phantom. In Celtic astrology the planet Venus, ruler of this sign, was known as Gwena, meaning white or light. During the tenth lunar month of the Autumnal Equinox the fading light of the Celts' Sun-king Arthur was transformed into the lunar light of Queen Guinevere. 'White Swan' is also an archaic reference to the Cygnus constellation – the home, according to the Druids, of their great matriarchal Creatrix. The Autumnal Equinox was also considered a time of reconciliation between the Sun and Moon gods, which provides great insight into the duality of the psyche.

Vine character

You were born at the time of the year marking the twilight of the Sun-gods, when the rays of the Sun became a soft diffused light. The brightest light in the sky was moonlight, and consequently your notable characteristics are not always apparent, but a reflection of a hidden or inner light. The spiralling symbol of the vine marked the light of the Sun that would eventually disappear at the Winter Solstice into the spiralling tail of the Star-serpent, Sarph. As a Vine character you are therefore an odd mixture of joy and sadness. One moment you are full of enthusiasm and vitality, and the next you are full of suppressed anger or sadness. Your emotions will always run at a high level and yet you can appear remarkably cool in the face of opposition or crises. It is a mistake for others to underestimate your strength of character, as you are an instinctive organizer and a born survivor. However, you may find it hard to come to terms with a deep sense of uncertainty, and as a result you can become totally dependent on your partner or family.

Your inherited traits of character come from your mother's side of the family and they show a highly sensual nature and adeptness in love as well as in the social arts. You have refined tastes and appreciation of the finer things in life, and your tact and kindness can create a harmonious atmosphere. In personal relationships your passionate nature tends to let off steam more openly, and marriage can be a difficult relationship to sustain; much will depend on your choice of partner. Your weak point of character is a sudden inertia or lack of motivation, which in turn places undue stress on all relationships. Generally speaking, you will find it hard to accept the changing cycles in life, which stems from having to make difficult adjustments in your youth.

With 165, 179, 195, 201 or 258 your finest qualities are activated and you have a calm and gentle temperament. You are a popular member of society and your artistic potential is well expressed and directed. Happiness in marriage or partnerships is almost guaranteed and there is a harmonious balance operating within your whole psyche. With 172, 177, 194, 211, 224, 226 or 259, all these aspects will frustrate your plans of finding happiness in love, achieving financial security and realizing your true potential. But if with 167, 168, 181, 186, 187 or 219 these aspects will strengthen your will-power and lift your spirits – positive influences that help to stabilize your emotions and help you focus upon your objectives in life. Overall, your feelings of uncertainty or apprehension require a great deal of emotional and material security, but you will inevitably experience great swings of good and bad luck during your lifetime. The position of your Moon will clarify your strengths and weaknesses with greater insight and will also put into perspective the karmic influences in your life. Your Basic Paragraph is thus extended

109

Vine
....
Moon in
Aries

You have a natural self-confidence and fiery temperament that cancels out any feelings of insecurity. But you can overplay your hand or overstate your abilities on occasion. Your Shadow self is a projection of your unconscious mind, a lunar dimension of character that dislikes conventional behaviour because it represents a lack of personal freedom. You have an adventurous spirit that prefers to explore all the possibilities in life, which in turn provide opportunities for advancement. As a Vine character you are likely to be highly motivated – indeed you have a mental and physical vitality which, if well channelled, can be regenerated at will. However, you need to control your impulsive nature and lack of patience; these traits of character can also become intensified if you react angrily or aggressively. Your emotions or feelings are inclined to be less refined, and can degenerate into coarse or rude behaviour. With 170, 179, 189, 195 or 201 your harsh traits of character are considerably mellowed and your artistic potential has positive merit. With 159, 166, 180, 185, 196 or 202 all your great strengths are activated and you should achieve your objectives in life. Overall, your lunar position reveals a natural competitor in life, which negates your reliance on others for support.

Hidden agenda

Your hidden agenda is to balance your needs with those of your partner or people with whom you are on intimate terms. While you have the strength of your convictions, you can also become indecisive at critical periods during your life. With your lunar position in the degrees that can form a polarity with the Autumnal Equinox, you are learning the basic levels of self-consciousness or a singular identity. Your apparent self-confidence can therefore be easily shattered, which relates to a residual memory of betrayal by a partner. During your lifetime you will, as a result, strive to find a relationship where your hidden light or potential is recognized. In your current life you are struggling to escape from a chrysalis state of being into a beautiful butterfly which symbolizes the following sign of the ivy. Your karmic lesson is to develop a sense of tranquility rather than a sense of self-survival. Your psychological profile also reveals a conscious need for self-development, and while this may take longer than you would like, hence your impatient nature, you are a quick learner on a karmic level.

110

Vine
. . . .
Moon in
Taurus

You have stable emotions and your perception in life is enhanced with an appreciation of the natural world and the inspired artists who try to capture its spectacular beauty. Your Shadow self is a projection of your unconscious mind, a lunar dimension of character that endorses the finer traits of the vine sign. You have what could be described as aesthetic taste, and yet you also appreciate simple designs with a functional use or purpose. You have strong powers of endurance and are considered reliable and trustworthy by friends and work colleagues. Your affections are warmly expressed, and all personal relationships tend to become lasting commitments. The insecurity associated with the vine sign is, however, deeply rooted, and you have an instinctive sense of self-preservation that makes you a shrewd investor in property or solid business schemes. Your need for possessions can also be directed towards your partner, and this can cause a few problems if it is compounded with fits of jealousy.

With 165, 179, 189, 201 or 258 you have natural charm and social graces. Your harmony within creates harmonious relationships in turn. Your artistic potential is also fully activated. With 177, 194, 211, 214, 222 or 259 these aspects frustrate your ambitions and limit your expression of feelings by adding an unrealistic note to all your objectives. Overall, your lunar position reveals great inner strength.

Hidden agenda
Your hidden agenda is to 'lighten up' in the sense that you are too inward-thinking, which can cast a dark cloud over your head. You can become a prisoner of your own mind and emotions if you continue to adopt entrenched viewpoints, which relates to past-life behaviour. In your current life you are being confronted with some of the most difficult karmic lessons of having to restructure your value system from top to bottom; from the base level of the lower mind to the higher-mind level of enlightenment. The spiralling inward projection

of your Shadow self is touching upon your hidden desires and natural instincts, which have been suppressed and must now experience a process of transformation that will regenerate your whole psyche. Your psychological profile shows a normal behavioural pattern on the surface, but you have a secret inner life that has profound meaning to you on an intuitive level. You therefore have the ability to transcend through meditation to a higher-mind level during your lifetime.

111

Vine
············
Moon in
Gemini

The light and dark side of your nature is very pronounced. You know how to use your insight into the mysteries of life with the skill of a juggler or magician. Your Shadow self is a mirror image of your unconscious mind, a lunar dimension of character that recognizes the duality of the psyche as an alternating source of power or strength. As a Vine character you are therefore a guide or messenger who can communicate on many levels of intelligence. This ability is a residual ancestral wisdom and knowledge of the forces of nature which have become alien to suburban or city dwellers. Your emotional nature, however, is inclined to be fickle, and this in turn can permeate your thinking capacity. As a result you have a changeable mind and can find it difficult to concentrate on one thing at a time. But if your Moon is well aspected you have a truly amazing capacity to retrieve obscure knowledge and present it in a coherent manner. With 164, 188, 197, 203 or 204 you have a high degree of intelligence and the ability to lecture on a variety of subjects. These are positive aspects that provide even greater insight as well as mental stability. With 171 or 208 your fickle temperament is compounded with worthless ideas. Look for positive aspects to Saturn and Jupiter for mental strength and expansive thinking. Your lunar position overall adds a sparkle to your personality and character that increases your popularity.

Hidden agenda
Your hidden agenda is to reach conclusions rather than leaving things up in the air. Only then you will understand the fundamental mainspring of the rational mind that can put things into perspective and actually expand your imagination. While you have a boundless curiosity, which is essential for acquiring knowledge, if allowed to run wild it creates its own confusion and superficial values. During your lifetime you will meet many fascinating people and their experiences will mirror your own. But you have the ability to interpret the symbolism attached to life experiences, and by acting as a guide or teacher you will fulfil your karmic quest. Psychologically speaking, your behavioural pattern is always changing as you catch the mood of the moment or prevailing influences affecting humanity.

You have a keen memory that provides a powerful intuitive link with ancient archetypal gods. This has greatly influenced how you perceive people and events in life. Your Shadow self is a projection of your unconscious mind, a lunar dimension of character that has recourse to past lives and ancestral knowledge. You are a very resourceful individual who will backtrack or improvise in order to achieve your objectives. While you have a high level of emotions, which can become intense in personal relationships, you are also cautious with regard to making friends and forming intimate relationships. You are basically extremely sensitive, which makes you vulnerable to emotional blackmail. On the other hand you are capable of playing the martyr when it suits. As a Vine character you are also concerned with emotional and financial security, and will work hard to achieve it. Providing your protective feelings do not become claustrophobic, you will cherish your partner and family and they will mutually support you. With 160, 167, 181 or 186 you have a more outgoing personality and your compassion and charity is extended to a wider circle of friends or strangers. With 161, 175, 182 or 198 you suffer from depressive moods and

may retreat into the dark and gloomy side of your nature. Look to Venus and Mars for positive aspects that can provide inner harmony and greater vitality. Overall, your lunar position reveals an enterprising nature that can overcome any setbacks in life, providing you have the love and support of your family.

Hidden agenda
Your hidden agenda is to develop your inner resources into conscious self-growth or awareness. While you are intuitively following these karmic lessons, you invariably continue to ask why people do not treat you with the respect that you feel you deserve. Your inner sense of dignity is a residual memory of past lives where you held positions authority and power. During your current lifetime you will therefore experience a few setbacks that can be quite demeaning. Your psychological profile reveals a surfeit of emotional energy that is often repressed. This is another example of trying to rationalize your intuitive emotions when you should in theory accept them for what they are. After all, you are a creative individual with the ability to achieve material success by using your instincts and shrewd mentality.

112

Vine
....
Moon in
Cancer

You have a powerful ego that can dominate your feelings and personal ambitions. While it provides great incentive and creative talents, it can also encourage intolerance and pompous behaviour. Your Shadow self is a projection of your unconscious mind, a lunar

dimension of character that courts the limelight through flamboyant behaviour and power dressing. This pronounced flair for drama reveals a sense of theatre and is usually accompanied by striking physical attributes. As a Vine character your artistic potential is powerfully activated,

113

Vine
....
Moon in
Leo

and your need for public recognition confirms a deep psychological sense of insecurity or uncertainty. Apart from the theatre, the need for role playing is an intrinsic part of human behaviour; because you need to play a leading role you will be drawn to the management side in business or, failing that, self-employment, where you can at least be your own boss. With 158, 170, 179, 189, 195, 201 or 258 you have immense charm, sincerity, generosity and natural warmth that people respond to. You can achieve success in the arts and lead a glamorous lifestyle. You are fortunate in love, but your expensive tastes can become ruinous if not checked. With 177, 194, 211 or 259 these aspects will frustrate your dreams and show an imbalance operating within your psyche that usually manifests as personality clashes with your family members and work colleagues. Overall, however, your lunar position reveals star quality.

Hidden agenda

Your hidden agenda is one of the less complex or mysterious ones. Your strong need to assert yourself is actually a karmic lesson designed to build up your self-confidence in a conscious manner to redress past-life experiences of self-effacement. Your fundamental urge to express yourself is therefore vital for self-development, but you do risk taxing the patience and good will of others if you overplay your part. During your lifetime you will therefore attract people who will try and put you down or diminish your ego. Also, because you are right on the boundary of legitimate self-assertion, you can also inflate your own worth. Your psychological profile unsurprisingly reveals a problem of low self-esteem, hence your strong need for the approval of your peers. But your natural talent for acting or taking leading roles is real enough, and people will always respond kindly to your warmth and enthusiasm.

114

Vine
....
Moon in Virgo

You have very precise attitudes that never vary or extend to open discussions. In your mind you have already analysed the facts, and the same applies to your emotions. Your Shadow self is a mirror image of your unconscious mind, a lunar dimension of character that remains inward-looking. Though you have a sense of humility and a conscious need to serve humanity, your lack of warmth or spontaneity can make personal participation very difficult. As a Vine character you are always trying to find a more balanced outlook, and your lunar position endorses a need to find a compensating aspect of

character in order to develop your full potential. You are, however, a hard worker in your field and a perfectionist, which considerably improves your chances of promotion or recognition. The pronounced duality associated with your sign has manifested as an imbalance, which is why you are inclined to work at home or in a solo position at work that provides privacy. You are basically a very private and reserved individual. With 167, 185, 188, 197 or 203 your personality and character is more fully developed and you have wider interests all round. You are more philosophically minded and your emotions are less repressed. With 157 you remain dogmatic in your opinions, and with 161, 182 or 198 your physical and mentality energy lacks vitality. Overall, your lunar position reveals a tendency towards the sciences rather than the arts. But if other aspects confirm artistic ability it would most likely take the form of being an art critic or an expert craftsperson.

Hidden agenda
Your hidden agenda is to develop greater independence, but in doing so not succumb to everyday pressures by becoming a recluse. While some kind of retreat is necessary in order to recharge your batteries, if too prolonged it can actually weaken your spiritual and physical vitality and result in nervous depression. Too much inward-thinking generally can be the root cause of psychosomatic illnesses. Vine people are prone to worry about their health and often become vegetarians or health fanatics. During your lifetime you may meet people who are clinically depressed, either in a professional capacity or just socially. 'Like attracts like' is a popular cliché, but it has profound meaning in the law of karma. Such meetings are highly significant and synchronistic by forcing you to confront previous lives' strengths and weaknesses, which highlighted a spiritual depth that lacked breadth or an overall perspective. Your psychological profile shows a high degree of intelligence and an insatiable curiosity.

Y ou have a charming and courteous manner which people find engaging. You are also inclined to be indecisive and easily influenced by others. Your Shadow self is a projection of your unconscious mind, a lunar dimension of character that is greatly influenced by the waxing and waning Moon, which represents great highs and lows on an emotional level. It can also affect your physical energy and motivation. As a Vine character your life can revolve around having to make rapid adjustments, but your lunar position can provide balance and harmony if the Moon and Venus are well aspected. The artistic potential associated with your sign is activated and the pronounced duality of light and darkness can also form a harmonious union. Your weak point, however, is a tendency to rely on others, and this can place you in some very awkward situations both financially and emotionally. With 158, 167, 179, 189, 217 or 258 the scales of Libra are nicely balanced and your sense of justice and inner harmony provides stability and greater peace of mind. Your artistic potential is highly creative and emphasizes a powerful sense of colour. With 173, 190, 214 or 222 these aspects promote disharmony generally and indicate low energy and vitality. Look for positive aspects to Jupiter for compensating influences. Overall, your lunar position reveals an idealist with a winning manner.

Hidden agenda
Your hidden agenda involves some painful self-analysis. Because you are what could be described as an elusive individual,

115

Vine
....
Moon in Libra

people are never quite sure of your motives, and for that matter your actions are not always aligned with your true feelings. In past lives you lacked staying power and tended to change allegiances if it suited your own plans. During your lifetime your ego can be easily dented but it can also recover fairly quickly as your own sense of reality reasserts itself. Having been born around the time of the Autumnal Equinox your sense of reality and unreality can merge as one, and this is why you find it difficult to make decisions. Your psychological profile reveals superficiality that can also be misleading, as you have a serious side to your nature that can remain hidden. Ultimately you must learn to trust your own judgement and re-evaluate your motives – a karmic lesson in wisdom and truth.

116

Vine
· · · · · · · · · · ·
Moon in
Scorpio

You are a powerfully motivated individual with passionate emotions and desires that can be equally intense in business dealings as in personal relationships. Your Shadow self dwells in your unconscious mind, a lunar dimension of character that is drawn to the dark side of the Moon. For some people darkness has a fearful connection, but to the Druids it contained a 'dark seed' or source of germinal life that dwelled in the spiritual realm of Annwn, a mystical temple in the Celtic Underworld. Descent into Annwn was an act of initiation and transformation that allowed souls to be reborn or regenerate annually at the time of the Winter Solstice. As a Vine character you have a penetrating insight into the mystery of Creation, and understand the liberating influence of Pluto or Pwyll, the Celtic god of the Underworld. You also understand the duality of light and darkness associated with your sign; you draw strength from darkness in order to maintain your creative skills and sense of purpose in life. With 167, 170, 186, 189, 264, 267 or 287 your passionate feelings and creative talents are positively channelled and you have a liberated spirit that brings light or knowledge into the world. With 172, 190, 265, 271 or 277 these aspects bring out the ruthless qualities of your nature, hence there is a danger you can become cruel and underhand. Look to Jupiter and Venus for mitigating aspects. Your lunar position overall reveals a powerful imagination and premonitions of the future.

Hidden agenda

Your hidden agenda is to develop your inner strength for pending transformations that will occur during your current life. You must also learn to study the manifestations of your unconscious desires so you can learn how to control them, and this is your karmic lesson. During your lifetime the intensity of your karma will bring you into contact with many trapped souls who have led decadent lives for many incarnations. You have the healing power to help these people, but it is crucial to your own protection that you first undergo deep meditation or psychoanalysis in order to cleanse any remnants of inner corruption. In past lives, while you were deeply involved in occult studies, you kept a low profile in order to remain a respected figure in society. Your psychological profile reveals an ability for positive reasoning; a rational mind that provides the stability for studying the occult objectively, or any subject that demands analysis. High finance may also be your forte.

Y ou are an optimist with an open mind that encourages a wide range of interests and activities. Your great sense of humour can dispel any dark clouds that may suddenly appear on the horizon. Your Shadow self is a projection of your unconscious mind, a lunar dimension of character that reveals a restless spirit which stems from a need for freedom or independence. As a Vine character you are self-assured and able to make rapid adjustments with ease. Indeed, you relish challenges of any kind. The powerful duality associated with your sign is drawn towards the light, hence your search for higher-mind development. You thrive on intellectual stimulation, and this is an important factor in partnerships. You also need to channel your high level of physical and emotional energy into outdoor activities that require great stamina, such as mountaineering or rugged sports. Early on in life you will find it hard to settle down or remain in the same job. Even when you do, you will remain a free spirit. With 160, 167, 181, 186, 197 or 203 you are a whirlwind of activity and your search for knowledge can bring high honours and personal merit. You are drawn to philosophical studies and religious beliefs. Your strong moral character and fair judgement denotes priests and judges. With 174, 191 or 208 you are blindly optimistic and also excessively self-indulgent. Overall, your lunar position reveals an uplifting influence that unifies your whole psyche.

Hidden agenda
Your hidden agenda is to find your true identity through higher-mind development. You are standing at the crossroads of a very important self-discovery; read the oak tree sign for greater analysis on the sacrificial ego. Your karmic lesson is one of self-sacrifice in order to discover the radiant nature of your soul. In past lives you have only skimmed the surface of real knowledge. However, in your current life, providing you don't waste your time on worthless ventures, you can develop the true vision of a sage. But you will not reach the first stage of this process until you have experienced your first return of Saturn, which occurs during your twenty-eighth year. During your lifetime you will meet great souls who will guide you towards your goal. Your psychological profile shows that your cheerful disposition and robust physical health provide great insurance against illnesses or neuroses.

117

Vine
. . . .
Moon in
Sagittarius

118

Vine
············
Moon in
Capricorn

You are a person of substance. You typify old-world values and traditions, and thus you create an aura of respectability and authority. Your Shadow self is a projection of your unconscious mind, a lunar dimension of character that nobody can upstage. While you appear to have little – if any – emotions, this is also a projection that is designed to keep people at a distance so you can observe their motives. As a Vine character you show little apprehension, and though you can make heavy going of having to adjust to certain phases in life, you continue to slowly climb to the top of your mountain, just as the winter Sun begins its ascent after the Winter Solstice. With regard to the duality associated with the vine, you identify with the dark phase of the Moon, which occurs approximately four days before the New Moon. As a result you have an introspective way of thinking, which nevertheless produces profound enlightenment. With 160, 167, 181, 186 or 197 you have a well-adjusted personality and character, and you are also a fair-minded individual with a high degree of intelligence and honesty. Your vitality and enterprise is greatly increased, and this in turn adds a more spontaneous trait of character. With 161, 182, 198 or 209 you

are taking life far too seriously, and this encourages a lack of social contact that can create a very lonely existence. Look for positive aspects to Venus and Uranus. Your lunar position overall reveals a great deal of self-reliance and ambitious objectives.

Hidden agenda

Your hidden agenda is to consciously develop a meaningful direction in life, which can release you from always having to conform to the standards or ideals of others. You are inclined to obey rather than question the dictates of society or authority. Time to break the mould, which has been cast by parental influence and family karma in past lives, and this is your karmic lesson to achieve in your current incarnation. During your lifetime you will probably reach senior positions of authority, and how you respond is the key to unlocking your true potential as a progressive thinker. You have a chance to be reborn rather than just perpetuating outdated theories. Your psychological profile shows a surprising immaturity or naivety when it comes to accepting your self-imposed limitations. On the rare occasions that you do 'act out of character', this is the time to reflect upon your intuitive responses rather than your carefully prepared script.

119

Vine
············
Moon in
Aquarius

You have your own vision of the future and it involves taking an independent stand against narrow-minded people who try to hinder natural progress. While they have a complexity of justifiable reasons, their basic instinct is fear of the unknown. Your Shadow self is a

projection of your unconscious mind, a lunar dimension of character that promotes a fearless campaigner for human rights and free speech. You are therefore inclined to rock the boat rather than trying to maintain a balance or even keel. The duality associated with your sign is thus transformed into a concerted effort of confrontation, albeit a rather unpredictable format that suddenly changes tack or direction. Your way of handling things is to keep people guessing, which gives you the time to invent another ruse. But while you enjoy the exciting spectacle of seeing people wrong-footed, you are nevertheless a sincere and serious advocate of humanitarian values. With 162, 169, 183, 188, 199 or 205, while you are an extremely radical individual, you will win the respect of your opponents with your brilliant ideas and originality. In personal relationships you can be difficult to live with, but if also with 165, 170, 179 or 189 you are more socially integrated and willing to make compromises. With 176, 193 or 210 your cranky behaviour can become totally unacceptable. Overall, your lunar position reveals high ideals and a certain self-containment that is not altogether incompatible for enjoyment in life.

Hidden agenda
Your hidden agenda is to evolve your vision and transform it into a source of great enlightenment. Your lunar position marks the Celtic Festival of Brigantia, a significant influence for spreading light around the world at a time when darkness still maintained a firm grip on people's imagination. While a certain amount of self-restraint is necessary to protect you from cynical adversaries, you must not let it isolate you from the rest of humanity. In past lives you had many confrontations with authorities that suppressed free speech or new ideas that upset their own religious or political policies. Your karmic lesson, therefore, is to overcome your sense of superiority and insular mentality. During your current lifetime you will undoubtedly stir up a few hornets' nests, but the sting of reality serves as a sharp reminder that progress is not merely the exclusive possession of idealists. Your psychological profile reveals a mixture of kindness and an obstinate insistence that your opinion or vision is beyond question. As a result, though you are a fascinating as well as dynamic character, you may not always endear yourself to supporters and critics alike.

You have an impressionable mind that absorbs information and your natural senses are equally sensitive. How you interpret it all is another matter. Your Shadow self is a projection of your unconscious mind, a lunar dimension of character that becomes more assertive after the Autumnal Equinox, when the Moon provides the source of inner light. This continues until the Sun becomes the source of conscious light after the Vernal Equinox.

As a Vine character the powerful duality of light and darkness has a more spiritual meaning for you. Because you are a highly sensitive individual, your experiences in life are attuned to the invisible or parallel world of spirit rather than the world of matter or physical existence. But you have the ability to move from one to the other, and this provides great insight into human nature. While this ability may only be known to you on the subliminal level of

120

Vine
....
Moon in
Pisces

consciousness, it does explain periods when your behavioural pattern becomes confused or disorientated. You are also so susceptible to drugs, medication and alcohol that you would be wise to abstain altogether. With 170, 189, 200 or 206 your artistic talents are activated and you have a mystical quality that confirms a pronounced spirituality. With 163, 177, 189, 194 or 211 your tendency towards escapism through drugs or alcohol is a cause for concern, and it impairs creative abilities. Look for positive aspects between Saturn and Neptune, and Mercury with Jupiter and Saturn. Overall, your lunar position reveals highly psychic abilities that require firm control and training.

Hidden agenda

Your hidden agenda is to find a definite path that encourages your latent spiritual faculties to develop. This may take the form of realizing a vocation that contributes to the welfare of the community through enhancing daily life. But during your lifetime you will find it hard to focus your attention on specific goals. While you may be an expert in solving hypothetical problems, you also need to extend this skill to everyday or mundane events. This will then provide a solid basis for conscious self-growth. In past lives you were inclined to lead a spartan existence in order to achieve a sense of purity. Your karmic lesson is to elevate this unique insight into practical realities. Your psychological profile reveals a propensity for addiction, and a personality that will lean on others – only to find that they will eventually turn the tables on you. In other words you cannot reap any rewards unless you have sown the seeds. Your strongest asset is, however, a firm belief that life has no meaning unless it addresses the spiritual nature of humankind or one's conscience.

Celtic moon sign: Ivy

Lunar Symbol: Butterfly

The lunar symbol of the *Butterfly* became synonymous with Celtic 'Fairy Faith' and is worn as a brooch by the Celts as a mark of respect for their ancestral spirits and ancient gods. The fairies represent a time warp of ancestral memories and the psychic phenomena associated with the supernatural world. The source behind the butterfly symbol is found in the Irish myth of Etain in Fairyland. The lovely Etain lived in the Otherworld realm known as the Land of Youth, and she was an immortal being or fairy. King Midir ruled this mystical kingdom, and when he married Etain it provoked a jealous rage in his first wife, Fuamnach. She was a powerful sorceress and turned Etain into a beautiful butterfly, and then raised a tempest to drive Etain out of the fairy kingdom. Etain was blown into the castle of an Ulster chieftain named Etar, where she fell into the drinking-cup of Etar's wife, who swallowed the draught and Etain. Being an immortal, she was then reborn as their daughter and grew into maidenhood knowing nothing of her real nature or ancestry. Eventually she was restored to her husband, and the delicate butterfly thus became a beautiful Celtic symbol of the metamorphic process of reincarnation.

During the eleventh lunar month the flowering ivy was used by the Celts to decorate the sacred shrines and altars of their Moon-goddesses. Ivy is an evergreen and symbolizes the perennial aspect of nature and the immortality of the human soul. Persephone, ruler of this sign, has a twin nature. She was an Earth-goddess during the summer months, and during the dark winter months she became the wife of Pluto, the pale-faced Hecate, and thus became Queen of the Underworld and a dark Moon-goddess. Persephone resembles the mysterious and elusive Celtic Moon-goddesses Arianrhod and Etain, and all have a similar mythology associated with hidden wisdom.

Ivy character

You were born at the time of the year when the dark night sky formed a dramatic backcloth to the light of the Moon and the stars became more dazzlingly radiant in the Northern Hemisphere. According to the Druids this is when the Full Moon casts its own dark shadow or polarity towards an invisible Moon-goddess. In the Celtic lunar zodiac the Moon, ruler of the willow, forms a polarity with your sign. While Persephone remains an undiscovered or hidden planet, many astronomers have already referred to a missing planet whose orbit is said to lie between Pluto and Neptune, and the name Persephone fits into the mythological sequence of planets in our universe. As an Ivy character you have the dual nature associated with your archetypal goddess, and your two most notable traits of character are great personal stamina and personal talents that could be described as 'fairy gifts', as they are rarely learned from books. You also have a pronounced artistic temperament with a conflicting set of moral and material values.

Personal relationships are the most sensitive and highly emotional experiences for the majority of people, but for you it can involve some dramatic encounters. While this is largely due to your tendency of falling in and out of love at regular intervals, when you do decide to settle down you can become overly possessive, clinging on like the creeping ivy that can overwhelm trees and plants. But providing that these extremes can be reconciled at some stage, you have a greater chance than most of finding a perfect match and a truly harmonious relationship.

With 165, 170, 179, 189, 195, 201 or 258 all your finest qualities are activated: you have natural charm and diplomacy, and your uncommon talents are positively engaged. You will also be more fortunate in love and finances. With 177, 194, 211, 224, 226 or 259, all these aspects are detrimental to your happiness and success generally. You are inclined to lose heart too easily, and to weave a web of fantasy in order to survive the harsher realities of life. But if also with 167, 181, 186, or 219 these aspects will increase your luck and will counterbalance any negative aspects. Overall, you are an extremely charming and well-intentioned person, but also have a subtle way of manipulating people to do your bidding. The position of the Moon will clarify your strengths and weaknesses with greater insight and provide relevant information on the karmic influences in your life. Your Basis Paragraph is thus extended.

121

Ivy

·············

Moon in
Aries

You take a direct approach in all things – there's no mistaking what you think – and you can become aggressive if you lose the advantage. But you are a generous and lively individual whom others sit back and observe with bated breath. Your Shadow self is a projection of your unconscious mind, a lunar dimension of character with an uneven temperament that stems from a quick and changeable mind. You are a highly energetic person who needs to be fully occupied at all times. As an Ivy character your great stamina is enhanced, but your energy can suddenly plummet unless you learn to pace yourself more effectively. In personal relationships your tendency to fall in love too quickly is emphasized and, as the saying goes, you are inclined to 'marry in haste and repent at leisure'. You are basically an impetuous person with a spontaneous and enterprising nature that ensures an exciting lifestyle. With 170, 189, 195 or 201 you are fairly laid back, and though you will follow your own path through life you are a caring partner and parent. With 159, 166, 180, 196 or 202 you are a human dynamo who appears never to sleep. While your energy is well channelled, you must learn more patience and tolerance if you are to accomplish your objectives. Look for positive aspects to Saturn and Jupiter to provide stabilizing and educating influences. Overall, your lunar position reveals a powerfully motivated individual who likes to be in full control.

Hidden agenda

Your hidden agenda is to find balance in your life, and this is intrinsically linked to fulfilling your karma. The poetic phrase 'Captain of his fate and master of his soul' is a nautical metaphor that captures the essential message from your unconscious mind, wherein lies the residual memory of past lives. Your conscious self-awareness in your current life is newly born in the sense that you have few guidelines to follow, hence your hectic activity in trying to establish a position in life where you feel more secure. During your lifetime you will therefore reach many crossroads with misleading signposts. Your psychological profile reveals an erratic behavioural pattern that is a result of finding yourself in a number of unwanted situations. The key to greater awareness is to place more value on the steadying influences of a partner or children and, in some cases, a career that demands reliability and responsibility, and this is your karmic lesson to learn.

You have the stability and endurance that provides a solid basis for success in life. You are also a person of refined tastes with an appreciation of the arts and social etiquette. Your Shadow self is a projection of your unconscious mind, a lunar dimension that ensures emotional and material security. With this kind of insurance you can set to work and produce a meaningful contribution, both at home and in the workplace. As an Ivy character you have tremendous stamina and tenacity. You are adept in business, and the luck associated with your sign mirrors your own input – or, in other words, you are capable of making your own luck. With such strengths it is difficult to see where you could fail, but weak points are always to be found – even if they are well hidden. But then again, so-called weaknesses can become one's greatest strengths. Your single-minded focus produces results, but it can also limit wider knowledge. With 160, 167, 179, 181, 189, 201 or 258 you have great charm and magnetism. Your intellect is vastly superior, and any artistic skills find great perspective. With 177, 194, 211, 214 or 222 these aspects identify pressure points or confusion in your chart, which can undermine your true potential. They create an imbalance of emotions and priorities. Look for positive aspects between the Sun and Moon, and Venus with Jupiter. Overall, your lunar position reveals a hopeful and positive outlook combined with practical skills.

Hidden agenda

Your hidden agenda is to fully activate your true potential. With so much action still controlled by your unconscious mind it is difficult to assess how much self-growth is possible during your current life. While you are following a very steady course through life, it can lack a certain imagination or spontaneity. This can, however, be due to gross self-indulgence or time-wasting in past lives. As a result you are inclined to overreact and obsessively pursue your objectives to the letter. Your intuitive mind is highly developed and you have sound common sense, but the area that requires special development is your higher mind. This is the key to conscious growth, which can enliven your whole psyche, and is your karmic lesson to achieve. Your psychological profile reveals a behavioural pattern that has been formed early in life, largely through family influence, and it colours your perception and consciousness more than ongoing life experience.

You are a witty and a highly amusing conversationalist. People enjoy your company, but never know when you are being serious. And there is a very serious side to your nature. Your Shadow self is a mirror image of your unconscious mind, a lunar dimension of character that has a duality all of its own. Your emotions can run hot and cold, and though you appear to hold some strong views, you can suddenly take a very different line the very next day. On the surface it can appear that while you have learned some basic facts, your real knowledge remains superficial. This is not entirely true, as although you have a highly curious mind that can store a great deal of information, by the natural process of awareness it inevitably evolves into higher-mind concepts. As an Ivy character your duality is also more stable, due to the earth element, and your intuitive knowledge more accurate. With 164, 188, 197, 203 or 204 your higher mind is activated and you are deeply philosophical; mastering difficult subjects is your forte. Also, your communication skills and ideas are well presented and directed. With 174, 177, 191 or 208 your ideas lack coherent perspective and you can become a compulsive liar in order to cover up your lackadaisical standards. Look for positive aspects to Saturn and Venus for concentration, honesty and less fickleness in relationships. Your lunar position overall guarantees an interesting and highly active lifestyle.

Hidden agenda
Your hidden agenda is to establish a definite link between the dual dimensional worlds of consciousness. You are a time traveller in the sense that your mind works effectively on both levels and thus provides great freedom of thought. At some stage, however, you must become more clear in your mind that your current life is an important karmic lesson of integration rather than division. In past lives you tended to see things in black and white without qualification. Dualistic thinking can become polarized if allowed, but as an Ivy character you have an ability for mind control that is highly advanced by modern-day standards. During your lifetime you may be naturally drawn to the study of language as a means of greater self-expression. Your karmic lesson is to learn how to communicate on all levels of expression in order to centre your whole psyche. Your psychological profile reveals a subtlety of mind which can become manipulative, and your behavioural pattern is not easily defined or analysed – elusive as your archetypal character Persephone.

124

Ivy
··············
Moon in
Cancer

You have a sympathetic and loving nature, and friends and family will come to rely on your support and advice. Your Shadow self is a projection of your unconscious mind, a lunar dimension of character that instinctively responds to the needs or anxieties of others. While you are inclined to worry unduly over financial or emotional security, you are basically a very sensitive soul who is easily upset by any form of criticism. As an Ivy character your moody nature is less pronounced, providing that your Moon is endowed with positive aspects. Your emotions are fairly evenly balanced and your intuitive mind is greatly advanced with an insight into human nature and the mysterious phenomenon of Nature itself. You have the latent powers of a mystic or medium, which puts you in touch with the Otherworld of fairies or ancestral spirits. Because you have a strong interest in ancestry and history, you should uncover some very interesting information. With 170, 189, 206 or 288 your intuitive insight is activated and creatively employed. With 161, 175, 182 or 198 you are inclined to sink into deep depressions and retreat inwardly. If also with 160, 167, 181 or 186 these aspects are great confidence-boosters and will draw you out of your shell. Look to Jupiter and Saturn for positive aspects which provide greater enthusiasm and enterprise. Overall, your lunar position reveals a tenacious individual with a strong survival instinct.

Hidden agenda
Your hidden agenda is to develop your latent powers of intuitive wisdom. In your current life you are inclined to be self-righteousness, whereby you often privately condemn the actions of others. You also have a tendency to bear grudges, which stems from a residual past-life memory in which you experienced attacks on your self-esteem. This was due to being extremely opinionated or too proud to compromise. During your lifetime you will learn your karmic lessons of tolerance, compassion and humility largely within your family and close friends. In family or group karma the reverse-role situation is highly significant, so if you find yourself suffering unwarranted criticism it recalls a time when you showed a lack of compassion or judged others too harshly. Your psychological profile reveals a hidden depth of character that needs to be brought to the surface or exorcised. Your tendency of collecting or storing things away in garages or attics is symbolic of your hanging on to past-life vices.

125

Ivy
. . . .
Moon in Leo

You are a self-assured person with plenty of charm and a courteous manner. Basically you bring a little sunshine into people's lives merely by your presence. Your Shadow self is a projection of your unconscious mind, a lunar dimension of character that radiates light or warmth even on dark cloudy days. You are a highly creative and enterprising individual who enjoys being in control of any given situation – and being an excellent organizer, this presents few problems. As an Ivy character you have a nicely balanced blend of human qualities, and your broad-minded attitude provides scope for continuous learning throughout your life. Though you are inclined to hold some strong opinions, you have a magnanimous outlook that overcomes any personal prejudices. You have affectionate and demonstrative feelings but you do tend to place your partner on a pedestal, which can have disastrous results if they do not live up to your standards or ideals. With 165, 170, 179, 189, 195, 201 or 258 your artistic potential is activated and you have great flair and personal style. You are a very colourful Butterfly character whom others tend to watch with fascination – one of the 'beautiful people' of society. With 177, 194, 211 or 259 your ambitions remain unrealized because of your vanity and self-indulgence. Look to Jupiter and Saturn for positive aspects that will serve to strengthen your resolve. Overall, your lunar position reveals a natural aptitude for glamorous careers.

Hidden agenda

Your hidden agenda is to develop your capacity for love – an issue that confounds the vast majority of people. But you have your finger on the pulse, so to speak, as you are inclined to make great sacrifices for loved ones. In affairs of the heart you are also more likely to suffer betrayal or unfaithfulness, yet you remain eternally optimistic that love will conquer all. In past lives you developed the principles of fairness and equality. However, in your current life you are now applying them to your family, only to find that they have their own ideals. Your karmic lesson, therefore, is to develop your conception of love to the higher plane of universal love that extends to the rest of humanity, including yourself. Your psychological profile reveals a distinct behavioural pattern that has all the hallmarks of great leadership.

126

Ivy
....
Moon in
Virgo

You have a high degree of intelligence, well grounded in practical application and elevated enough to reach intellectual status. You have a very discerning mind and emotions. Your Shadow self dwells in your unconscious mind, a lunar dimension of character that provides the focus for concentrated learning and stability in all your endeavours. It is a powerful influence generally that can, however, limit your social life because of your need for strict routines and eagerness to prove your self-worth. As an Ivy character it can strengthen your position in life, but it can also block your inspiration. It's a question of your rational mind trying to control your intuitive insight – or, in other words, whether your Butterfly spirit remains a colourless moth. The aspects to your Moon will help to clarify whether this imbalance is already entrenched or if there is room for expansion and transformation. With 158, 160, 167, 170, 188, 189, 197, 203 or 206, all these aspects provide inspiration and activate an appreciation of the arts as well as the sciences. You are also more outgoing and your highly intuitive mind contains a wealth of knowledge. With 157 you have an inflexible attitude, and with 161, 182 or 198 your high degree of nervous energy is not creatively channelled, which can result in mental and physical fatigue. Overall, your lunar position reveals that there is too much emphasis on self-interests, but this can be avoided provided you work more closely with others or a partner.

Hidden agenda

Your hidden agenda is to see clearly the truth of all things your analytical mind is capable of studying. In past lives you have allowed yourself to be deceived by your own confused thinking and by the promises made by others. This is why in your current life you are developing your ability to discriminate, but you must avoid becoming cynical or overly critical. If carried to extremes, it can also become counter-productive if you deny your own needs and those of others close to you, and this is your karmic lesson. During your lifetime you will experience first-hand the insincerity of people you have tried to help, but you will gain tremendous insight into human nature and your own psyche. Deep down you are a very sensitive soul who would prefer to lead a quiet life, and

your natural reserve typifies a refreshing modesty. Your psychological profile reveals a set behavioural pattern that rarely changes: everything you do or say has a measured response.

You are a born diplomat, anxious to avoid any upsets or discord in your home or at work. In trying to please everyone, however, you can suddenly find that you are being squeezed by both sides, which places you in a personal dilemma. Your Shadow self is a mirror image of your unconscious mind, a lunar dimension of character that swings between two extremes, but your instinctive response is always tempered with justice and mercy. As an Ivy character your hidden wisdom can rise to the surface on occasion and provide ideal solutions or compromises. But for the rest of the time, if in doubt your instinct is to do nothing. This can often be the right decision, strangely enough. So while you are temperamentally indecisive it can be to your advantage, as things do seem to 'turn up' for you, even though you walk on a knife-edge. Your belief in providence or in 'fairy luck' mainly pays off. With 158, 167, 179, 189, 217 or 258 you have great charm and magnetism, a person of refinement and artistic talents. You have a subtle mentality that few can compete with. If with 257 there is an imbalance operating within your psyche that can limit your true potential. With 190, 214 or 222 these aspects promote discontent and

indulgent behaviour. Look for positive aspects between the Sun and Moon, and Venus with Mars or Jupiter. Overall, your lunar position reveals a romantic nature and sophisticated tastes.

Hidden agenda

Your hidden agenda is to develop more self-reliance or personal responsibility. In your current life you are inclined to change your allegiances if you feel your own position is being undermined. Your karmic lesson is particularly difficult to accept because it means coming to terms with your strong ego that refuses to yield, despite your conscious efforts to the contrary. Every compromise you do make is a projection of how you wish to feel inwardly, but it is your ego that rises to the surface. As a result you have to feel in control, yet at the same time you are not prepared to give with a full heart. During your lifetime your experiences in personal relationships, especially with partners, will be extremely testing. Your psychological profile reveals a behavioural pattern more complex than you perhaps realize. You like to think that you are an easygoing individual, but people close to you are never sure which way you will react.

127

Ivy
. . . .
Moon in Libra

128

Ivy

....

Moon in
Scorpio

You are inclined to be a fatalist by adopting the view that some things are somehow ordained and therefore irreversible. Your Shadow self is a projection of your unconscious mind, a lunar dimension of character that has penetrating insight and knowledge of the unknown regions of the mind and soul. While this can be a useful tool for psychoanalysis, you are very wary of using it. You can therefore remain a highly superstitious character unless you train your mind to a professional level. As an Ivy character you have tremendous physical and mental stamina that thrives on harsh conditions or dangerous situations. Psychologically speaking, it takes the form of personal initiation rites that give you a sense of superiority. You are naturally drawn to power struggles where you can become a ruthless competitor. If your Moon has constructive aspects, your objectives in life will be for the greater good of humanity. With 167, 170, 186, 189, 264, 267 or 287 these aspects will raise your spirits and sights to a higher level of desire and thinking that is morally sound or just. Your knowledge could become a source of regeneration for yourself and others. With 172, 190, 265, 271 or 277 your secretive nature and ambitious strategy creates an uneasy atmosphere, and your capacity for ruthlessness is activated. Overall, your lunar position will either sow the seeds of self-destruction or transform your whole psyche. In order to achieve the latter you must learn to channel your emotional energy into creative projects.

Hidden agenda

Your hidden agenda is an intense form of self-development that requires persistent effort and commitment. While you do not lack will-power and endurance, it is the nature of your self-development or karma that presents some difficult choices. It means eliminating a residual need to feel powerful, and this can only be done when you have discarded a greater part of yourself – or rather, what you 'think' you are. During your lifetime you may experience sudden falls from grace, but when you pick yourself up and begin again you should feel a remarkable transformation. The Butterfly spirit symbolizes a soul that has taken flight from an Earthbound existence. Your transformation is equally exotic in that it frees you from the material world and allows your creative skills to find new direction, and this is your karmic lesson. Your psychological profile reveals inner fears of loneliness that may actually manifest during your transitional periods.

129

Ivy

....

Moon in
Sagittarius

You are a restless individual with the world to explore both in your mind and in the context of travel. Your search for knowledge and adventurous journeys should make fascinating reading. Your Shadow self is a mirror image of your unconscious mind, a lunar dimension of character that already dwells in the Otherworld realm of fantasy and mystical beings. As an Ivy character you have great physical and mental stamina – a high energy level that requires creative outlets as well as plenty of physical activity. While you are a very straight-talking individual, there is also an elusive quality present which manifests as a need for personal freedom. You are a natural philosopher of life and your curious mind will approach any subject or issue from several angles in order to obtain a wider picture. Though you may overlook certain details, once your mind is disciplined and focused you have enormous potential for any kind of professional career that demands high standards. With 160, 167, 181, 186, 197 or 203 your potential can be fully realized and you also have great personal qualities of honesty, humour, generosity and sound judgement. The extreme nature of these aspects, however, can encourage self-indulgence – but then you are a 'larger than life' character after all. With 174, 191, 194, 208 or 211 you are a time-waster and your intuitive insight can lapse into mental confusion, thus weakening your vitality in the process. Look to Saturn for positive aspects that will help strengthen your resolve. Overall, your lunar position provides a vibrant energy that boosts your spirits and also promotes moral standards.

Hidden agenda

Your hidden agenda is to integrate your dual identity by raising it to the spiritual dimension associated with your sign. The polarity operating between your Sagittarian Moon and Gemini can become a contest of lower- and higher-mind activity. Once they are harmoniously balanced you have the capacity for rapid self-growth and spiritual wisdom. In past lives you have relied on clever tactics and lived on your wits rather than accepting responsibility. In your current life you are still inclined to roam free, but this time round you are making an effort to widen your knowledge – a karmic lesson. Your psychological profile reveals an uncomplicated personality and straightforward behavioural pattern. You are also not the worrying type, which is evident in your optimistic attitude, and thanks to your frank and open mind, you do not tend to develop psychological problems.

130

You are a serious contender in life for positions of power or authority. In fact you can take life far too seriously on occasion. Your Shadow self is a projection of your unconscious mind, a lunar dimension of character that is greatly affected by the Moon's cycles. Your best work is usually done between the New Moon and the Full Moon, but during the waning period and dark phase of the Moon you can become strangely depressed. As an Ivy character you are also sensitive to the lunar eclipses. These events should be carefully monitored, as they expose hidden problems that have been causing inner stress. However, having come to the surface they can then be expelled, thus encouraging renewal or self-growth. Your latent psychic abilities and intuitive knowledge is also activated around the Full Moon. But you are a very practical, down-to-earth person who is not given to fanciful ideas or imagination, and this is your greatest strength when faced with supernatural phenomenon. With 160, 167, 181, 186 or 197 these aspects adjust the imbalance operating within your psyche by providing an uplifting source of energy that dispels depressive moods and recharges your batteries when you need it most. They also increase your intelligence and vitality. With 161, 172, 182, 198 or 209 your mood swings can reach the depths of melancholia, and you may retreat into your lonely world of solitude. These aspects denote extreme difficulty in forming any personal relationships; look for positive aspects to Saturn and Venus. Overall, your lunar position reveals great discipline.

Hidden agenda

Your hidden agenda is to release your 'Butterfly spirit' by letting go of your inner fears, which take the form of disturbing and recurring dreams. While they largely relate to childhood experiences, they also represent a residual memory of rejection in past lives. You are a very sensitive soul who has always experienced problems in relationships and has compensated by concentrating on work. But in doing so you have created a void of emotional feelings, which explains your cautious nature in your current life. Your karmic lesson is learning to trust others without conditions attached. During your life you will resist your karma, as your residual memory is a powerful influence. But during your twenty-eighth and fifty-sixth year you will experience a surge of emotional energy that transforms your whole psyche. Your psychological profile reveals an introvert character that nevertheless has an intriguing personality.

131

Ivy
· · · · · · · · · ·
Moon in
Aquarius

You have a highly inventive abstract mind and can dream up extraordinary perceptions of the future. Your strong humanitarian beliefs, however, are soundly based on your experience of life and the need to alleviate suffering. Your Shadow self is a projection of your unconscious mind, a lunar dimension of character with a powerful conscience. Though your have a dispassionate nature and prefer uncomplicated relationships, as an Ivy character you should eventually become a loyal and loving partner. You also have great physical and mental endurance when it comes to pursuing just causes. This can become a major issue in your life, as you have a liberal mind and a reforming spirit. While you are intellectually inclined, you are an idealist who can identify with New Age thinking regarding environmental issues. The planet Earth figures strongly in your sign, and you respect all wildlife and the natural world. With 162, 169, 183, 188, 199 or 205 you are a brilliant campaigner and organizer, highly intelligent with the ability to talk people round to your ideas. Your personal relationships may prove to be less compatible, but if also with 165, 170, 179 or 189 you are a very charming and persuasive lover. With 176, 193 or 210 your personal eccentricities may prevent the opportunity for any lasting relationships, and your objectives in life are too bizarre. Overall, your lunar position provides a unique vision of the natural and supernatural world – an excellent influence for a science-fiction writer.

Hidden agenda

Your hidden agenda is to develop conscious control of your erratic ego. It manifests in your current life with a personal quest to slay metaphorical dragons, but you must be careful that they are not your own invention. In past lives you may very well have been a crusader or a missionary. Your residual memory certainly has a fanatical zeal that relates to high ideals that were not always appreciated. During your lifetime you will continue to experience disillusionment with the governing bodies of society or authorities in general. Your greatest support will come from other like-minded people who are no longer in the minority as the New Age sweeps away outdated prejudices. Your psychological profile reveals an unpredictable behavioural pattern, but on closer analysis you are a fairly self-contained individualist who has written his or her own script. Your inner vision and knowledge provides the source.

You are in essence the true spirit of the Butterfly. You have an inner wisdom that others do not always appreciate or even understand. But that is because it represents an elusive ideal that cannot materialize fully on the physical plane. Your Shadow self dwells in your unconscious mind, a lunar dimension of character that dissolves in daylight and is reborn at midnight, the magical hour of darkness. You are a gentle and compassionate person who is highly sensitive to suffering or pain in others. As an Ivy character you have great stamina that belies your fragile body and spirit. While this may draw you to the healing professions, your sensitivity to beauty and colour can make you a fine artist or musician, a writer or poet. The expressive movement of dance or the illusive world of film are other options – a vocational occupation rather than just a job. There is a secretive side to your nature that creates a certain mystique. Though you can become vague or easily confused, this is not surprising considering you are naturally attuned to the Otherworld dimension. With 170, 189, 200 or 206 you are a true mystic and your artistic talents are dramatically activated. You have great charisma and style. With 166, 177, 189, 194 or 211 these aspects are extremely hazardous to your health and general well-being. Your true potential may never flower. Look for positive aspects to Jupiter. Your lunar position overall, however, provides a source of great inspiration.

Hidden agenda

Your hidden agenda is to develop your artistic talents and spiritual nature. The two are intrinsically linked to conscious self-growth, which has been a difficult karmic lesson in past lives, but one that you must now learn. Because you are a highly sensitive soul you have retreated from the harsh realities of life, and this residual memory still haunts you. You were also inclined to be critical of others, and though you are being drawn towards fulfilling your karma in this life, your need for caution is greater. During your current lifetime your trusting and vulnerable nature can attract deceitful or immoral people who will lead you back into darkness or chaos. You have the potential for making a perfect transition to your higher mind in your current life, hence your struggle to free yourself from negative influences. Your psychological profile reveals a passive nature – a quietly spoken individual who doesn't like to cause a fuss. Time, perhaps, to argue your case more effectively.

Celtic moon sign: Reed

Lunar Symbol: White Hound

The lunar symbol of the *White Hound* is attributed to the ghostly spectre of the white hounds that belonged to King Arawn, an archaic ruler of Annwn, a lunar mystery temple located in the Celtic Underworld. Dogs, namely Cerberus and Anubis, guarded entrances into the mystery temples of the Underworld in ancient Greece and Egypt; in Celtic myth the White Hound was the guardian of the spiritual realm of Annwn. The Otherworld and Underworld are often confused as being the same place, but they represent a dual-time dimension. The Otherworld was a kind of Celtic heaven to which their gods returned and where the Sidhe (fairies) resided. The Underworld was a primal place of creation that contained Annwn from whence all spiritual life was formed and reformed during the process of human evolution. Pwyll, Lord of the Underworld, formed a special relationship with Arawn after undergoing a number of initiations. Pwyll, or Pluto, thus became Lord of both kingdoms and, in Druidry, a saviour of the human race. Though Pwyll was regarded as an awesome deity, he had the power of regeneration that transformed death into rebirth or reincarnation, a Druidic belief that the Hellenic Greeks and Romans never contemplated, as Hades was regarded as a place of no return.

During the twelfth lunar month the Fire Festival of Samhain was celebrated. It was a festival for honouring the dead and the past year, and it was the time when the boundaries between the natural and supernatural worlds dissolved – a time for divination, but also a time for purification with the burning of effigies that symbolized the terrors of the past. The reed has dense growth and a submerged thick root like a tree, and that is why the Celts identified it with a hidden dryad or an Underworld god.

Reed character
You were born at the time of the year when twilight and the jet of night moved together, which according to the Druids represented the outermost darkness ruled by Pwyll, or the planet Pluto. The reed month in the Celtic ritual calendar was a

time when the roar of the sea and the east winds whistled bleakly through the reed-beds of the rivers. As a Reed character the revolutionary influence of your ruling planet Pluto (Pwyll) brings to the surface and into the light the hidden wisdom concealed by Persephone or Arianrhod. Reed characters are the duality aspect of the Ivy sign. Persephone and Pluto form a unifying aspect of the psyche, which nevertheless is full of drama and passion. While you have a powerful personal presence similar to ivy people, you are more forceful and less inclined to compromise; you have a role to play that excludes any weaknesses or indecisiveness. You act as a catalyst rather than a competitor in life, and you are concerned with transforming the whole pattern of life rather than just certain aspects.

Your inherited traits of character and talents come mostly from your father's side of the family, but your mother remains the most powerful influence in your life. In Jungian psychology, Pluto and Persephone represent the 'animus and anima', which symbolizes the masculine and feminine development of the personality and represents a doorway leading to the collective unconscious. The persona is the bridge into the world of consciousness, a psychological analysis developed further under *Hidden agenda* in all signs. With so much of your personality and character suppressed or hidden, you remain an enigmatic individual. However, what does surface clearly are your passionate emotions, suspicious nature and your tendency towards fatalism, the reason being that you enjoy the intrigue and drama in life and in personal relationships. But anyone brave enough to become involved with you will find that you are immensely caring and a highly imaginative lover. Career-wise, the cut and thrust of the business world may attract, or any avenue where personal drive and a penetrating mind is required for research or investigation. Your fearless attitude also indicates a favouring of dangerous occupations.

With 264, 267, 269, 270, 273, 278, 279 or 287, all these aspects are positive influences, bringing to the surface all the hidden traits and thus introducing a new dimension of your personality and character. Read them under *Paragraphs of Conjunctions and Aspects (see page 156)* and discover your true identity. Likewise any negative or difficult aspects, such as 265, 268, 271, 277, 283, 286 or 289, will also introduce a new dimension of character. But if also with 167, 181, 186 or 204 these aspects help to counterbalance any negative ones and will lift your spirits and strengthen your moral character. Overall, you strive for complete power – not only within yourself, but endeavouring to influence others in the process. The position of your Moon provides greater insight and relevant information on the karmic influences in your life relating to the Druids' belief in reincarnation. Your Basic Paragraph is thus extended.

133

Reed
....
Moon in Aries

You are an enterprising and highly energetic person who hates restrictions of any kind. You are eager to start new projects but have trouble completing them, as you are already moving on to greener grass elsewhere. Your Shadow self is a projection of your unconscious mind, a lunar dimension of character that is inclined to overreact due to an impetuous nature and uneven temperament. Basically you have the courage of your convictions, even when they can be rather foolhardy or ill-conceived. As a Reed character you are relatively unsubtle in your methods, but your adventurous spirit adds great force to your personality and character. You are also a person who likes to feel completely in control of any situation, and while you are a loyal friend you are also a sharp competitor, inclined to look after your own interests. Having said that, if the lunar aspects are positively activated you are a fearless champion of the oppressed. With 159, 166, 180, 196, 202 or 276, while you are a forceful individual your passionate nature is more controlled and you will push yourself to the limit in order to achieve success, which can be extremely profitable and win public acclaim. With 176, 190, 207, 222, 265 or 277 your quick temper will land you in trouble, and these aspects can undermine even your best efforts as well as sow the seeds of discord in personal relationships. Overall, your lunar position endorses a need for challenges that can be dangerous, which relates to the character of your sign. However, providing you adopt a more cautious approach generally, your sense of survival remains a source of strength and ingenuity.

Hidden agenda
Your hidden agenda is to look deeply within yourself in order to find out why you are such a restless soul. Your hectic lifestyle and frantic activity is a smokescreen that confuses no one but you. In past lives you built up a lot of resentment about other people's successes, and this residual memory has made you determined to be a winner in your current life. You also made sacrifices for others that you felt were not appreciated – hence your problems in marriage or partnerships, as you now tend to look after your own interests first. During your lifetime you will find yourself in isolated positions. But while you don't mind being alone, you don't necessarily like *living* alone. A successful partnership should help you to find your true identity, and this is your karmic lesson. Your psychological profile reveals a fear of being totally alone.

134

Reed
....
Moon in Taurus

You are a practical and reliable person with astute business skills. Everything you do is well planned and executed. Your Shadow self is a projection of your unconscious mind, a lunar dimension of character that provides a source of stability and endurance. As a Reed character you are therefore even more persistent and determined to reach positions of power or authority. The ruthless side to your nature is, however, greatly modified and controlled, but your passionate nature can become excessively jealous and possessive. Generally speaking, your lunar position is considered to be an extremely positive influence, particularly in the expression of feelings or emotions. So unless it is badly aspected, you are an affectionate and caring partner or parent. There is inflexibility operating between your conscious and unconscious mind, which can narrow your vision or imagination. It stems from a stubborn nature with a resistance to change and a preference for strict routines in life. With 160, 167, 179, 181, 189, 201 or 279 you are more broad-minded and your higher mind is positively activated, which promotes wider knowledge and interests. With 172, 177, 194, 214, 259, 263, 268, 271 or 274 these aspects undermine your strength of character and can bring out your ruthless side. Overall, your lunar position provides creative skills and self-reliance.

Hidden agenda

Your hidden agenda is to resist some of your most passionate desires, as they represent a residual memory of past-life experience when you caused a great deal of pain to yourself and those close to you. There is, still in operation, a kind of intensity that your family and friends can find unnerving. Your concern with financial security can become an unhealthy obsession that creates problems in your domestic life. At best your actions are directed at securing a comfortable lifestyle for your family, but the underlying motive is often being able to justify your need to own or possess things, including your partner. During your lifetime you will experience conflict and crises that represents a very basic struggle for survival. It's a question of learning moderation, as you are inclined to excessive self-indulgence; this is your karmic lesson, which is more difficult to achieve than you may think since you have extreme reactions and intense emotions. Your psychological profile reveals a behavioural pattern that can swing between a very placid or very aggressive response.

You are a very modern-minded person, always up to date with new ideas and fashions. Your vivacious personality and apparently carefree attitudes belie deeper emotions and ambitions. Your Shadow self is a mirror image of your unconscious mind, a lunar dimension of character that responds quickly to any situation in life. You are a person of 'many parts' who enjoys out-manoeuvring more pedestrian people. As a Reed character you have greater flexibility generally, especially when you need to communicate your ideas and feelings. Your weakness is an emotional one, as you are inclined to change your feelings, which in turn influences your decisions and results in a lack of drive or motivation. The position of Mercury in your chart holds the key to mental stability, and if placed in Libra you have good reasoning powers but are slow in making decisions. If in Scorpio you rely on intuitive thinking, but your powers of concentration are excellent. If in Sagittarius your concentration is weakened, but you are more tolerant and sincere in

135

Reed
. . . .
Moon in Gemini

all your endeavours. With 167, 169, 181, 188, 197, 203, 204 or 279 you have an intellectual mind, and these aspects provide positive motivation and moral virtues. Your need for power is directed towards charitable causes and helping others. With 171, 177, 208 or 271 you tend to lack commitment and stubbornly avoid change. Overall, your lunar position reveals a high nervous energy that sparks off your passionate nature.

Hidden agenda

Your hidden agenda is to find an inner focus and evolve your perception of life to a higher-mind level. You basically lack integrity, which leaves you wide open to superficial values and false friends. In past lives you avoided social obligations or cooperation and acted on primal instincts only, which encouraged coarse or unrefined behaviour. In your current life you are frantically trying to cultivate your mind by adopting sophisticated attitudes. During your lifetime you may continue to act the innocent when it comes to explaining your involvement with unsavoury customers. However your karmic lesson is precise: evolve by acquainting your mind with higher learning or principles, otherwise you will backtrack into a world of grey areas that fudge all attempts at honesty. Your psychological profile is, not surprisingly, fairly complex, as your behavioural pattern is difficult to interpret. But providing you find the right doorway, your conscious and unconscious mind can step onto a higher plane of intellect.

136

Reed
....
Moon in Cancer

You have a keen memory and a powerful imagination that requires creative outlets. You are a kind and thoughtful individual who people find extremely supportive in times of crises. Your Shadow self is a projection of your unconscious mind, a lunar dimension of character that is highly sensitive to the Moon's fluctuating cycles of energy and emotions. You are inclined to dwell in the past rather than facing up to changes that affect the future. As a Reed character you are not likely to forgive or forget personal slights or criticisms. But there is a rapport operating between your lunar position and tree sign that strengthens your resolve and enterprise. You are also a canny business person who is able to rise to positions of power in banking and insurance, or high finance generally. Your intuitive mind or 'gut feeling' will prove invaluable, not only in your career but in life in general. With 170, 189, 206, 264, 267 or 288 you have a very compassionate nature and your intuitive and rational mind are nicely balanced. You have a more charming and gracious manner altogether. With 177, 182, 184, 194 or 289 these aspects weaken your character and your intuition is highly suspect; better stick to professional advice. If also with 160, 167, 181 or 186 these aspects provide luck or good fortune just when you need it most. Read all aspects very carefully for more conclusive evidence. Overall, your lunar position reveals a highly emotional person who has great tenacity and will-power.

Hidden agenda

Your hidden agenda is to learn to be more grateful or gracious in accepting help from others whom you tend to regard with suspicion. In past lives you were inclined to be miserly in a material and emotional sense, giving nothing away unless you were repaid in full. During your current life you are now trying to make amends by helping others, but you will experience some heavy family burdens that relate to your karma. Group or family karmic lessons are often difficult to fulfil with an open heart, as there are strong residual memories of being abandoned or left to fend for yourself. Your karmic lesson is to learn to forgive others, and through absorbing their pain it will actually release your own. Your psychological profile reveals a highly charged behavioural pattern that contains a lot of anger or resentment. Family feuds will continue to rage until you can rise above it all and transform your negative attitudes.

137

Reed
....
Moon in Leo

You have great personal style that impresses people. You are always well dressed and well groomed, and your charming manners epitomize a leading figure in society. Your Shadow self is a projection of your unconscious mind, a lunar dimension of character that responds to the limelight. You are a highly creative individual and a very competent organizer and promoter. As a Reed character you have greater finesse and sophisticated interests, but you are not merely a figurehead and have set your sights extremely high. One way or another you will use influential friends and may resort to bullying tactics to achieve your goals. You have a very passionate nature that is difficult to fully control, hence you are inclined to have numerous and torrid affairs, but you manage to sail through any scandals with dignity. Acting or politics might very well suit your temperament. With 166, 167, 179, 185, 195 or 278 these aspects help to bring out your best qualities in different ways, and you will achieve a high degree of success and public recognition. With 177, 194, 259, 271, 274 or 277 your true potential is undermined by vanity, pompous attitudes and grandiose thinking. Look for positive aspects to Jupiter and Venus for compensating balance. Overall, your lunar position reveals a fiery temperament, but you are a very warm and considerate person who enjoys life perhaps a little too much on occasion.

Hidden agenda

Your hidden agenda is to develop more humility. You are bordering on megalomania in your current life, which is an overreaction to low self-esteem in past lives. While you need to take charge of your life, you are inclined to exhibitionism despite your nonchalant manner. You are not an easy person to understand as you also have a penchant for sedition or scheming. In addition you lack self-discipline, and this can undermine your finest traits of character. During your lifetime you will attract people who flatter your ego, and these people mirror your own weaknesses

– a karmic lesson designed to make you look more closely in the mirror of truth. Your psychological profile reveals class prejudice or snobbery that is well concealed, although you are inclined to be a social climber. There is a secretive side your nature that will remain with you in future lives.

138

Reed
....

Moon in
Virgo

You are a most discreet person who can quickly analyse a situation and act accordingly. While you find it hard to relax completely, your *idea* of relaxation will seem like hard work to others. Your Shadow self is a mirror image of your unconscious mind, a lunar dimension of character seeking a perfect ideal. Your perspective on life is therefore highly focused on impersonal notions or philosophies, and takes little account of human nature. As a Reed character your passionate feelings are less demonstrative and you are inclined to be overly critical, both of your partner and in all emotional relationships. Your passions will be expressed more verbally in intellectual debates or in the competitive arena of business where your subtle mind can diminish any rivals. You would also make a fine investigative reporter or journalist. With 160, 164, 167, 169, 189, 197, 269 or 279, all these aspects provide inspiration and confidence that will improve your mind, and generally help to integrate your feelings and thoughts, thus making you more amenable and sociable. With 161, 182, 198, 209 or 271 the hard side of your nature is activated and your schemes may fail simply through bad luck or mistiming. Overall, your lunar position endorses a fine head for business, but exerts a repressive influence for the expression of feelings. Read all aspects very carefully, as you have a contradictory set of ideals which require positive or hamonizing influences.

Hidden agenda
Your hidden agenda is to develop a conscious attitude to say what you really feel and think, but in doing so you must also take other people's feelings into account. In past lives your lack of achievement was largely due to pinning your hopes on the good will of others. In your current life you also retain a powerful residual memory of sexual frustration. By learning the karmic lesson of not being dependent on others, you will also learn compassion if you are willing to help others. During your lifetime you may suddenly distance yourself from events or personal relationships that you find draining, and, not wishing to hurt others' feelings, you have developed the art of subtlety and subterfuge. You are ultimately developing a filtering system that allows you to make critical decisions without being swayed emotionally. Your psychological profile actually reveals excellent potential for becoming a psychiatrist or psychologist.

You are a very amenable person who works hard to achieve a pleasant lifestyle and a harmonious atmosphere at work and at home. Personal relationships, especially with partners, can be highly influential in either supporting or upsetting this fine balance. Your Shadow self is a projection of your unconscious mind, a lunar dimension of character that has a genuine desire to please everyone, and this is why you can actually end up pleasing no one. As a Reed character you have reverted to charm and diplomacy in order to achieve your goals, and as a result your subtle mind can become extremely manipulative. The position of your Moon is, however, a powerful influence for making fair judgements, and this can raise your mind to higher levels of intelligence and intuitive wisdom. Your emotions are more sensual than passionate, and more romantically inclined. You also have an appreciation of the arts and a more refined temperament. With 158, 167, 179, 195 or 273 you have sincere feelings and genuine concern for others, and you have artistic talents that should be encouraged more. You would make a fine diplomat or artist. With 177, 194, 214, 222 or 274 these aspects are negatively engaged in frustrating your dreams and desires, and you can become anti-social as a result. Your lunar position overall reveals a pleasant temperament and a will to compromise.

Hidden agenda

Your hidden agenda is to cultivate more meaningful relationships. In your current life you are experiencing great shifts of consciousness that swing from one extreme to another. In past lives this imbalance had swung towards selfish actions and self-interests. Consequently you are now trying hard to compensate by listening to other people's views and feelings and, while this is a new experience, you are inclined to resent their interference, which is why you may suddenly change your mind and withdraw your support. You have a very strong ego underneath that easy-going nature, and though it is essential for Reed characters to be strongly motivated, it can also encourage a natural tendency towards jealousy or bitterness. Your karmic lesson is keyed into the Autumnal Equinox, a period of self-growth that relies on a bridge being formed between your conscious and unconscious minds – a bridge that can be constructed by taking the middle road or pathway towards spiritual enlightenment. Your psychological profile reveals you are a person seeking a new identity.

139

Reed
. . . .
Moon in
Libra

You have a magnetic personality and sexuality that people find intriguing, attractive or rather threatening. Either way your presence can cause a stir of emotions that are base instincts or primal reactions. Your Shadow self dwells in your unconscious mind, a lunar dimension of character that is highly psychic and attuned to the occult or hidden mysteries of life. You have intensely passionate emotions and can totally dominate your partner by sapping their will-power. As a Reed character you need to be very careful not to abuse your power over people, as this could lead

140

Reed
. . . .
Moon in
Scorpio

to scandals and criminal activity. This will have more force and impact if your Moon conjuncts your Sun, as this places extra stress on the powerful Reed characteristics and causes a transformation of the positive and negative into what some would regard as supernatural powers. This could be even more potent if Mercury is also positioned in Scorpio; if positioned in Sagittarius or Libra you should be able handle this power more wisely. With 160, 167, 186, 189, 264 or 267 these aspects instil a sense of morality and fair judgement that allows access to your higher mind. Your source of knowledge is transforming for yourself and others. With 173, 190, 209, 265, 271 or 277 your passionate nature can revert to mental cruelty because you are forced to become more ruthless due to blocking influences. Overall, your lunar position has over-complicated your powerful motives and desires. To simplify your objectives you must refrain from becoming involved in emotional blackmail or subversive activities.

Hidden agenda
Your hidden agenda is to see yourself clearly in a very dark mirror. Fulfilling your karmic lesson can be a very painful purification rite, as you are experiencing a total transformation of both your conscious and unconscious mind. This will mean learning a new set of personal values and becoming more self-reliant. In past lives you had amassed a great deal of material wealth but it did not bring personal happiness, as is so often the case. During your current lifetime you may initially experience great hardships or even poverty, but as you begin to appreciate the kindness and generosity of others in similar circumstances, your transformation will rapidly change your whole perspective on life. Psychologically speaking, you have a dominant personality, but you are also extremely honest and have a depth of character that people regard as a strength or virtue rather than a weakness.

141

Reed
....
Moon in
Sagittarius

You have a vibrant energy that is highly charged, but you tend to scatter it in many directions. As a result, while you have sown many seeds of thought, you will only begin to reap them in later life. Your Shadow self is a mirror image of your unconscious mind, a lunar dimension of character that raises your spirits at critical moments in your life. You are an honest individual with a highly developed intuitive mind. As a Reed character your powerful sense of purpose and perspective is enhanced with a philosophical approach and openness. The secretive side of your

nature is therefore less pronounced and your passionate nature and high energy levels are directed into physical and intellectual challenges. Your attraction to dangerous sports or activities is activated and you will be drawn to careers that require physical and mental stamina – a soldier of fortune, perhaps? You are not in a hurry to settle down, and marriage or permanent relationships should take into account your need to continue with your various exploits. With 160, 167, 181, 186, 197, 203, 278 or 279 these aspects activate your immense potential and you could become an honourable student of any faculty or university. Generally speaking, you will make a popular figurehead in your community. With 174, 191, 194, 208, 211 or 280 you may set your sights too high, thus weakening your motivation and strength of character. Look for positive aspects to Saturn to improve your self-discipline. Overall, your lunar position broadens your horizons.

Hidden agenda
Your hidden agenda is apparent for all to see, because you personify a powerful character who seeks a place in the history books. Your karmic lesson, however, is to make a definite commitment to yourself and others. In past lives you achieved only minor recognition, hence your residual memory of missed opportunities and less taxing challenges. During your lifetime you will encounter a number of people like yourself who appear to be running away from situations they can't or won't handle. These mirror images should give you pause to reflect upon your weaknesses. You have a mission in life that can become an obsession, but your karmic lesson and your quest for higher education are, fundamentally, a search for truth – a truth ultimately found in yourself. Your psychological profile reveals a robust character who doesn't believe in doctors or medical advice.

You are a truly formidable character in the business world or in careers that require one hundred per cent commitment. You have an austere nature that others regard as almost superhuman. Your Shadow self is a projection of your unconscious mind, a lunar dimension of character that responds dramatically to the Moon's cycles. Around the waning dark phase, just before the New Moon, you may experience dark depressions that can briefly immobilize you. As a Reed character your passionate nature is repressed emotionally, but is directed to powerful ambitions and material status in life. As a result your social and personal life can become almost non-existent. However, people with Capricorn Moons tend to seek partners who can bring out their hidden sense of humour and personal qualities not always shown in public. You have a depth of character that takes time to manifest, but when it does you appear to grow younger as layers of psychological blockages begin to disperse. With 160, 167, 181, 186, 197 or 278 these aspects not only help to dispel depression, but will increase your zest for life and broaden your intellect. With 161, 182, 198, 209, 224 or 283 you are on a downward spiral of emotions and dark thoughts that makes life pretty gloomy. Look to Mars, Saturn and Venus for positive aspects that can help to reverse things. Overall, your lunar position adds greater inner strength, but it also promotes a lack of sensitivity.

Hidden agenda
Your hidden agenda is to transform your inner strengths into a source of great ideals or moral ethics rather than perpetuating material values. While this may

142

Reed
. . . .
Moon in Capricorn

not be your last rebirth on Earth, you are standing at the threshold of a karmic judgement that will greatly influence future incarnations. In past lives you have reached this point many times, but your inability to let go of rigid attitudes and self-righteous behaviour has been a stumbling block. During your current life you are therefore placed in positions that require you to make judgements of others; this can be on a minor scale of employing people or on a higher moral level as a judge or juror. The compassionate act of mercy will help to release your own residual memories of unfair treatment, and this is your karmic lesson to learn. Your psychological profile reveals a behavioural pattern that has been formed early in life and needs to evolve in order to fit in with society.

143

Reed
....
Moon in
Aquarius

You are a militant campaigner of just causes and you will forcefully argue your case. But this can also take the form of writing to people in authority without actually resorting to anarchy. Your Shadow self is a projection of your unconscious mind, a lunar dimension of character that has an unpredictable nature, which is why your chart is quite difficult to analyse. As a Reed character your sense of purpose can therefore suddenly waver, but your need to exert influence is dramatically increased. While you will be more intellectually inclined and foster many original ideas, there is a danger that your need for independence can become a fanatical fixation. Your passionate nature and sexuality can also become highly unconventional, and your emotions can lack warmth. You are, however, a great humanitarian who is deeply interested in improving the quality of life for the underprivileged. This is where you can certainly make a difference, particularly as a sociologist or an administrator of charities. With 162, 169, 183, 188, 199, 205 or 285 these aspects will activate your humanitarian nature and you have a powerful intellect that promotes inventive and highly original projects. Though you are likely to have a number of eccentricities, you would make an affable professor. With 176, 193, 210 or 286 your unconventional behaviour can become perverse and your quick temper uncontrollable. Look for positive aspects to Saturn and Jupiter. Overall, your lunar position provides great inspiration and vision for self-growth or higher-mind knowledge.

Hidden agenda

Your hidden agenda is to develop greater practical or common sense, otherwise you will waste a lot of time on unworkable projects or ideas. In past lives your intense pride and rebellious nature cast you adrift from society and precluded happiness in personal relationships. This time round you must learn moderation in all things. During your lifetime you will encounter much prejudice as you are a 'person out of time' in the sense that you are a visionary with ideas far beyond other people's comprehension. The purification rites associated with your sign are ones of cleansing your mind, body and spirit of lust. This is why you are experiencing your karmic lesson of keeping your distance emotionally, but this can be transformed into genuine love.

Your psychological profile reveals fears of impotency, and though it can manifest as a physical reality, it is controlled emotionally and spiritually.

You have great sensitivity, and in this capacity you appreciate art and beauty. Your compassionate nature also draws you towards the healing professions. Your Shadow self is a projection of your unconscious mind, a lunar dimension of character that knows humility. As a Reed character this can make you a healer with extraordinary powers of insight that provide accurate diagnosis for finding cures. You could also become a natural spiritual healer. You are a curious mixture of gentleness and strength, and this contrast relates to the dual nature of your Piscean Moon, which shows two interlocking personalities that react completely differently. Inwardly you are often shocked at your own behaviour, and yet there is another side that applauds your ability to throw a few punches. People who have a dual nature also have an understanding of the dual cycle of life and death, and therefore you have access into the mysteries and reincarnation. In short, you are a spiritual person. With 170, 189, 206 or 288 your spiritual nature has a mystical quality that draws you into the psychic realm of Dwyll, or Pluto. Your artistic potential is activated, and so are your powers for healing. With 177, 194, 211 or 289 these aspects are extremely negative influences that can demote your spiritual nature to

whimsical fancies or dangerous illusions. Look for positive aspects to Jupiter and Saturn. Overall, your lunar position softens the nature of your sign.

Hidden agenda
Your hidden agenda is to develop your inner access to the spiritual realm. This will provide a truer vision than relying solely on religious teachings that can contain a polluted stream of dogma. Your karmic lesson relates to the Druids' belief that the soul continues to evolve through many lifetimes by its own volition. In other words this is something you must do for yourself and not rely on other people's vision or experiences to guide you, for each soul has a separate path. In past lives you remained firmly entrenched in obscure religious orders, and as a result met few truly enlightened souls. During your current lifetime, however, you will experience many strange encounters with people who suddenly appear in your life as messengers or guides at critical periods when your faith begins to falter. You will make much progress through meditation and leading a simple life. Your psychological profile reveals a high degree of emotional tension that can affect your health. Quiet retreats can help you to find your inner strengths.

144

Reed
. . . .
Moon in Pisces

Celtic moon sign: Elder

Lunar Symbol: Black Horse

The lunar symbol of the *Black Horse* is the mystical persona of Pryderi, son of the Celtic Horse-goddess, Rhiannon, and Pwyll, God of the Underworld. The symbolic rebirth of Pryderi on the day of the Winter Solstice acknowledges the primeval power of the Celts' Moon-goddess, whose battle for supremacy with solar deities eventually reached a compromise. All goddesses were regarded as personifications of their great Moon-goddess Ceridwen, and Rhiannon, personified as the White Mare at the Summer Solstice, confirms their ancient matriarchal culture. Pryderi's name means 'trouble' or 'care', and he was aptly named, as his disappearance caused his mother to suffer an unjust penance and loss of faith in the Moon-goddess. His timely return seven years later restored the ancient autocracy of the matriarchy, and confirms the authenticity of an ancient Celtic lunar calendar and zodiac.

The elder tree has held a mysterious aura since megalithic times, when its leaf-shape was delicately etched on funerary flints to symbolize death and rebirth. In the ritual zodiac of the Druids it marked the critical stage between life and death at the time of the Winter Solstice. The Druids had placed Saturn, known as Sadorn, at the end of the lunar zodiac because it marked the imprisonment of the Sun or solar spirit. Astrologically speaking, Saturn governs all formative processes and is 'Lord of the mineral kingdom' in which the source of all life and light is imprisoned. The Druids' cosmology therefore confirms an accurate knowledge of the planetary positions and influences. During the thirteenth lunar month the Druids celebrated the solstice with elderberry wine, which symbolized the last sacred gift of their Earth-goddess. It was said to regenerate the body and spirit, and produced powerful dreams of prophecy.

Elder Tree character

You were born at the time of the year when Earth was enveloped in dark nights. With only the mystical light of the Moon to guide them it was a time of silent uncertainty but great spiritual awareness. As an Elder Tree character you will therefore continue to struggle onwards, despite tremendous odds against you, and achieve ultimate victory in your endeavours. Your greatest strength is your integrity and instinctive knowledge in knowing when you are right and when other people are wrong – a moral judgement rather than a materially minded decision. In your youth, however, you are inclined to waste much time and energy on wild adventures, and your free spirit doesn't take kindly to discipline or authority. Consequently your education can suffer. You will nevertheless begin to command respect and exert a powerful influence as you grow older, and continue to improve your knowledge with extended learning.

Your inherited traits of character come from your father's side of the family, but your mother, or her family, provided the support and encouragement for pursuing your own course through life. It is from her side of the family that you have inherited a certain wildness, the untamed spirit of the 'black colt'. You are an outspoken person and at times inclined to speak without thinking, which can be an easy way out of a situation in your mind; you sometimes feel that if you speak bluntly, people will learn to keep their distance. But when you feel deeply moved on a serious issue, you can sway people with great oratory or noble action. Your search for fame and fortune will take you to many foreign places, only to discover that your true destiny lies much closer to home. The study of ancient cultures and philosophies will be your guide, and even if you never travel physically, the journeys in your mind are extremely exciting and vivid. You are a very energetic person who needs constant physical and mental stimulus. Your personal life is an open book, as you will never make commitments until you are ready to do so.

With 160, 167, 181, 186, 197, 203, 242, 258, 278 or 279 these aspects positively activate your best qualities and provide a source of good luck fortune that allows you great leeway in life. You have moral integrity and intellectual ability, and should reach positions of influence with greater ease. With 168, 187, 204, 239 or 282 you are a more serious character whose progress may be slower, but you have a more reasoned logic and strategy. If with 161, 182, 192, 209 or 283 these aspects are repressive influences that can block your efforts by decreasing your vitality and will to overcome any obstacles in life. Overall, you are a most flamboyant individual with a sense of humour and optimism that projects light and inspires others. The position of your Moon provides greater insight and introduces the karmic influences in your life. Your Basic Paragraph is thus extended.

145

Elder
··············
Moon in
Aries

You are a quick-witted restless individual who lacks patience and perseverance. But make no mistake, you will be up and running when other people are still asleep in their beds. Your Shadow self is a projection of your unconscious mind, a lunar dimension of character that responds with great enthusiasm and daring when confronted with any obstacles in life. As an Elder Tree character your pioneering spirit will break new boundaries and set in motion numerous alternatives as a challenge to the more conventional way of doing things. You are so impulsive that you may find yourself in dangerous situations without realizing it. But this is when you are at your best, and your aggressive tactics and sharp reflexes can win the day. You can have a very satirical sense of humour or wit that can also sting your opponent's ego. Your own ego, however, is inclined to be self-centred, and can become deflated if people ignore you. With 166, 185, 202, 217, 232 or 276 you are more controlled in your passions, and direct your energy to well thought-out schemes and ventures. A sign of achievement through concerted effort is identified with these aspects. With 176, 190, 207, 222, 265 or 277 your aggressive nature and selfish ambitions are activated, and you can become a bit of a bully and an impossible person to work or live with. Look for positive aspects to Jupiter and Saturn. Overall, your lunar position endorses a restlessness, but increases your will to win.

Hidden agenda

Your hidden agenda is to develop a controlled level of consciousness. There is an imbalance within your psyche which manifests as a high level of emotional and physical energy that lacks mental or cohesive direction. In past lives you had difficulty making concrete decisions without the support of others. In your current life you are determined to 'go it alone', and this is why you can appear to be self-orientated. During your lifetime you may find yourself in isolated positions for short periods, in order to gather your strength and adjust your perspective. As a result you should discover a new sense of identity that works better by cooperating with others. It is particularly significant in personal relationships, and if you can find a partner who provides the support and guidance you are seeking, your whole psyche can be harmoniously transformed. This is basically your karmic lesson. Your psychological profile reveals an erratic behavioural pattern denoting a lack of conscious control, but this can change when you reach emotional maturity, which is longer than most.

146

Elder

·············

Moon in Taurus

You have strong powers of endurance and a firm set of values that is inclined to be materialistic. Your appreciation of the arts, however, promotes aesthetic tastes and standards. Your Shadow self dwells in your unconscious mind, a lunar dimension of character that provides emotional stability with affections warmly expressed. Your love of the good things in life can become excessively self-indulgent, but you are a generous host. As an Elder Tree character your need for emotional and financial security will restrict your movements, but you will certainly enjoy a more contented lifestyle. Your interests will also be directed to the arts, in business ventures or investments.

Your lunar position can encourage a resistance to change, and this is a conflicting influence to a person with such a free spirit and expansive mind. This will not be as strong if your Mercury is in Sagittarius and not in junction with the Sun. With 165, 167, 179, 181, 186, 189, 201 or 273 you have charm and personal magnetism, and all the social attributes. While you have more refined tastes and are less inclined to waste time on impractical projects, your humanitarian principles will eclipse your materialistic outlook. With 161, 172, 177, 182, 209, 214 or 271 these aspects will block your expression of feelings, encourage narrow values and limit your success. Look for positive aspects between Mercury and Jupiter, and Jupiter with Saturn. Overall, your lunar position is steadying influence that provides artistic and practical skills

Hidden agenda

Your hidden agenda is to consciously develop your intellect, as you are inclined to give way to indulgent excesses or passionate desires. This is linked to a residual past-life memory when your powerful sex drive compromised your moral integrity. Subsequently in your current life you are being drawn back into relationships that gratify your ego but are destructive and encourage a negative form of hypocrisy. During your lifetime, therefore, you will have to moderate your appetites: you may not become overweight physically, but rather it's a reflection of your lower mind struggling to get off the runway in order to reach your higher mind. Your karmic lesson is learning discrimination and overcoming your envious nature. Your psychological profile reveals a character less prone to anxieties or neuroses of any kind.

Y ou are a busy person, with never enough time to fit in all your dates in your diary. You have a flair for writing and languages, as communication is an essential part of your personality. Your Shadow self is a mirror image of your unconscious mind, a lunar dimension of character that never sleeps. Even your dreams are full of vivid events and streams of people who will cross your path. As an Elder Tree character you have an extremely restless nature with a high degree of nervous and physical energy. You are intellectually inclined and keen on improving your mind; you are an avid reader and your curious mind enjoys delving into every subject imaginable. As a journalist or broadcaster you are a font of information. Your emotions or feelings, however, are so changeable that permanent relationships are difficult to sustain. But this doesn't really bother you, as there are always new people to meet and places to go. With 167, 169, 188, 197, 203 or 204 you have a brilliant intellect and the capacity for learning difficult subjects with ease. You are an inspired and highly creative writer. With 171, 177, 208 or 210 you have a superficial or shallow mind given to gossip and exaggeration. Look for positive aspects to Jupiter and Saturn. Overall, your lunar position increases your restlessness, but adds great wit and logic to your search for knowledge.

Hidden agenda

Your hidden agenda is not to lose sight of your main objectives, as you are inclined to miss the obvious in your hasty entrances and exits. The symbolism here is highly significant because you always appear to be leaving or arriving – a kind of temporal replay, which relates to your karmic lesson. In past lives you had unrestricted freedom, like a wild horse, but you eventually decided that company or personal relationships could be more fun. Therefore in your current life this residual memory draws you to interact with others by means of frantic communication, and

147

Elder
. . . .
Moon in
Gemini

relationships are still regarded as being fun. During your lifetime you will have to consciously make up your mind whether you are staying or going. If you decide to stay you should find that your nervous tension will disappear, and that words have an important meaning rather just being the means of conversation, and this is your karmic lesson to learn. Your psychological profile shows an erratic behavioural pattern, but you appear to thrive on constant movement and change.

148

Elder

....

Moon in
Cancer

You are a highly emotional person, despite your attempts to persuade yourself that you don't care what people think. You have a kind and sympathetic nature and a genuine concern for other people's feelings. Your Shadow self is a projection of your unconscious mind, a lunar dimension of character that responds to the changing cycles of the Moon. The waxing period is when you feel most optimistic, but during the dark phase just before the New Moon your energy can suddenly drop to low levels. As an Elder Tree character you are cautious and resourceful. You are also more likely to settle down earlier in life, as you have strong maternal or paternal instincts. You are, however, a fairly complex individual and your mood it is not always easy to gauge. Your search for knowledge will be directed around ancient cultures, history and antiques. You have a keen sense of history, coupled with intuitive insight that draws out the explorer in you to visit ancient sites. With 170, 186, 189, 197, 204 or 242 these aspects activate your best qualities of compassion and a balanced blend of emotions and intellect. Your versatile skills are also activated. With 161, 177, 182, 194, 209 or 211 your mood swings can descend to depression, and these aspects undermine your true potential. Look for positive aspects to Jupiter for compensating influence. Overall, your lunar position provides a more reflective influence that can aid your reasoning.

Hidden agenda
Your hidden agenda is as complex as your nature. Your lunar position marks the period close to the Summer Solstice when the turning of the solar year meant having to sacrifice one's ego in order to evolve on a spiritual or higher-mind level. But before beginning this journey you must establish a firm foundation from which to evolve. In past lives you were a demanding parent by being overly ambitious for your children, because of your own success. In your current life this residual memory remains a powerful influence, and your karmic lesson is to develop a new conscious attitude and emotional behavioural pattern. This will help to free your trapped ego, and eventually you will learn that by focusing upon your own objectives your free spirit will begin to evolve without the emotional shackles you have attached to it. Your psychological profile indicates a highly sensitive individual who is prone to mood swings and who dislikes taking advice, especially medical advice.

You have superb organizing skills that allow you to live life to the full. You have great personal style and flair, which sets you apart from others. Your Shadow self is a projection of your unconscious mind, a lunar dimension of character that is highly creative and indicates warm expression of feelings. You always 'think big', having an expansive vision and high ambitions. As an Elder Tree character your leadership ability is pronounced, which should encourage responsibility for your actions early on in life. Though you remain a free spirit, your self-indulgent nature can become extreme, as you enjoy spending money on lavish gifts and gourmet food and drink – so much so that you will probably become a connoisseur. With all this good living you can, however, become snobbish or pompous and at worst a patronizing individual. But generally speaking you are very loveable and people enjoy being in your company. With 165, 167, 179, 186, 195 or 242 you have all the social graces and your artistic ability is well activated. You have good fortune on your side and you will also be lucky in love. With 177, 182, 194, 209, 245 or 259, all these aspects are undermining influences that activate your

weaknesses of vanity, laziness and intolerance, and generally have the effect of demotivating you. Look for positive aspects to Mars and Saturn. Overall, your lunar position reveals a fiery individual who never takes a back seat.

Hidden agenda

Your hidden agenda is to consolidate your exuberant energy before it evaporates and thus depletes your strength. In your current life you have an opportunity to create your own lifestyle and, in a karmic sense, your own destiny. But your high-octane level of energy is not only extremely explosive but also inclined to rapidly burn out. In past lives you tended to wish your life away with dreams of castles in the sky. As a result this residual memory becomes a distracting influence in your current life. During your lifetime you will experience major turning points involving children; you can relate to their world of fantasies, but you should then discover that your own dreams have actually stopped you from realizing your true potential. Your psychological profile reveals you are a 'Peter Pan' character, and can remain an immature adult for a greater part of your life.

149

Elder
....
Moon in
Leo

You are inclined to worry inwardly even when things are going well for you. This is because you read the 'small print' of any contract or commitment, each of which always carries a warning or disclaimer. Your Shadow self is a mirror image of your unconscious mind, a lunar dimension of character that has a

measured response to life. While you have a discerning nature, it does tend to lean towards a critical view of others and self-flagellation. As an Elder Tree character this can deflate your ego, but in a positive sense it provides a more focused perspective and you are less inclined to waste time and energy on risky ventures. Your

150

Elder
....
Moon in
Virgo

natural vitality can also be affected, and this is a more serious matter to contend with. If your Mercury is placed in Capricorn it could completely change your personality and character into a more serious and sober-minded individual. If in Sagittarius it will widen your horizons and control your critical nature. If in Scorpio your search for knowledge will uncover obscure and profound information. With 160, 164, 167, 169, 189, 197 or 242 these aspects override the negative aspects of your lunar position and provide a rounded perspective by integrating your mind and your emotions. With 161, 182, 198, 209 or 245 you are working at half speed, and your hopes or dreams are easily dashed or may never be activated at all. Look for positive aspects to Jupiter and Mars. Overall, your lunar position is a restrictive influence, although it does curb your excesses and sharpen up your attitudes.

Hidden agenda

Your hidden agenda is to develop a rapport between your unconscious and conscious natures. In past lives your conscious mind was always rushing ahead of your physical and emotional stamina, and consequently you suffered from ill health. This residual memory still haunts you, and explains why you are currently learning to pace yourself more efficiently. Your karmic lesson is accepting more responsibility for your actions and helping people with more serious or severe handicaps. During your life you will come into contact with people who – despite their disabilities – lead full and active lives. Their tremendous motivation and independent spirit should make quite an impact on you. Your psychological profile reveals a deep sense of vocation. This is also linked to family influence, which suggests that an ongoing association with medical or health care is a karmic link.

151

Elder
· · · · · · · · · · ·
Moon in Libra

You have an easy-going nature and a courteous manner. This helps to create a congenial atmosphere at home and at work. Your Shadow self is a projection of your unconscious mind, a lunar dimension of character that appreciates the beauty of nature and the finer things in life. You are basically an idealist who believes the world would be a better place if people were more romantic and less aggressive. As an Elder Tree character you have charm and diplomacy, which helps you to see other points of view. Your search for knowledge is directed towards the arts rather than the sciences. Your weakness is indecisiveness, and you can become emotionally manipulative. Personal relationships are also highly significant with this lunar position. Because you dislike arguments or emotional discord, your choice of partner can be crucial to your personal happiness. Your need for personal freedom is also compromised in personal relationships. With 165, 167, 179, 195, 213 or 219 these aspects activate the finer side to your nature and your personal charisma denotes a social leader. While it may slow down your quest for knowledge, it does provide some pleasant diversions. With 177, 194, 211, 214, 222 or 223 your idealistic nature will take a battering and your self-indulgence is difficult to control. Look for positive aspects between Jupiter and Saturn, and the Sun or Moon with Saturn. Overall, your lunar position provides emotional sensitivity and a more balanced outlook.

Hidden agenda

Your hidden agenda is full of hidden meanings or symbols. In order to interpret them you need to develop your intuitive or abstract mind. In a recent past life you made a list of things that you felt you needed for a contented life, but the list continued to grow so that in the end you never achieved anything. This residual memory is enshrined in your unconscious, and this is why the symbols have become abstract – because they were never achievable in the real world. This kind of abstract thinking is akin to the ancient Egyptians' belief that if they memorized a long list of the names of all their gods, it would provide safe passage through the Underworld and into the 'Boat of Ra' – a seat with the gods. Your karmic lesson is to be self-sufficient, and as you begin to achieve it you will find great harmony within and consciously develop greater self-awareness. Your psychological profile shows you will realize your own self-worth.

You have a very intriguing personality, and despite your hectic lifestyle you are a very private individual. Your Shadow self dwells in your unconscious mind, a lunar dimension of character that has passionate emotions and highly psychic abilities. You have a smouldering intensity that exudes sexuality. As an Elder Tree character your resolute sense of purpose is directed towards improving your mind and channelling your high physical energy into activities that demand great stamina and fitness. Your intuitive perception and analytical mind is capable of penetrating the root of any problem or mystery in life. As a result your search for knowledge will probe the depths of human experience. Your need for independence can be compromised by a very complicated love life. You are not a person suited to playing second best, and if your jealous nature is roused you are inclined to react with extreme anger. If Mercury is placed in Scorpio and badly aspected this is more likely to occur. Careful study of the planetary aspects should reveal more. With 160, 167, 186, 189, 264, 267 or 279 these aspects are extremely beneficial and will raise your mind and morality to higher levels. You are a caring, generous person with a marked degree of intelligence. With 190, 194, 209, 210, 265, 271 or 277 the darker side of your nature is activated, which can be very unpleasant for others. These aspects generally weaken your moral fibre. Look for positive aspects between Jupiter and Pluto, and Pluto with Mercury, Uranus and Saturn. Overall, your lunar position endorses a great sense of survival.

Hidden agenda

Your hidden agenda is to develop a conscious level of greater self-control and sensitivity to the feelings of others. You are experiencing an inner battle that has raged in many past lives. In your current life you may experience a number of traumatic incidents, but you will recover because this is a karmic lesson designed to open your eyes to the dangerous pinnacle to which you have been clinging by not letting go of your anger. Your interest in the occult or spiritual teachings should give you access to how to achieve a complete transformation. It's a question of tuning into your inner wisdom or higher mind. But until this transition is complete your current life can descend into chaos or anarchy. Your psychological profile reveals you are a person who likes to play with fire. This usually stems from an overly strict parent who curtailed your freedom during your childhood.

153

Elder
....
Moon in Sagittarius

You are an extremely optimistic individual – almost blindly optimistic on occasions. But you have such a vivacious personality and inner radiance that it rubs off on others and creates a sense of hope. Your Shadow self is a mirror image of your unconscious mind, a lunar dimension of character with highly developed intuitive powers that can be quite prophetic. You are philosophical and quickly learn from your mistakes or errors of judgement because you have a magnanimous nature. As an Elder Tree character you have an extremely restless mind that needs time to focus on relevant issues. You will therefore find it hard to study any subject in great depth until you become an adult. Nevertheless, as a student your curious mind and versatility will greatly impress your tutors. Your vibrant energy and enthusiasm denotes an all-round player, with particular emphasis on outdoor sports as well as intellectual interests. With 160, 167, 181, 186, 197, 203, 204, 242 or 278 these aspects are enormously beneficial for promoting your potential and you are top-class material. The only thing to watch is that tendency towards blind optimism and extremism in the sense of being 'over-programmed'. With 174, 191, 194, 208 or 245 your true potential can be blocked through a lack of motivation or too much self-pride. These are difficult aspects in any chart. Look for positive aspects to Saturn and Mars. Overall, your lunar position emphasizes all your strengths and weaknesses, which encourages a zest for living an exciting life.

Hidden agenda

Your hidden agenda is to free your conscious mind from compulsive learning. While you are a seeker of truth, you are inclined to be mentally overloaded with useless information. It is a question of selective study rather than learning subjects that may impress your peers. Your fear of being misunderstood or intellectually inferior is a residual memory from past lives, but it has created a need for self-improvement. As you begin to expand your own knowledge you will develop more faith in your own abilities, and this is your karmic lesson. Travelling will broaden your whole perspective, and you will find ultimate success either abroad or through the influence of a foreigner. Your psychological profile reveals a rather promiscuous behavioural pattern that is directly linked to your emotional fear of being trapped. It has created a claustrophobic mentality in trying to free itself. However, your ability to adapt generally means that you will quickly resolve any negative thoughts or fears.

Y ou have a conventional mind and emotions, but on the inside is another personality trying to break away from a very traditional upbringing. Your Shadow self is a projection of your unconscious mind, a lunar dimension of character that provides self-discipline and patience. You are relatively serious-minded and less inclined to self-indulgences – a mature Elder Tree character who has developed a 'wise head on young shoulders'. While your feelings are undemonstrative, you make up for it with faithfulness and reliability in all personal relationships. The ambitious side of your nature is directed towards achieving material success. But this is where problems can occur, as you are always torn between your career and family obligations. However, as you become more successful these tendencies will diminish, and you will become more generous in your affections. The position of Venus in your chart is the key to unlocking a part of your psyche that has become isolated. With 158, 160, 167, 170, 179, 181, 186, 189 or 195 your repressed emotions are released and your potential intellect and creative skills are activated. You should be fortunate in love and also successful in your career. With 161, 182, 198, 209, 224 or 245 these aspects are extremely negative influences that knock your self-confidence and discipline and generally increase inhibitions and depressive moods. Look for positive aspects between the Sun and Moon with Jupiter and Uranus. Overall, your lunar position provides stability and self-determination.

Hidden agenda
Your hidden agenda is to come to terms with a heavy family karmic debt that goes back generations and hasn't yet been resolved. Therefore, in your current life you are experiencing on the very deepest levels parental responsibilities that include your own parents. In an effort to free yourself from your parents' influence and demands you then moved into a more intense karmic situation in which you are on the receiving end of complex emotions from your partner and possibly your children, too. Nearly all your emotional energy is spent trying to understand their problems. During your lifetime you must learn to develop the patience of Job, and eventually a day will dawn when you suddenly find yourself on the outside looking in. This usually occurs in your twenty-eighth and fifty-sixth years, and is linked to the returns of Saturn, Lord of Karma in esoteric astrology. It releases trapped energies and marks a 'coming of age', both emotionally and spiritually. Your psychological profile reveals a repressed ego that is seeking a new identity.

154

Elder
··············
Moon in Capricorn

155

Elder
············
Moon in
Aquarius

You are a very independent person and completely unconventional. You are determined to make your way through life under your own steam, ignoring authority or the status quo. Your Shadow self is a projection of your unconscious mind, a lunar dimension of character that needs personal space in order to pursue idealistic causes and ingenious schemes. As an Elder Tree character you have a highly progressive mind attuned to New Age philosophies. Your vision of the future can be extremely fascinating and highly original. Your advanced level of inventiveness and scientific ability, combined with a need to explore, means that you may well become an astronaut or test pilot of prototype planes. Your search for knowledge has certainly lifted off the runway and is rapidly soaring ahead. You also have a natural aptitude for astrology, astronomy, computer technology or anything to do with modern science. With 162, 169, 183, 199, 205 or 243 you are well on your way to achieving recognition for your highly original work. You are a great humanitarian with a quest to improve humankind's knowledge and the environment in which we all live. With 176, 193, 210 or 246 your true potential is blocked by a lack of self-control and rebellious attitudes or wild ideas that win few friends or respect. Look for positive aspects to Saturn for more inner strength. Overall, your lunar position provides great inspiration but your need for independence can destabilize personal relationships if you do not take care.

Hidden agenda

Your hidden agenda is to develop a greater sense of reality. This applies equally to personal relationships and your work. While you have great originality of thought and vision, you can too easily become locked into an idealistic world that is currently a world of the future that doesn't yet exist. In past lives your inventive nature achieved a degree of success, but this success quite literally went to your head. You were also sexually amorous to such an extent that you never became personally committed to anyone but yourself. It has manifested in your current life as a powerful ego, hence your need for total independence and your tendency to distance yourself emotionally. While it gives you time to reflect, your karmic lesson is to ultimately make some personal sacrifices for your partner and family. Your psychological profile reveals you have a built-in discontent that influences the way you behave, which is to challenge or change the rulebook.

156

Elder
············
Moon in
Pisces

You have a kind and sympathetic nature that is trying to come to terms with society in general. You often feel extremely vulnerable to outside forces, but you are also very adaptable to change. Your Shadow self is a duality that operates in the unconscious mind, a lunar dimension of character that responds with sensitivity to other people's feelings and fears. You are highly intuitive and receptive on the psychic level. As an Elder Tree character you are a reflective and romantic individual, drawn to helping others in a quiet but practical way. You are especially drawn to the arts, and your search for knowledge takes a more spiritual route. You have very deep emotions and you are less inclined to roam in search of wild adventures. But there is another side to your personality that is more pragmatic, and you have an inner strength of purpose that is vocational rather than intellectual. You are a natural healer and mystic. With 170, 189, 206 or 244 your artistic potential is activated and your powers of healing and spirituality are highly advanced. With 177, 194, 211 or 247, however, these aspects impair your creative talents and your spiritual nature can be easily duped by people who pretend to be your friends. In effect, your vulnerability is overshadowed by negative influences. Look for positive aspects to Jupiter and Saturn. Overall, your lunar position provides a simple faith and love of humanity.

Hidden agenda

Your hidden agenda is to develop an inner strength that can cope with the physical world. Your sensitivity is both an asset and, at times, your Achilles heel. In past lives you gathered your strengths by living a simple lifestyle and following a spiritual path. There are strong links with religious orders or missionary schools. This residual memory was carried over, and you see a world in chaos with people being manipulated by greed and corruption – an apocalyptic vision. During your lifetime you will come into contact with some of your worst fears, but as you begin to realize your own frailties you will begin to fully integrate your powerful duality – a difficult karmic lesson to achieve but you have an inner faith that records an old soul. Your psychological profile reveals inherited weakness that can be related to physical or mental disorders, but you also have amazing powers of recovery.

Paragraphs of conjunctions and aspects

The following interpretive paragraphs refer to planetary aspects. Read the information relating to your Basic Paragraph before consulting the information in this section.

Paragraphs of conjunctions and aspects

157 Moon Conjunction Mercury

This aspect is commonly found in charts of highly intelligent people, and those who show a marked degree of sensitivity and imagination. There is also a high degree of nervous energy that needs to be positively channelled. The Moon is a planet of fluctuation and response, and therefore its effects are coloured by the planets it makes contact with, rather than the other way around. If the conjunction is well aspected with 167, 168, 203 or 204 the nervous system is strengthened. With 165, 170, 201 or 206 your imagination is inspirational and creatively channelled through the arts – excellent aspects for Rowan, Ash, Willow, Holly, Ivy and Reed signs, in particular.

158 Moon Conjunction Venus

Emotions are calm and feelings are affectionately expressed. Charm and personal magnetism attracts many admirers, but there is a tendency of vanity or too much self-love. There is also an appreciation of the arts and aesthetic tastes, but a love of luxury and rich foods can develop into self-indulgence. With 168 or 219 there is more self-discipline and a practical outlook on finances. With 174 or 223 these aspects encourage extravagant spending and extreme self-indulgence, including numerous love affairs. Overall, however, this conjunction does provide a sense of harmony and social popularity.

159 Moon Conjunction Mars

The energy levels are high and so are personal ambitions. There is also an emotional need for independence, and if freedom is denied it can evoke an aggressive response. Generally speaking, there is a tendency for vigorous debates or arguments and an inclination to take risks; the aspects, therefore, need careful analysis. If forming squares with the Sun and Uranus there is physical and financial recklessness. But if with 168 or 232 time and energy is constructively employed. If found in the charts of the Alder or Reed signs it requires special study, as it can make the difference between success and failure; your other aspects should help you to assess what the influence is likely to be.

160 Moon Conjunction Jupiter

There is enormous energy and vitality attached to this conjunction, and this is usually directed through a flair for business and an exciting personal life. A liking for pleasure demands a high standard of living and a high income, but overall it is an excellent influence that bestows generosity, honesty and magnanimity. There is also a sense of fair play combined with moral ethics. The extreme nature of Jupiter can, however, encourage a tendency towards self-importance and vanity. If with 223 or 235 vanity and blind optimism can cause financial bankruptcy and there is often no compunction in gambling away income and any inheritances. With 242 or 279 all resources are well managed.

161 Moon Conjunction Saturn

This is a powerful conjunction that provides an ability to work very hard and a strong sense of duty. There is a propensity to self-denial and thrift, and little praise is given to others because there is usually a craving for perfection that can become an obsession. Emotions are not readily expressed, and this can result in loneliness or depression. Such a sombre influence does, however, provide stability and endurance. With 165, 167 or 242 the nature of this conjunction is greatly improved and feelings are more openly and sincerely expressed. With 172, 224 or 245 powerful inhibitions stem from a difficult childhood where affection or encouragement may have been denied by parents.

162 Moon Conjunction Uranus

A high level of emotional tension is attached to this conjunction together with an overwhelming dislike for conformity or conventional rules. Children with this planetary influence are difficult to cope with, and even as adults there is a marked degree of independence that can become extremely perverse if thwarted. There is, however, a genuine feeling for humanitarian causes and a visionary mind that has a high degree of intelligence, and which – if properly trained – has the capacity for brilliant and truly original ideas. With 169, 205 or 243 emotions are more stable and the mind is more tolerant and raised to higher levels of thinking that are deeply philosophical. With 210 or 237 an explosive temper can undermine true potential, as it becomes a liability rather than an asset.

163 Moon Conjunction Neptune

The emotional level is high and there is an attraction towards mysticism or spiritual matters. People with this conjunction are natural mystics and artists, as there is a powerful imagination that draws upon a love of nature and beauty. While there is much sympathy and compassion shown to others, there is a vulnerability to negative influences that can cause confusion or instability. With 164, 168 or 251 emotions and imagination are well controlled and strengthened by reasoned thinking or common sense. With 211, 226 or 247 these aspects show gullibility and a strong tendency to live in a world of unreality.

164 Moon Trine Mercury

Common sense and intelligence are indicated with this conjunction. Freedom of movement and expression promotes a fluent talker and uninhibited body language. A curious mind that quickly absorbs information and facts reveals an aptitude for a wide range of subjects. The prime motive is always being up to date with the latest trends, but because it operates on a minimal effort, real depth of knowledge can be lacking. However, this is compensated by a certain cleverness and ability to make logical deductions. With 167, 203 or 204 there is more incentive for improving the mind, and a good head for business. With 177, 208 or 271 these aspects impede knowledge with unrealistic ideas, errors of judgement and dogmatic opinions. Overall, it is a positive aspect for broadening the mind, and excellent for all signs.

165 Moon Trine Venus

An excellent aspect for marriage or partnerships. Feelings are affectionately expressed and very supportive when difficult situations arise that require loyalty and full cooperation. Tastes are inclined to be expensive, but there are usually a number of artistic talents expressed through craftwork or skills that can make the home look very luxurious on a reasonable budget. Unless badly aspected by Saturn this Venusian influence is extremely beneficial in all charts, especially the Willow, Vine and Ivy signs.

166 Moon Trine Mars

This is usually a sign of robust good health and quick responses, both mentally and physically. But there is a tendency to take risks with little regard for the consequences. While emotions are largely controlled, the mind can be sharp and prone to satire. Here is a natural competitor with powerful ambitions. On a level playing field the odds are always favourable, but when faced with unfair tactics or disloyalty, verbal attack is directed with devastating accuracy at opponent's weak points. With 231 or 232 there is a more thoughtful and constructive approach in operation. But if with 236 or 237 misfortune is often the direct result of bad judgement or a bad temper that incurs strife and a disharmony. Overall, however, this aspect does increase personal motivation.

167 Moon Trine Jupiter

A very beneficial influence that shows a pleasant temperament, good humour and a generous spirit. This aspect is a sign of popularity and high achievement through expansive vision. Idealist qualities are shown, and a fair-minded approach that allows for weaknesses in others. Overall, this aspect remains a powerful and positive influence, but the extreme nature of Jupiter can be directed towards excessive self-indulgence, and positive aspects generally need the challenging negative aspects in order not to become complacent or inert. It is an excellent influence for Birch and Elder signs, and people with this aspect often benefit from living abroad at some stage.

168 Moon Trine Saturn

Ability to organize and take responsibility is shown, but such abilities can be limited through a lack of imagination and concentration. There is, however, a sense of duty and of making considerable self-sacrifices in order to fulfil obligations. While life can be short on fun, this aspect strengthens the potential to achieve successful objectives. It provides a very sobering influence in charts that require a more rational outlook. There is basically a natural reserve or cautious response in operation that denotes an autocratic nature – a steadying influence for Alder, Hawthorn and Elder signs.

169 Moon Trine Uranus

This aspect often appears in the charts of astrologers. It denotes a high degree of intuitive knowledge and visionary insights. While tolerance and humanitarian principles are shown, there is also a strong need for independence. Nervous energy is high but well channelled into exciting projects. Life is never dull or routine and often leans towards unusual and perhaps bizarre interests. Radical thinking denotes a dislike for conventional theories or authority, but any exchanges are usually confined to philosophizing rather than dramatic actions. In the charts of all the tree signs it provides visionary inspiration.

170 Moon Trine Neptune

The imagination is powerful and drawn towards wanting to do something rather special in life. A vocational calling may provide a sense of inner contentment. Personal magnetism and a graceful manner that attracts attention are shown. This aspect is often found in the charts of artists, natural healers and people with a spiritual mission. Because of a strong sensitivity to the pressures of society or any disharmony in personal relationships, there is a need to find quiet retreats in the country where the beauty of nature provides a calming influence. An appreciation of music and the arts is another relaxing medium. This aspect provides excellent influences for Ash or Ivy signs, as long as there are stabilizing aspects of Saturn.

171 Moon Square Mercury

While there is an astute intellect, the mind can become cunning or underhand and there is a strong tendency to gossip. Basically there is a great deal of restless thinking, which encourages inconsistency and nervous tension. But there is also a sharp wit that provides ready-made answers, and this facilitates careers where quick thinking is required, especially sales promotions and selling in general. Overall, there is a tendency to speak without regard for the consequences. If with 203 or 204 these aspects will add more breadth and depth of character and raise the mind to higher levels of intellect.

172 Moon Square Venus

There is a lack of ability to express feelings that can lead to unhappiness and disappointments in personal relationships. As a result incompatibility can occur in marriage or partnerships. A strange moodiness is present, and judgement can be weak. An over-assertive manner often conceals shyness or an inferiority complex. If with 217 or 221 these aspects help to boost self-confidence, and sensitive feelings are more openly expressed with affection and sincerity. If with 214 or 226 there is a cold indifference that can be anti-social, and problems can arise over financial security. Overall, a difficult aspect for personal relationships in any chart.

173 Moon Square Mars

There is a tendency to become aggressive and quarrelsome, which stems from over-excited emotions that respond with irritable, impulsive and combative reactions. Mars is considered a combative influence rather than passive one, but if badly aspected there is usually an inner frustration that relates to limited opportunities. While self-respect and self-control must be carefully developed, there is usually a high degree of intelligence and enterprising ambition. With 236 it's a question of bad planning and a need to reorganize your lifestyle. If with 237 your uneven temper is explosive and uncontrollable, which can be enormously destructive and result in nervous breakdowns. Look for positive aspects between Mars and Jupiter or Venus and Saturn for counterbalances.

174 Moon Square Jupiter

While popularity and good humour are present, inner conflicts can centre around moral or religious beliefs. Financial judgement is usually weak and there is a tendency towards idleness. Health can suffer from self-indulgence affecting the liver. However, this aspect is often found in the charts of successful people because of the will to live life to the full. It is necessary, however, to judge the strength of Saturn, which can steady the more extreme tendencies. Ideal aspects are 168 or 242, which enforce greater self-discipline. If with 191 or 245 judgement remains weak and success is restricted.

175 Moon Square Saturn

This is a very potent aspect that can provide the key to success or failure in life. It is identified with struggle and self-determination that is destined for ultimate success, but the strength of the individual is paramount. It invariably causes depression, initially through a basic lack of confidence that is linked to a difficult mother–child relationship. The lack of a mother figure in turn leads to choosing partners that are older. This can result in the storing up of problems for the future or later on in life. Look for positive aspects between Saturn and Jupiter, and the Sun and Moon with Venus and Jupiter. If found in Birch, Holly, Reed or Elder signs it provides the necessary inner strength to evolve to higher levels of consciousness.

176 Moon Square Uranus

Real talent and intellectual ability is combined with stubbornness and fanaticism. The positive traits need strength and direction from other planets to combat inevitable restlessness and wilfulness that manifests in disruptive displays of anger or resentment. There is a high nervous tension bordering on genius and perverse thinking, both being difficult for complete integration into society. With 188 or 243 these aspects add stability and strengthen the mind and body. With 210 or 237 fanaticism, intolerance and a bad temper are raised to dangerous levels that can result in violent confrontations with authority or the police. It is an extremely volatile aspect that requires careful study; look for stabilizing aspects that will counterbalance its effect.

177 Moon Square Neptune

There is much self-deception associated with this aspect, and this can manifest in unrealistic schemes for making money or becoming famous. Complications may occur in emotional relationships, which are extremely difficult to unravel or understand. The predisposition to wishful thinking can weave extraordinary stories that may become very real to the individual concerned. This type of confusion effectively impairs any creative talents, and generally speaking this aspect remains a weak point in any chart.

178 Sun Conjunction Mercury

The only aspect the Sun and Mercury can make is a conjunction. While this conjunction confirms mental stability, the thought process is inclined to be dogmatic and prejudiced. But the mind is not detached from personal feelings or self-expression, and a great deal of thought or consideration is usually directed in this area. If badly aspected, however, there is a tendency towards too much introspection. With 185, 186 or 203 these aspects broaden the intellect and expand your perspective of life. With 182 or 209, however, the mind becomes inward-thinking, which in turn encourages personal inhibitions.

179 Sun Conjunction Venus

This is considered to be an excellent conjunction to have in a chart. It shows genuine affection, generosity and a charming disposition. There is a strong inclination towards arts and music, and refined tastes in general, as well as a highly sensual personal magnetism that attracts many admirers. People with this conjunction in their charts usually have a striking or glamorous appearance, which can lead to a career as an actor or model. But there is, however, always the danger of exploiting one's looks at the expense of developing depth of character.

180 Sun Conjunction Mars

The Sun and Mars have a special relationship, as both are sources of energy and self-growth. While Mars is more aggressive in action, the Sun provides a radiant source of conscious growth. This conjunction shows a hard worker in his or her chosen field, but there is a tendency to work to breaking point, brought about through sheer physical exhaustion. Enthusiasm tends to run wild which can result in minor accidents occurring, with injuries to the head being commonplace. But if this additional energy is well directed it is an excellent aspect to have, especially in the charts of the Ash, Alder and Elder signs. With 187 or 232 energy is constructively organized and creatively channelled.

181 Sun Conjunction Jupiter

This is an extremely fortunate influence and, providing the conjunction is free from negative or depressing aspects, the individual concerned should have the best attributes in the book. These include a well-developed and cultured mind, and a sense of humour with a satirical slant if Mars is well placed. There is great optimism and generosity that lifts the spirits of others. Material luck is always present, even if events conspire to create financial difficulties. Overall, there is a vibrant energy and vitality that permeates the whole psyche. With 242 or 243 these aspects confirm a high degree of success that wins personal honours. With 245 or 247 a lack of ambition is shown, and a tendency to drift along in life with no coherent direction.

182 Sun Conjunction Saturn

Of all the aspects, the ones relating to the Sun and Saturn can provide the necessary 'anchorage' or stability in all charts. While a certain amount of personal limitation and frustration can be felt with all Sun/Saturn aspects, in the Celtic lunar zodiac they represent conscious growth that can only evolve through letting go of past-life behavioural patterns that manifest as negative traits of character. A conjunction can mean considerable worldly success, but it is always a hard-won success that equates with a self-made individual. Difficult relationships with parents, particularly with your father, provides the will to overcome all obstacles, and though life can be short on fun, sacrifices are willingly made. Serious direction of energy and effort is shown by other planetary aspects. Look to Mars, Jupiter and Venus for positive aspects. Any negative aspects between Saturn and Jupiter or Saturn and Mars should be most revealing.

183 Sun Conjunction Uranus

This conjunction can be the source of considerable talent if its unsettling nature can be controlled. There is often a flair for 'modern' careers, in the sense of newly created systems or methods of work. Also present is a natural aptitude for astrology and astronomy. A high degree of intelligence exists which, if properly trained, can become quite brilliant, as it is already touching upon visionary concepts that are years ahead of conventional thought. The undermining weakness is erratic and unpredictable behaviour and a perverse self-will that must be curbed if successful personal relationships and social acceptance are to be achieved. With 186, 189, 255 or 258 these aspects provide great support and direction – particularly the one between the Sun and Moon, which creates an inner harmony that inspires all natural talents.

184 Sun Conjunction Neptune

This conjunction is especially excellent for artistic creativity in relation to ballet, poetry, theatre or cinema. It is also the sign of a natural mystic. Because the influence of Neptune is considered nebulous or somewhat difficult to define, there is a mystical and spiritual influence in operation that creates a very soporific energy and aura. Strange wavelengths are activated that have an 'Otherworld presence' or hypnotic effect. An excellent aspect for Holly, Ivy and Reed signs, providing that there are positive aspects to Saturn somewhere in the chart.

185 Sun Trine Mars

This is a dynamic aspect of tremendous energy and vitality. It is often found in the charts of athletes, racing drivers or military service people. Action is the name of the game, and while an aggressive nature is indicated, it is usually well directed into highly competitive arenas that require strict training and discipline. If badly aspected by Saturn or Neptune it can be limited or weakened, but generally speaking it is a highly motivating aspect that can produce winners through sheer persistence and will-power. This aspect is a sign of strength and good health, and is excellent for the Birch, Alder and Elder signs.

186 Sun Trine Jupiter

This aspect has direct links with such professions as the law, publishing and the church. It is a very fortunate aspect in the sense that it provides a kind of safety net or insurance against poverty or misfortune. In personal terms it denotes self-confidence, generosity of spirit and a cheerful or jovial nature. It is an excellent aspect for self-growth or studying classic subjects. People with this aspect in their chart are inclined to be unspoiled by material wealth, as they prize intelligence or intellectual ability above all else. Overall, it provides tremendous scope for creative and versatile talents.

187 Sun Trine Saturn

While success is likely through hard work and patience, there is great emphasis on a well-organized and moral life. Longevity is also associated with this aspect, which is often found in the charts of senior statespeople or those that gain great respect as they grow older. There is an enduring quality of tradition and worldly success associated with most positive Saturn aspects, and this particular aspect is linked with old ancestral roots in the Celtic lunar zodiac. If found in Birch, Holly or Elder signs, family inheritances are also more commonplace.

188 Sun Trine Uranus

There are excellent powers of leadership associated with this aspect, especially if well aspected to Jupiter. It shows a broad vision and powerful humanitarian principles. While there may be a lack of tact on occasions, this can be overlooked as blunt speaking or honest dialogue – an abiding feature of strong leadership.

This aspect is also associated with longevity that usually runs in the family. It stems from progressive thinking or continuous self-growth. There are also considerable inner reserves of emotion that provide a source of passionate ideals, originality and inspiration. If found in Rowan, Alder, Hawthorn or Elder signs it can be a major influence in career choices.

189 Sun Trine Neptune

There is a harmonious rapport operating between the conscious and unconscious mind, or between mind and emotions. Personal charm combined with a strange magnetism creates an air of mystery and an elusive personality. Intuition is highly developed and coupled with an artistic temperament. But this aspect will not realize its full potential unless there is support from other planetary influences. If positively aspected to Saturn it provides the ability to bring ideas, inspiration and artistic potential to a successful fruition. On its own, nevertheless, it does show a strong appreciation for the arts, and people with this aspect in their charts are regular visitors to art galleries and exhibitions. An excellent aspect for Ash, Hawthorn, Vine and Ivy signs, but in all charts it provides harmony and balance.

190 Sun Square Mars

A high energy level can be misdirected with this aspect, resulting in impulsive and hasty actions that cause injuries through being 'accident-prone'. Risk-taking generally can become a way of life simply for the sheer pleasure or thrill it tends to excite. With 166, 204 or 232 energy and passions are controlled and risks are carefully weighed against the benefits. With 236 or 237 there is an urgent need to reflect quietly on the real motives behind your behaviour, and self-discipline is needed to control a quick temper.

191 Sun Square Jupiter

There is a negative form of restlessness in operation that is a most trying character trait. A blind optimism prevails, and an urge to do just as one pleases without due thought or consideration of the consequences. Pretentious behaviour and an attraction to making fast money becomes a risky way of earning a living. Health can also suffer, due to a liking for rich foods. Negative Jupiter traits can, however, be modified by a strong position of Saturn in the chart, especially Sun and Moon conjunctions.

192 Sun Square Saturn

This aspect is often found in the charts of successful people, as there is an inner strength that provides tremendous motivation and a will to overcome personal limitations. But self-expression or communication with others remains limited – a self-consciousness that stems from a sense of inadequacy. While general health can suffer from a lack of vitality, this is often compensated by persistent effort and a well-organized lifestyle. With 181, 231 or 242 these aspects revitalize the energy and extend the boundaries of personal limitations. With 198 or 245 you become more easily depressed and inclined to take a sombre outlook on life.

193 Sun Square Uranus

This aspect is an indication of considerable nervous strain and a self-willed perversity that can get out of hand. People who have this aspect in their charts often attempt to impose their moral and religious views on others, sometimes in fairly extreme ways. There is a craving to be 'different' that indicates a powerful ego, and basically a genuine frustration at not being understood by your peer group due to having a totally different perspective of life and future progress. With 169, 243 or 258 these aspects provide stability and restore a sense of balance and inspiration. With 176 or 286 explosive tempers and fanatical beliefs do not help matters.

194 Sun Square Neptune

This is a very debilitating influence. There is an almost disproportionate amount of psychological confusion that weakens the character, especially if there is already a high level of emotion present. This is Neptune in its 'chaos' mode, which opens up all the wrong channels or wavelengths that contain weird and unreliable contacts. Attraction to strange cults or religions can prove disastrous. Drugs and alcohol should be avoided, too, as they can be just as dangerous. It's a question of choosing friends wisely, as there is gullibility and naivety present. Look for strengthening moral aspects of Jupiter and Saturn.

195 Mercury Conjunction Venus

This conjunction is a delightful combination of idealism and artistic appreciation. It provides a calm mental outlook and a natural talent for singing or public speaking. It is highly beneficial for people engaged in work where the expression of beauty is conveyed through the hands – dress designers, musicians or hairdressers, to name but a few. But other aspects can either strengthen or stifle any creative talents. With 165, 189 or 219 artistic talent is of a high order and well applied. With 182, 209 or 224 artistic potential is stifled in order to pursue more material careers, and this may be due to a lack of funds from an early age.

196 Mercury Conjunction Mars

This conjunction provides quick mental and physical reflexes. There is a sharp satirical wit that can be highly amusing. There is also the ability for serious intellectual or mathematical studies and, if a writing skill is shown, this can develop into a very individualistic style. If the conjunction is badly aspected it can encourage bitter disputes that can affect mental health. With 186, 187 or 232 these aspects strengthen the mind and provide a sense of purpose and direction in life. With 209, 236 or 237, people with these aspects can become their own worst enemy by adopting aggressive tactics and not listening to sound advice.

197 Mercury Conjunction Jupiter

This conjunction provides optimism and a high degree of intelligence, though real potential and ability are usually developed through further education and life experience. It's really a question of finding a clear framework from which to work, as people with this conjunction are extremely versatile and multi-talented. Success in the arts and literature or the law is likely, and in some cases, if there are positive aspects to Neptune, religion holds a great interest. Other planetary aspects will also provide a clearer direction. There is a tendency to philosophize and hold strong moral views. Overall, it shows an open and curious mind with fine ideals and humanitarian principles.

198 Mercury Conjunction Saturn

There is a very sobering mental influence attached to this conjunction that shows a profound thinker who can take life far too seriously. People with this conjunction are inclined to abide by the law and regard moral conduct as a code for clean living. Learning, however, can be a slow process, and children with this placing should not be forced into studying against their will. With careful supervision and encouragement they can produce some thoughtful ideas and worthwhile contributions to society in their adult years. Since there is a tendency towards depression, look to Jupiter and Mars for positive aspects.

199 Mercury Conjunction Uranus

People with this conjunction must be allowed to live life their own way, as it denotes a wilful nature and a highly independent mind that refuses to accept conventional values. There is a strong identification with new trends in science, and real potential bordering on genius that needs space and freedom to develop. Conjunctions are not considered positive or negative; it depends on the aspects they make to other planets. With positive aspects to Saturn and Jupiter this conjunction becomes a source of great inspiration and vision. Any positive aspects to Uranus are commonly found in the charts of astrologers. The planet Uranus is associated with space travel, modern science, aeronautics, astronomy and astrology. Because of its erratic axial inclination, it is identified with eccentric or cranky behaviour.

200 Mercury Conjunction Neptune

This shows a powerful and creative imagination, and is often found in the charts of poets, musicians and composers. It denotes a kind and gentle nature that is inclined to be 'unworldly', and because there is a tendency to experience delusions and uncontrollable impulses, some kind of protection or conscious awareness must be in place. With 164, 244 or 288 these aspects provide common sense, mental vigour and clear insight. With 177 or 209 there are weaknesses of character and dark moods, which are very difficult to overcome.

201 Mercury Trine Venus

This aspect is very similar to 195, but with the emphasis now on expanding the artistic potential to a wider audience. Positive aspects to Jupiter indicate involvement in the literary world or theatre; Saturn, the administrative side of the arts; Neptune, the cinema or fashion world; Uranus, modern music and arts; and Pluto or Mars highlight passionate affairs and passionate ideas generally.

202 Mercury Trine Mars

This aspect is extremely beneficial to the nervous system and stimulates the mind. There is often a marked literary ability, and people with this aspect are excellent in debate and make assertive public speakers. But there remains a rashness and a tendency to take unnecessary risks. Eyesight, hearing and reflexes are usually very good, so flying and driving can be either a pastime or a profession. Direction in life, however, needs to be firm and decisive, as there is a propensity to race through life without a clear or constructive plan. Look for strengthening aspects of Saturn that provide practical planning.

203 Mercury Trine Jupiter

This aspect shows an active mind, but it can lack ambition. While the necessary drive may be missing, the mind is of a high calibre and writing ability is a prominent trait that usually finds success in publishing. It also shows an excellent sense of humour. For the cut and thrust of positive aspects look to Mars and the ambitious strategy of Saturn. Any positive aspect to Jupiter always provides a source of luck or good fortune and remains in place throughout life.

204 Mercury Trine Saturn

This aspect shows no lack of ambition, and the general outlook is serious and practical with a regard for honesty and morality. A depth of thought and good reasoning powers is combined with ability to organize. It is a stabilizing influence to have in any chart, especially in business or careers requiring careful analysis of facts and figures. An excellent aspect for Birch, Hazel, Vine and Elder where the individual potential requires strong support.

205 Mercury Trine Uranus

There is a progressive outlook here, and the mind is highly intuitive and dextrous. There is also a high degree of self-reliance and an excellent memory. It shows a complete individualist with extremely original ideas that have a deep vein of brilliance. The content is the same as for 199, but trines often need the hard aspects of Mars and Saturn to fully activate the true potential.

206 Mercury Trine Neptune

This shows a powerful imagination easily developed and expanded through poetry, dancing or acting. If creativity is revealed in the chart it will greatly influence the way your mind works, as it is highly sensitive to external influences. Positive aspects to Jupiter bring out the showmanship traits, while negative aspects to Saturn can actually strengthen the mind. Overall, there is a highly spiritual content that leans towards mysticism.

207 Mercury Square Mars

This aspect shows a quick mind and a sharp tongue. There seems to be an inborn irritability or prickly nature linked to overworking or exhaustive routines. Finding fault with others is often a ploy to cover up your own mistakes brought about by trying to work against the clock. With 166, 231 or 232 these aspects help to control the temper, expand the mind and provide more constructive planning.

208 Mercury Square Jupiter

There is artistic and literary ability associated with this aspect, and this is shown through an original and fertile mind. However, people with this aspect in their charts must guard against indiscretions or exaggerating their abilities. There is also a tendency to be absent-minded, but the real weakness is poor judgement, especially if badly aspected by Neptune. With 168, 198 or 242 the mind is greatly strengthened and objectives are clearly defined. Look for other positive or constructive aspects of Saturn for compensating traits.

209 Mercury Square Saturn

There is a tendency to plot and scheme, which is part of a strict routine and rigid thinking. A dark cloud of depression is never far away and is linked to constant worries and fears about material security as well as an inner sense of loneliness. Reliability and patience is never in doubt, and there is a capacity for studying subjects in great depth, which can produce some profound philosophies or concepts. However, your mind has a harshness or lack of sympathy which can manifest as a form of mental cruelty to others. With 168, 181 or 242 these aspects will greatly improve mental and physical vitality and provide a wider perspective overall.

210 Mercury Square Uranus

There is a tendency here towards eccentricity and a lack of tact that can become extremely tiresome to others. It is generally linked to a strong belief of being 'superior' or in some way chosen to play a unique role in life. While there is great talent associated with this aspect, it is invariably undermined by such cranky behaviour. There is also a propensity to waste energy because of inner nervous tension and confusion. Look to Saturn and Jupiter for positive aspects.

211 Mercury Square Neptune

While your imagination is fertile and your intuitive perception of a high order, these traits are not always used positively. Worry and a lack of self-confidence is part of a circuitous approach that began with self-deceit and a scheming mentality, and so it continues to generate more and more mental confusion. There is, however, a fine appreciation of the arts and beauty, and if this can be employed constructively the circle can be broken or short-circuited periodically. With 181, 204 or 251 these aspects should help to break the chains of self-delusion and encourage a more positive use of talents.

212 Venus Conjunction Mars

Any aspects between Venus and Mars are highly significant as they reveal the intimate details of one's sex life and passionate desires. Mars is never truly compatible with any other planet in the way it is with Venus, as they represent the male and the female nature. In esoteric astrology Mars represents the 'animal soul' in humankind, and Venus is the 'human soul' that equates with the lower and higher mind. Eventually, the energy of Mars must gradually transmute into the higher vibration of Venus, therefore the synthesizing effect of their aspects to each other can also provide an insight into spiritual nature. A conjunction must thus take into account which planet is the stronger or more effective influence. If Venus has negative aspects to Saturn or Pluto it can inhibit the finer feelings of love, and with Mars in the dominant role, behaviour is coarsened in general. In short, look very carefully at any aspects to these planets. This particular conjunction, however, shows a harmonious blend of Venusian charm and Martian energy and denotes an active and enjoyable sex life. People with this conjunction are very attractive to the opposite sex as they have a magnetism that is hard to resist. On a spiritual level they are already a unifying influence in the psyche. It is an excellent aspect for Alder and Vine signs.

213 Venus Conjunction Jupiter

This conjunction is an excellent influence for business partnerships, especially between members of the opposite sex. There is great charm and generosity that leads to personal popularity. People with this conjunction in their charts are fortunate in the sense that both planets are considered 'beneficial' ones that on their own stand as a source of creative talents and together implement luck or good fortune that provides greater opportunities for success. Also with this conjunction is a set of ideals that remain in place despite difficult or negative aspects. Overall, it conveys a gentle nature and humanitarian attitudes.

214 Venus Conjunction Saturn

All aspects between Venus and Saturn limit the affections and indicate self-sacrifices. They have nothing in common and are never compatible. The conjunction has the effect of delaying marriages or personal commitments and is linked to inhibitive psychological factors. Sometimes, however, the causes are not related to the person with this conjunction but rather to their choice of partner, and this has a more complex psychology. If affection was not shown between your parents when you were a child, for instance, it could influence you to choose someone who is either much older than yourself or not demonstrative emotionally. The consequences are counter-productive to achieving long-term happiness. Overall, there is a powerful sense of duty that takes precedence over personal feelings and can be sublimated for the sake of an elderly parent or relative.

215 Venus Conjunction Uranus

If artistic talent is shown in other areas of the chart this conjunction contributes much originality, especially through new and exciting artistic trends. While there is a need for peace or harmony, there is also much highly strung tension than can be externalized through the arts. This is a very powerful force of energy and, if it finds no positive outlets, emotions can build up to uncontrollable levels resulting in wild and eccentric behaviour that has little regard for personal reputations. With 188, 243 or 255 these aspects are positive influences that can steady the emotions and direct creative talents more effectively. Overall, however, there is a predisposition to unconventional relationships.

216 Venus Conjunction Neptune

Any aspect between Venus and Neptune brings out the romantic nature of both men and women.

With regard to harmony within the psyche, Neptune is said to be the 'higher-octave chord' or spiritual vibration. A conjunction confirms artistic ability and a romantic nature. Such a vibration has a mystical and magnetic aura that permeates the whole psyche. People with this conjunction in their charts have the inspirational gifts or talents associated with the Otherworld realm of the unconscious. But it does need some positive aspects of rational Saturn and creative direction of Jupiter to maintain a steady course through life, otherwise such potential remains in the dream-like state of existence. If found in Ash or Ivy signs this is particularly significant.

217 Venus Trine Mars

Feelings are fully expressed with this aspect and so is the enthusiasm for love affairs, which can be either extra-marital or simply promiscuous. Other aspects such as 219 or 232 can, however, encourage loyalty to one partner . But overall there is a need for freedom of expression, otherwise it can generate a great deal of nervous and emotional strain. People with this aspect are nevertheless inclined to make love-matches that stand the test of time and any conflict of emotions.

218 Venus Trine Jupiter

Read also 213, as the same influence is in operation, but trines extend the positive or beneficial influence to higher levels of the mind. In this case it integrates artistic expression with the mind and/or the intellect. People with this aspect are therefore equally conversant with the arts and academic knowledge. However, the extreme nature of Venus and Jupiter is fully activated, and self-indulgence and extravagance must be kept in check. This aspect is an excellent inspiration for all tree signs, especially the Rowan, Ash, Holly, Vine and Ivy.

219 Venus Trine Saturn

Saturnian influence on Venus always chills the expression of feelings, and the artistically creative talents associated with Venus never flow freely. Social life is often lacking and relationships generally can lack fun or spontaneity. At best this aspect does show a good business head and successful financial investments. Look for compensating influences in other planetary aspects, in particular positive aspects between the Sun and Moon with Venus, Mars and Jupiter.

220 Venus Trine Uranus

This aspect usually involves an artistic talent, and musical ability is top of the list. People with this aspect in their charts generally have a genial nature and are inclined to have numerous friendships and acquaintances. They are basically highly sociable and most probably members of various societies or clubs. They also have a romantic and highly sensitive nature. This extends to sympathy for the so-called 'misfits' in society, and as a result they usually attract a strange mixture of friends.

221 Venus Trine Neptune

There is a great deal that is ephemeral or unworldly about people with this aspect. While artistic talent is usually present, it needs to be encouraged as it may easily drain away or lose its fragrant quality. But there is much glamour and refinement shown that always remains throughout life. Look for support and encouragement with aspects to Jupiter or Saturn

222 Venus Square Mars

Although feelings are warm and affectionately expressed, this aspect shows intense sexual relationships that are often marred by quarrels caused largely by a flirtatious nature. Emotions are inclined to be hypersensitive, and this can put a strain on family relationships as well as partnerships. Read 212 on the relationship between Venus and Mars. This negative aspect does prevent a sense of inner harmony, but look for other compensating aspects as described with 212.

223 Venus Square Jupiter

This aspect shows extreme levels of feelings and a craving for the luxuries in life. There is and exaggerated sense of drama and a tendency to become involved in love affairs. With 219 or 242 feelings are more reasonably balanced and self-indulgences are curbed. Finances are also more solvent. Overall, this aspect does require strong controlling factors in the chart; check the position of the Sun and Moon, and if they form a positive aspect with each other this will also provide greater harmony within the whole psyche.

224 Venus Square Saturn

First read 214, which reveals the nature of these two planets in any aspect to each other. A square is much of the same, but the emphasis is on financial prospects. This is often a sign of lost inheritances, and bad luck can dog finances or investments. Look for positive aspects to Mars and Jupiter for greater luck and self-reliance.

225 Venus Square Uranus

This aspect has the same content as 215, but with the square there is more emphasis on choice of friends or business partners. Extreme caution and care is required, as disastrous relationships can occur that can be very difficult to recover from. Look for the same compensating aspects as shown with 215 and check whether Saturn is strongly aspected for overall support.

226 Venus Square Neptune

This aspect shows high ideals, but they need to be carefully analysed as they can be extremely unrealistic. Disappointment often occurs in emotional relationships because of unreliability in the partner. There is also a tendency to be secretive about love affairs. Care must be applied in the area of business and finances. Read 216 for further information on the relationship between Venus and Neptune, and the same compensating aspects should help to provide a more practical perspective.

227 Mars Conjunction Jupiter

This conjunction forms a powerful alliance of creative and assertive energy. All objectives are pursued in a positive and energetic manner. People with this conjunction in their charts are always open and frank about their ambitions and, while they may become involved in disputes, they are extremely fair-minded and magnanimous – win or lose. Making difficult decisions doesn't present a problem, as their ability to see the wider picture or potential opportunities allows them to cope with any change of plans simply by tackling the situation from another angle. They are perhaps the greatest opportunists and entrepreneurs in the business world as luck is usually on their side. With such a powerful force in operation a square is needed in the chart to ensure that success is not short-lived. With 175 or 192 these aspects provide great inner strength and motivation that, if anything, increases with time. If with 242 – a trine between Jupiter and Saturn – this also provides enduring success.

228 Mars Conjunction Saturn

This is a very potent conjunction. It is often a sign of considerable suffering that is linked to physical handicaps or disabilities caused by accidents. They can be minor or major, depending on the other aspects in the chart. A trine between the Sun and Moon provides an inner sense of harmony, but it also needs a few squares that have the effect of not accepting any limitations. With 175 or 192 the will to overcome any obstacles is simply quite amazing. Overall, this conjunction presents a demanding challenge, but it is often found in the charts of people who win great respect by surviving difficult conditions.

229 Mars Conjunction Uranus

This is a very powerful conjunction that shows a high but tense level of energy, which is always near to breaking point. People with this conjunction are highly productive individuals in the sense that they push themselves to the limit of physical and mental endurance. They are basically exciting people to observe, as their lifestyle is usually full of drama and controversy. A volatile temperament is shown, which is often associated with great artists or entertainers rather than conventional careers. Look for both stabilizing and creative aspects so that this energy and potential can be fully realized; positive aspects to Venus, Jupiter and Saturn are ideal counterbalances.

230 Mars Conjunction Neptune

This conjunction is always difficult to define. The fiery nature of Mars confronts the nebulous influence of Neptune, a watery element that is fluid and, like the sea, has inner turbulence and changing tides that can suddenly become either calm or tempestuous. In personal terms it indicates plenty of enthusiasm that can be carelessly directed, and your energy reserves are never high. It can, however, produce creative interpretation in the arts, and your imagination is extremely powerful and intuitively directed. There is also psychic ability that can manifest as power or influence over other people's minds. Mars is a self-assertive force, which does need careful direction. Look for moral and less selfish motivations with positive aspects to Venus, Jupiter and Saturn.

231 Mars Trine Jupiter

First read 227, which provides the substance of these two planets' contact with each other. This aspect is working from the same content, but a trine shows a more harmonious blend of traits and the high energy level is directed evenly towards both physical and intellectual pursuits. A strong will-power is shown, along with great optimism and the ability to enjoy life. Overall, a very positive aspect to have, and one that is linked to good health, wealth and a contented marriage or love life.

232 Mars Trine Saturn

This is a 'tough' aspect identified with tremendous endurance and the ability to live through harsh conditions. Found in the charts of mountaineers, explorers, elite military-service people and those with careers that involve harsh conditions or control over large groups of people – the type of person who leads by example. People with this aspect have sound judgement and know exactly what they want from life – and what they have to do in order to achieve it. An excellent aspect for Alder, Oak or Elder signs.

233 Mars Trine Uranus

This conjunction shows an ability to make quick decisions and a high energy level that thrives on impossible challenges. While similar to the above aspect, people with this aspect in their chart are drawn to modern engineering or technology that requires an original and inventive mind capable of solving difficult problems. They make excellent drivers and pilots, or people who enjoy dangerous speed-sports.

234 Mars Trine Neptune

First read 230, which explains the nature of these two planets. This aspect has the same content but operates on a higher-mind level. It emphasizes a spiritual nature with a disciplined mind and body, which suggests a militant crusader with firm religious convictions. There is also a strong attraction to mystical cults or healing groups, and the nautical world. Imagination and intuition are highly developed and there is a natural ability to keep ahead of others, which may be linked to mental telepathy. There is certainly a high level of mental power attached to this aspect.

235 Mars Square Jupiter

This aspect indicates blind optimism and impulsive actions. Much care and forethought needs to be developed as the energy level is high, but positive outlets are not easy to find. Reckless and rebellious behaviour can be difficult to curb once it takes hold. There may also be a lack of temperance that can become a serious problem. Overall, this aspect shows a restless energy that requires self-discipline and moderation in all things. With 232 or 242 these aspects provide ideal counterweights, but look for further support in the chart with aspects of a similar nature.

236 Mars Square Saturn

This aspect can undermine the true potential in any chart. Enthusiasm and interest in new projects can quickly wear off, and this is associated with a difficulty in maintaining an even flow of energy. People with this aspect can be very energetic one minute and totally lethargic the next. It's a question of either overestimating their own capabilities or never tackling the real issues, which results in a lack of purpose and a tendency to drift through life. With 166, 185, 231 or 242 these aspects will greatly improve matters, but there may always be a propensity to shirk responsibility if the going gets tough.

237 Mars Square Uranus

This shows an explosive temper, intolerance and a tendency to always contradict the ideas or views of others. There is a high degree of nervous tension combined with uncoordinated reflexes, and this usually manifests as accident-proneness. Self-control needs to be developed on all levels, as there is a disturbing vibration in operation within the whole psyche. Look for positive aspects between the Sun and Moon and also between Jupiter and Saturn.

238 Mars Square Neptune

There is great sensitivity shown with this aspect, which can be the Achilles heel in any chart. While it shows leadership potential, there is also a tendency towards escapism through either drugs or alcohol – a dangerous pastime, since sensitivity or an allergic response to medicines – even prescribed medication – is also indicated. This aspect is often found in the charts of actors and sailors. Both are drawn towards the watery realm that symbolically represents the illusionary world or a place in which to make interesting voyages of discovery.

239 Jupiter Conjunction Saturn

Jupiter and Saturn represent two extreme opposites of planetary influence. While Jupiter is the largest planet in our galaxy and symbolizes the expansion of the mind, a highly creative influence, Saturn is identified with limitations. In ancient times Saturn was observed as the outermost planet in the known universe long before telescopes were invented. In modern astrology the rings of Saturn symbolize bonds and restriction. In the Celtic lunar zodiac Jupiter rules the sign of the Oak Tree, which marks the Summer Solstice. Saturn rules the last lunar month of the year (Elder Tree), marking the imprisonment of the Sun-king who would eventually be reborn on the day of the Winter Solstice. Jupiter and Saturn therefore symbolize different ends of the light spectrum observed by the Druids: the expanding light of the summer Sun and the contracting or limiting light of the winter Sun. This conjunction forms a very potent planetary relationship, and there is great potential coupled with a focused perspective and physical and mental endurance. There is considerable ability to achieve objectives, not only through hard work but also through a superb intellect if Mercury is well aspected in the chart. Overall, this conjunction forms a powerful source of strength and faith in oneself.

240 Jupiter Conjunction Uranus

This conjunction emphasizes a powerful need for personal independence, as both planets are identified with freedom of expression – Jupiter with creative intelligence and Uranus with progressive thinking. People with this aspect in their charts are therefore inclined to be restless and can become resentful if restricted in any way. While there is great potential that is inspired with vision and originality, other aspects are needed to fully activate this highly erratic creativity. With 169, 188, 198 or 242 this combination of planets forms a stabilizing influence and provides positive outlets for creative abilities. Look to the other aspects in your chart for similar combinations of strength or concentration and positive direction.

241 Jupiter Conjunction Neptune

Both planets are associated with creative talents and this conjunction is an excellent influence for bringing out the artistic potential shown in any chart. But it does require more tenacity or self-determination to fully realize this type of ethereal talent and higher-minded intellectual ability that leans towards literary skills. There is a high degree of idealism in operation, and intuitive perception combined with philosophical or religious beliefs. People with this aspect in their charts are compassionate and have strong humanitarian views with a love of animals, including sea creatures. Financial success is likely to be from unusual sources or in the form of a fluctuating income.

242 Jupiter Trine Saturn

This is the one of the best aspects to have in any chart as it shows successful progress in life through the steady application of constructive and creative ability. If Jupiter or Saturn are joined by positive aspects from the Sun, there is breadth of vision and conscious awareness of personal limitations that encourages greater adaptability and versatile skills. It remains a positive directive throughout life.

243 Jupiter Trine Uranus

This aspect is a positive blend of original thinking, leadership and compassionate ideals. There is a dislike of narrow values and all forms of conventionality, which encourages greater knowledge and learning. An excellent aspect for Rowan, Oak and Elder signs, but overall it provides greater scope and vision for all signs.

244 Jupiter Trine Neptune

First read 241, which provides the background of these two planets' contact with each other. Trines are considered to be integrating influences and areas of balance in the chart. Jupiter is associated with creative energy and linked to good fortune generally. Neptune is equally creative artistically and relates to the spiritual nature of humankind; it is less concerned with material wealth. This aspect shows a natural disposition to help the underprivileged, and involvement with charities or missionary work is most likely at some stage. There is also a psychological need to retire periodically from the mundane world and gather strength, as upholding such moral and spiritual standards can be taxing.

245 Jupiter Square Saturn

This aspect sets a difficult task. Personal restrictions or limitations are usually accepted with resignation, and it is often found in the chart of people who yield to more dominant forces. But all squares have a fascinating psychology, as they represent areas in the chart where more effort or strength is needed; in karmic astrology they therefore represent areas of potential growth. People with this aspect in their charts may have to decide whether to challenge authority or their personal limitations. If they are prepared to accept that their own weaknesses are responsible they will gradually learn more self-discipline, which is the object of the exercise. The only alternative is to revert to low self-esteem.

246 Jupiter Square Uranus

Jupiter and Uranus both represent a 'free spirit' and are associated with a need for personal independence from an early age. This aspect effectively brings out all the negative qualities of restlessness and outspokenness, which can become unbearable to others and ultimately mar or damage relationships. Financial losses are also likely to occur due to a mentality that ignores sound advice. Look for supporting aspects from the Sun and Moon to Jupiter and Uranus, and aspects that provide mental stability.

247 Jupiter Square Neptune

If the chart shows strength of character and practical ability this aspect will provide great sensitivity to suffering, and this can be positively directed towards actually alleviating suffering. But a strong attraction to strange religious cults can result in disastrous consequences, due to the negative self-indulgent nature of Jupiter being influenced by the negative Neptunian attraction to drugs or alcohol. Overall, it shows unrealistic ambitions, and financial affairs are best left to reliable professional advisers.

248 Saturn Conjunction Uranus

This conjunction represents a confrontation of the rational mind with the irrational mind, one being equally as strong or as influential as the other. While ambitions and self-reliance are present together with self-determination, these will tend to alternate with depression and nervous tension. These sudden changes, which affect the personality and character, can be rather difficult to come to terms with. But the position and aspects to Mercury hold the key when deciding if one is stronger than the other or whether they are well balanced and integrated. Mercury in Capricorn, Taurus

and Virgo confirms practical or rational thinking. In Aquarius the mind, though inclined to be irrational, has inspired vision. In Gemini it is inventive and versatile, and in Libra it has good reasoning powers but tends to be indecisive. In Aries it is quick-thinking and inclined to be outspoken and less rational at times. In Leo it indicates strong opinions but great optimism. In Sagittarius it shows broad-mindedness and, though restless, the mind is intellectually inclined. In Cancer it is shrewd and highly intuitive, but in Pisces it is flexible and easily impressionable. In Scorpio it is penetrating and analytical. The aspects provide direction and should reveal any strengths or weaknesses.

249 Saturn Conjunction Neptune

If the rest of the chart shows artistic ability this conjunction will provide constructive form to the imagination and inspiration. While there may be some conflict between materialism and idealism, Saturn stabilizes the nebulous quality of Neptune. There is often a flair for commercial business enterprises with this conjunction that works from an intuitive grasp of consumer needs. Spiritual nature is also inclined to be more orthodox and less mystical.

250 Saturn Trine Uranus

First read 248, which explains the different attitudes of mind associated with these two planets. If the powers of concentration are good, they will be strengthened by this aspect, which shows great initiative and will-power together with patience and caution. Success is likely in professional careers rather than mundane work, and scientific and administrative positions are favoured. An excellent aspect for Birch, Rowan, Hawthorn and Hazel signs.

251 Saturn Trine Neptune

While this aspect is similar to 249, a trine is more helpful in encouraging any artistic or creative talents, and the imagination and powerful intuition are put to good use. It also shows practical or common sense combined with good organizational skills. Spiritual nature, while less mystical, is nevertheless highly evolved, and this aspect confirms an old soul. People with this aspect in their charts therefore have the benefit of moral guidance and have sound judgement if involved in ethical problems.

252 Saturn Square Uranus

This aspect shows mental tension and depressive moods. These planets are also linked to wider-generation influences because their orbits stay in range of each other for long periods. This aspect indicates a generation gap that is highly pronounced, and therefore people with this aspect usually experience a clash of values with parents and, at a later date, their own children or the 'younger generation'. Look for positive aspects to Jupiter and read 248 for guidance relating to the position of Mercury.

253 Saturn Square Neptune

This aspect shows emotional strain and psychological inhibitions. Disillusion and personal disappointments can encourage a form of paranoia. There is a tendency to become involved with impractical projects that never get off the drawing board, but while it causes impatience or frustration, people with this aspect in their charts often fail to learn by experience. Look for positive aspects to Mercury and Jupiter for supporting strength and direction.

254 Uranus Conjunction Neptune

This conjunction has a remarkable influence as it only occurs approximately every 171 years. When in operation it adds to the number of truly great people or souls being born. The last time it occurred was during the 1820s and it began to form a conjunction in January 1989 until approximately March 1997. However, during this period, due to the retrograde motions of both planets, this conjunction slipped slightly out of place on occasion, but was at its most exact or potent during 1993. Overall, it shows much originality and kindness, and while a strong self-will is prominent it is directed towards serving humanitarian and compassionate causes.

255 Uranus Trine Neptune

This aspect remains in place for very long periods because of the slow movement of the outer planets in relationship to Earth. When it does occur, one of these planets will also be in contact with another major planet – a combination that provides great insight into the whole psyche and the psychological behaviour pattern. This aspect shows great intuition and sensitivity, and the mystical nature of Neptune is self-evident with a spirituality that is highly psychic and visionary.

256 Uranus Square Neptune

This aspect shows an intense level of emotions and a tendency towards self-indulgence. If one of these planets is the ruling planet of your tree sign (either the Rowan or the Ash), the potential associated with the sign needs to be encouraged. Look for support through the strengthening aspects of Saturn and creative direction through Jupiter. The relationship between the Sun and Moon should also be carefully considered.

257 Moon Conjunction Sun

This conjunction marks the New Moon period. It places an emphasis on being forced to make new beginnings in life every so often, since it symbolizes an inner imbalance which forms deep-rooted habits that need to be broken if self-growth and greater self-awareness are to evolve. The tree sign containing the Sun is an extremely powerful focal point in the chart, and if Mercury and Venus also occupy the same sign, which frequently occurs, this emphasis becomes an even greater imbalance with much stress on the strengths and weaknesses of character. Look at any Sun and Moon aspects for mitigating influences and check if the strength of Saturn and Jupiter can provide positive outlets.

258 Moon Trine Sun

This aspect forms a splendid integrating link between the conscious and unconscious mind. A general harmony of personality and character is emphasized, and manifests as a calm temperament and popularity. If, however, both the Sun and Moon form difficult aspects with Saturn or Venus it can detract a certain amount of popularity, but overall this is an excellent aspect to have in any chart. Any so-called negative aspects can actually provide greater motivation, as this aspect can encourage a lack of ambition since life has an element of luck and inner contentment, and this can result in complacency.

259 Moon Square Sun

This aspect reveals inner conflicts that can be linked to difficult relationships between parents and children. It can manifest as having been pushed into a career chosen either by parents or simply through a lack of positive direction that results in dissatisfaction in general. People with this aspect in their charts can also become arrogant or unwilling to take advice. However, it is often found in the charts of those with successful careers later in life as compensation for inner conflict or problems within the family.

260 Sun Trine Venus

This aspect never occurs, as Venus cannot move more than 48 degrees away from the Sun.

261 General Consideration of Aspects to the Sun

The Sun influences the conscious self, general vitality, self-expression and activities in life. If the Sun forms trines to other planets it shows a positive blend of traits associated with the particular planet and with the tree sign the Sun is in. But while trines are excellent aspects to have and indicate a certain amount of luck and opportunity in life, they usually require the cut and thrust of squares to fully activate the true potential, which can otherwise remain dormant.

262 General Considerations of Aspects to the Moon

The Moon governs the emotions, instinctive behaviour, which includes parental feelings, and the unconscious or intuitive, abstract mind. The Moon is a planet of fluctuation and response and, in the context of lunar aspects, it 'receives' rather than 'transmits'. It does, however, greatly influence the emotions during its monthly cycle of waxing and waning in everyday life. The aspects operate in the same way as shown with the Sun, but because the Moon relates to the unconscious, the influence of aspects is not always apparent unless shown openly through emotional behaviour. It operates on a deeper level of the mind, a lunar dimension that manifests as the Shadow self, which is referred to with the Moon's position in relationship to the tree signs.

263 Pluto Conjunction Sun

In astrology it is said that Pluto 'intensifies' the nature of the planet it comes into contact with. If you read the chapter on the Reed sign you will find deeper insight into this planet's own nature and influence. People with this conjunction may have a power fixation, and it can become an overwhelming influence to cope with in any sign. It can also manifest as drastic upheavals in life or dramatic overnight changes. The powerful nature of Pluto is, however, extremely self-regenerating,

and this conjunction provides the ability to survive even major disasters and begin anew. Outer planets such as Pluto are considered by most astrologers to exert external or generation influences rather than personal qualities or traits. But Pluto is a highly significant transforming influence on the subliminal level of consciousness, which manifests in the behavioural pattern. The regenerating influence can lay dormant for many years and has a complex nature. The following aspects are therefore brief cameo pictures relating to the magnetic power of Pluto on the mind and emotions.

264 Pluto Trine Sun

This aspect shows strong leadership qualities and a desire to live life to the full every day. People with this aspect have a powerful magnetism that is more attractive than with a conjunction or a square. It shows a positive use of all energy and the ability to make fresh starts with greater determination and without recriminations.

265 Pluto Square Sun

A great deal of hidden resentment is associated with this aspect, and power can become an obsession. While positive expression is not easy and inner tension can build up as a result, this aspect does show great sympathy for others, and people with this aspect can be very supportive to friends and family in their hour of need.

266 Pluto Conjunction Moon

This conjunction deepens and intensifies the emotions, and mood changes are likely to be explosive on occasion. When this does occur there is an overwhelming desire to destroy previous efforts or end emotional relationships. There is a depth of feeling that few can fully understand, but a partner with deeper insight can transform this inner turbulence. Choice of partner is therefore crucial for the well-being of the whole psyche.

267 Pluto Trine Moon

Emotions are controlled and feelings are honestly expressed. While a protective nature is shown, people with this aspect are less inclined to be jealous or possessive. An excellent aspect for all business dealings, there is an intuitive grasp of high finance that could lead to powerful positions in the money markets or to building up new businesses.

268 Pluto Square Moon

This aspect reveals a psychological blockage of emotions and there is a tendency towards emotional unrest and suspicious thoughts. Any sudden changes that take place are inclined to be emotionally upsetting because they are not by personal choice. Important karmic lessons are identified with this aspect, and they revolve around sexual problems and difficult family relationships. Professional counselling can be helpful.

269 Pluto Conjunction Mercury

This shows a deeply penetrating and analytical mind that solves difficult problems with superb logic. It also indicates an aptitude for research on subjects such as the occult, psychology, criminology and astrology. Overall, it shows an astute individual who prefers to find their own answers rather than accept the verdict or opinions of others. Psychic abilities are also linked to this conjunction.

270 Pluto Trine Mercury

Nervous tension is more easily released with this aspect, which is very similar to the above conjunction. Psychic ability is associated with Pluto, but with this aspect it can remain dormant for many years. Overall, it shows a constructive use of personal influence.

271 Pluto Square Mercury

This shows an inability to see things in their true perspective, which results in the making of verbal promises that are difficult to deliver. Communication generally may be a problem, and professional counselling is advised.

272 Pluto Conjunction Venus

There is a tendency to fall suddenly and passionately in love, but it may remain a secret affair. This conjunction requires positive or constructive aspects if the financial abilities are to succeed and sexual repression is not to become a serious problem.

273 Pluto Trine Venus

There is likely to be an exaggerated enjoyment of life, with self-indulgence leading to health or weight problems. But financial ability is strengthened if there are also positive aspects to Jupiter or Saturn.

274 Pluto Square Venus

Although there are some psychological inhibitions present that may curb strong sexual urges, they can also manifest as lustful fantasies. Financial problems may occur as a consequence of over-investing or taking one risk too many. Moderation is required in all things. Difficult relationships are often a projection of inner turmoil or passions.

275 Pluto Conjunction Mars

A quick and violent temper may be present which requires great effort to control. But there is tremendous physical stamina that directs energy towards powerful ambitions that can be highly successful. Criminal tendencies can occur, however, if both planets are badly aspected.

276 Pluto Trine Mars

This aspect indicates a passionately hard worker, and emotional and physical energy are positively controlled and utilized. There is a capacity for making new beginnings and taking adversity or setbacks in one's stride. Self-confidence and self-reliance are also emphasized.

277 Pluto Square Mars

This aspect shows that objectives can become an obsession and success can be at the expense of others with little regard for their feelings or loss. This can cause problems at work and at home, as there is much intolerance and aggression. Look for positive aspects between Mars, Mercury and Jupiter, and also Pluto with Jupiter and Saturn.

278 Pluto Conjunction Jupiter

This shows considerable ability to break with the past and assume another identity in the sense of being able to transform personality traits. Strong powers of leadership are shown, as well as the capacity to study serious subjects in great breadth and depth.

279 Pluto Trine Jupiter

This aspect is similar to the above, but with additional powers of intellectual ability. Objectives are also better organized and are motivated by an interest in helping others rather than by selfish reasons or a need for power over others.

280 Pluto Square Jupiter

This aspect shows a degree of fanaticism and a desire to exploit people. Religious conflicts may be at the heart of the matter, but material wealth is seen as a powerful lever of exploitation. Psychologically, it stems from personal inadequacies. If Pluto is placed near the solstices or positively aspected to the Sun or Moon, this aspect marks a transformation process that will overcome any personal inadequacies or limitations.

281 Pluto Conjunction Saturn

While this can cause deep-seated obsessional problems, it can also provide a constructive approach to objectives through careful planning and patience. This aspect is, however, regarded as a generation influence, so people with this aspect are likely to experience external pressures that are repressive to individual growth or liberty.

282 Pluto Trine Saturn

Similar to the above, but this aspect shows an ability to unite the opposing planetary influences into a coherent perspective. Any personal limitations or frustrations are therefore more easily overcome.

283 Pluto Square Saturn

This is identical to the conjunction, but negative traits can become more serious or out of control if there are conjunctions to the Sun and Moon. Look for the strengthening or weakening influences of these planets in order to determine this potent relationship.

284 Pluto Conjunction Uranus

This is an extremely dynamic conjunction with astounding potential. On a personal level children with this aspect require careful upbringing as this generation influence encourages revolutionary beliefs. They can grow up to create a new humanitarian society or equally destroy the very foundations of civilization. This conjunction last occurred during 1963–69.

285 Pluto Trine Uranus

This aspect shows an ability to direct energy in a dynamic and impressive way. It is a highly energizing influence to have in any chart. Although it shows unconventional behaviour and ideals, it provides powerful insight into the mysteries of life.

286 Pluto Square Uranus

Flash-point tempers that are sudden occur with this aspect, and while they develop as a result of repressed inner tensions, they can be highly destructive to self-interests and generally cause distress to others. Positive aspects to either planet can channel this energy into highly creative work.

287 Pluto Conjunction Neptune

Any planet forming an aspect to Neptune becomes more refined and softens any harsh traits of character, but it can also dissolve any strength. Working together, however, these two planets are able to dissolve deep-rooted inhibitions. Aspects to both planets should reveal more.

288 Pluto Trine Neptune

Same as above, but both planets are in greater harmony and psychic awareness is positively directed towards healing others and yourself – a positive use of occult traits.

289 Pluto Square Neptune

This aspect shows negative involvement with clairvoyance or psychic activity that stems from blocking influences inhibiting the normal flow of spiritual awareness. This can be traced to parents' strong religious beliefs that were based more on superstition or fear rather than compassion or love. People with this aspect should therefore avoid the above temptations and concentrate on building up their inner strengths for positive self-growth.

. . . .